# The Catechism Yesterday and Today

## The Evolution of a Genre

*Berard L. Marthaler, O.F.M.Conv.*

*A Liturgical Press Book*

THE LITURGICAL PRESS
Collegeville, Minnesota

Cover design by Ann Blattner

| 1 | 2 | 3 | 4 | 5 | 6 | 7 | 8 |
|---|---|---|---|---|---|---|---|

**Library of Congress Cataloging-in-Publication Data**

Marthaler, Berard L.
    The catechism yesterday and today : the evolution of a genre /
Berard L. Marthaler.
      p.  cm.
    Includes bibliographical references.
    ISBN 0-8146-2151-1 (perfect bound). — ISBN 0-8146-2353-0 (case
bound)
      1. Catholic Church—Catechisms—History and criticism.
    2. Catholic Church—Doctrines—History.   I. Title.
BX1959.M37    1995
238'.2—dc20
                                          95-15939
                                            CIP

# Contents

# Preface

*The Catechism Yesterday and Today* is the story of a book or, more accurately, the story of a book-genre. The popular image presents the catechism as a series of questions and answers compiled for the purpose of religious instruction. A history of the genre—even a short one such as this—paints a different picture. Archbishop John Thoresby of York commissioned *The Lay Folks' Catechism* of 1353 to combat the widespread ignorance of the clergy and to promote reform. In the sixteenth century after the invention of the printing press, reformers of all stripes, Protestant and Catholic, circulated catechisms. The genre came to include a variety of works of different lengths, styles, and purposes. Few were truly original; most were compilations adapted to the needs of a particular place and time. Some were source books for preachers and teachers; many were primers for children and the uneducated. Some served as vehicles of evangelization and inculturation in mission areas, and in Ireland they served political ends.

From the time of the Reformation catechisms have served both as confessional statements and pedagogical tools. This dual purpose gave them an importance beyond their intrinsic value and has caused catechisms to be judged by conflicting criteria and priorities. Ecclesiastical authorities and theologians tend to judge catechisms in terms of orthodoxy and completeness. Catechists and teachers, no less concerned about orthodoxy, give priority to the effective communication of the Christian message and evaluate catechetical texts by how well-adapted they are to the background and capacity of the learners.

The catechism was impressed on the hearts of the faithful long before it was set in type. From the earliest days of the Church, the story of salvation had been painted on the walls of the catacombs, etched in bas-relief on columns of Romanesque churches, and highlighted in the stained glass windows of medieval cathedrals. It was taught in sermons and homilies and celebrated in ritual and prayer. In these pages, however, my concern is the printed word. I single out examples of classic catechisms to illustrate how the genre came to be.

I describe the functions they were made to serve to show that even simple catechisms often had a complex mission. Given that my aim is to trace the evolution of the genre, my primary focus is on the form of catechisms, and I comment on their contents only in passing.

The *Catechism of the Catholic Church,* promulgated by Pope John Paul II in 1992, represents the latest stage in the development of the genre. Its publication spawned new interest in catechisms and has been the occasion for a reconsideration of the place of catechisms in the Church's pastoral ministry. By reason of its size alone, the *Catechism of the Catholic Church* shattered the popular image of the catechism as a series of questions and answers whose principal, even sole purpose was the religious instruction of children. Pope John Paul II describes the new catechism as "a statement of the Church's faith and of catholic doctrine . . . a sure norm for teaching the faith and . . . [an] instrument of ecclesial communion." He sees it as a means "of strengthening the bonds of unity" and of "proclaiming the faith and calling people to the Gospel life." John Paul, citing the example of the householder who cleans out his attic (Matt 13:52), says the *Catechism of the Catholic Church* "contains both the old and the new." It adopts the "old," structure that organizes catechesis around the Creed, Sacraments, Commandments, and Lord's Prayer, while at the same time presenting the contents often "in a 'new' way in order to respond to questions of our age."

Although *The Catechism Yesterday and Today* describes the new catechism as the latest stage in the evolution of the genre, my own interest in the history of catechisms began long before. Sr. Mary Charles Bryce, O.S.B., for many years a colleague in the department of Religion and Religious Education at The Catholic University of America, introduced me to the subject. I cite her several times in the later chapters, but her research and influence pervade the entire book. She convinced me as she did a generation of students that catechesis is a form of ministry of the Word, closely linked to the liturgy, and inseparable from the Church's mission to proclaim the Gospel and make disciples of all peoples.

Some of the material in chapters 2 through 6, 10, and 12 was published in *Professional Approaches for Christian Education* (PACE).[1] The chapter on the Irish catechisms borrows heavily from the doctoral dissertation of Patrick Wallace, long associated with the Mater Dei Institute of Religious Education and now a Dublin pastor. The account of the First Vatican Council draws on the Ph.D. dissertation of another former student, Michael Donnellan. I am also indebted to many colleagues at The Catholic University of America. Dr. Nelson Minnich, professor of Church history, made several suggestions that improved the chapters on the catechisms of the Reformation. Dr. Peter Phan, professor of theology, provided the information on Alexander of Rhodes that appears in chapter 5. Monsignor Kevin Nichols, former National Advisor on Religious Education to the Roman Catholic Bishops of England and Wales, read the chapters on the English catechisms.

My appreciation is due Ms. Carolyn Lee, curator of the rare book collection, who provided invaluable help in locating texts in the vast, but only partially catalogued, collection of catechisms in the Mullen Library at The Catholic University of America. And Mr. Bruce Miller, another member of the staff of the Mullen Library, helped trace down sources and made suggestions for the improvement of chapter 7. Maura Thompson Hagarty, Richard McCarron, and Morris Pelzel, doctoral students in the Department of Religion and Religious Education at The Catholic University, deserve special mention. They assisted at various stages in the preparation of the manuscript, checking references, entering the text into the word processor, proof-reading various drafts, compiling the index, and, in general, being at-hand when I needed someone to help me cope with the technology of the computer world. To all these and other colleagues and friends who go unnamed, I am grateful for their encouragement in writing this book and, as I contemplate retirement, for the generous support they have given me during the thirty-plus years that I have spent at The Catholic University of America.

Finally a word of appreciation for the Faculty Research Grant I received from The Catholic University of America that helped launch the project, and a grant from the Lilly Endowment, Inc. that facilitated its completion and publication.

The Catholic University of America
March, 1995

NOTE

1. Published by Brown-Roa, Dubuque.

ONE

# A Time of Transition:
# Catechisms for Lay Folk

The story of the catechism as we have come to know it begins in the late Middle Ages. Before it became enshrined in the pages of a book, the catechism was a series of oral instructions, usually in some form of sermon, given at set times in the liturgical year. By the thirteenth century the basic outline of the catechism was well established: the Creed, the Ten Commandments, the twofold precept of love of God and neighbor, the seven deadly sins, the seven principal virtues (faith, hope, charity, justice, prudence, temperance, fortitude), and the seven sacraments. The first time "catechism" was used to describe a book of instruction, however, was in 1357. In that year Archbishop John Thoresby of York directed that newly enacted ordinances governing catechetical instruction be translated into the vernacular for the use of the clergy and the benefit of the people, and thus was born *The Lay Folks' Catechism*.

## Medieval Catechesis

Before describing Thoresby's catechism and similar works, it will be helpful to give some background.[1]

In the first centuries of the Church catechesis was institutionalized in the catechumenate, a protracted period during which time candidates for baptism had their lifestyle scrutinized, memorized the Creed, and learned the Lord's Prayer. After the rites of initiation which included baptism, chrismation, and full participation in the Eucharist, the neophytes ("newly born") reflected on the mysteries (in Latin, the "sacraments") and heard further instructions as to what it means to be Christian. This last phase was known as *mystagogy* or *mystagogical catechesis*.

By the fifth century infant baptism had become more and more the common practice and the rites of initiation, both before and after baptism, more informal. Nonetheless vestiges of the traditional catechumenal practices are found in the instructions and homilies of Ambrose of Milan (d. 396) and Augustine of Hippo (d. 430). Two works in particular by Augustine shaped the catechetical tradition of the Middle Ages. *De catechizandis rudibus*, intended primarily as a practical manual, proposed methods and techniques for the catechist; it presents an introductory instruction for inquirers that is in fact a survey of salvation history. Augustine wrote *Faith, Hope, and Charity*, also known as the *Enchiridion*, in response to a request to sum up the essentials of Christian doctrine in the briefest possible form. Divided into three unequal parts, he used the baptismal Creed, the Lord's Prayer, and the twofold commandment of love to explain "what we must believe, what we must hope for, and what we must love." As will be seen, many modern catechisms continue to use this tripartite distribution of material.

By the ninth century provincial councils and synods, concerned about widespread ignorance of Christian beliefs and morals, directed that religious instruction be given in the vernacular. They formulated canons that required godparents for baptism to be examined as to whether they could recite the Apostles' Creed and the Lord's Prayer. Lists of virtues and vices provided the basic outline for moral instruction. The seven deadly sins, contrasted with the seven principal virtues (faith, hope, charity, prudence, justice, temperance, and fortitude, and their consequences) were the subject of sermons and admonitions in confession.*

Literacy was largely the privilege of clergy, and their ability to read was limited by their access to books. As is common in oral cultures the Middle Ages put great premium on lists, word associations, verse, and other aids to memorization. The *septenarium*, for example, was a genre that catalogued doctrines and practices in groups of seven. In the *Enchiridion* Augustine identified seven petitions in the Lord's Prayer, and in his explanation of the Sermon on the Mount he correlated them with the seven Beatitudes. [2] In the twelfth century Hugh of St. Victor (d. 1142), gave classic expression to the genre in his short *De quinque septenis seu septenariis*. Hugh's "five sevens" are the seven deadly sins, seven petitions of the Lord's Prayer, seven gifts of the Holy Spirit, seven virtues

---

*The use of sacramental confession as an occasion for catechesis gave rise to so-called confessional booklets. Intended originally for priests, they provided guidelines for interrogating penitents about their knowledge of the Creed and basic Christian practices. Later it was customary in many places to place posters in churches that could be used as check-lists to help people prepare for confession. After the invention of printing, the laity began to use booklets similar to the penitentials used by the confessors. According to Josef A. Jungmann, these confessional booklets were "forerunners of the catechism, except that the section devoted to the commandments dominated all others" (*Handing on the Faith. A Manual of Catechetics* [New York: Herder and Herder, 1959] 17).

(humility, meekness, compunction, desire for the good, mercy, purity of heart, peace), and the seven Beatitudes.[3]

The tenth canon of the Fourth Lateran Council in 1215, comparable to the Second Vatican Council in our own time for its extensive reforms, had far-reaching theological and pastoral ramifications not only for sacramental practice but for catechesis. It directed bishops to appoint preachers and provide catechetical sermons in the vernacular that could be put in the hands of parish priests. The best-known catechetical sermons from the thirteenth century are the series of short instructions preached by Thomas Aquinas in the Neapolitan vernacular during Lent of 1273. He explained the Apostles' Creed, the Lord's Prayer, the Hail Mary, and the Decalogue in the context of the twofold commandment of love. He followed the order proposed by Augustine in the *Enchiridion*. At the beginning of the sermons on the Commandments he said, "Three things are necessary for salvation, knowledge of what must be believed; knowledge of what be hoped for; and knowledge of what must be done."[4]

Although Church councils and prelates continued to lament the ignorance of laity and clergy alike, Christianity permeated every aspect of medieval life. A careful reading of Chaucer's *Canterbury Tales* provides a window on the religious life and practices toward the end of the fourteenth century. The social calendar followed the liturgical cycle. Sundays were highlighted; Advent, Lent, the principal feasts of Our Lord and the Blessed Virgin Mary were holy days; and the feasts of patronal saints were the occasion for processions and celebrations. Great cathedrals, pilgrimage centers (as for example, the tomb of Thomas à Becket at Canterbury to which Chaucer's pilgrims were headed), and wayside shrines gave people a sense of sacred place. Popes, bishops, parish priests, and lesser clerics, together with abbots and abbesses, monks and nuns, and mendicant friars, all easily recognized by their distinctive garb, were everywhere. Popular piety and the cult of saints were powerful forces in the shaping of religious attitudes and values.

The ordinary people came to know biblical stories from hearing them recounted in sermons and seeing them illustrated in bas-reliefs, stained glass windows, paintings, and tapestries. The few who had the advantage of formal schooling, for the most part boys destined to become clerics, learned to read from primers (forerunners of textbooks). Chaucer in the Prioress's Tale describes a "litel clergeon seven years of age."

> This litel child, his litel book lernynge,
> As he sat in the scole at his *prymer.* . .[5]

There is some dispute as to whether the name *primer* was derived from "prime," the first of the canonical hours, or simply refers to *liber primarius,* the first book that a child used in learning to read. In any case, the earliest known examples were prayerbooks for laity. They included the Little Office of the Blessed Virgin, the Office of the Dead (vespers, matins, lauds), and the "gradual psalms" (psalms 119–33), the penitential psalms, and the Litany of Saints. To these were added a selection of devotional prayers that varied widely. The simpler version for school boys contained basic prayers, the Pater noster, Ave Maria, and Creed, and was prefaced by the alphabet. (As late as the eighteenth century, the lexicographer Samuel Johnson still defined the primer as "a small prayer-book in which children are taught to read.")[6]

## Catechisms in the Cause of Reform

The Church's preoccupation with orthodoxy and the deep faith of the people notwithstanding, popular piety, a powerful force in the shaping of religious attitudes and values, was mixed with a good deal of misinformation and superstition. The reform-minded archbishop of Canterbury, John Peckham (1279–92), attributed the poor state of the medieval Church in large part to the ignorance of the priests. At the Council of Lambeth in 1281 he promulgated a series of canons that was to become foundational legislation for later medieval directives on catechetical instruction in England. He commanded that every parish priest should review the fundamentals of the faith "four times a year, on one or more holy days." Using the vernacular every priest should himself or through another explain to the people simply and clearly the fourteen articles of the Creed, the Ten Commandments, the twofold precept of love of God and love of neighbor, the seven works of mercy, the seven deadly sins with their consequences, the seven cardinal virtues, and the seven sacraments of grace.[7]

### The Lay Folks' Catechism

In 1352, John Thoresby, Lord Chancellor of England and cardinal of the Roman Church, was named archbishop of York and "primate of England." (The archbishop of Canterbury is "primate of all England.") Like John Peckham seventy-six years earlier, Archbishop Thoresby lamented the carelessness and ignorance of the clergy, and based his hope of reformation on better and more frequent catechetical instruction. In 1357 the Convocation of York approved a series of ordinances very similar to the Lambeth canons of 1281 that outlined the contents and frequency of catechetical instruction. In order to insure that the ordinances be remembered and observed, Thoresby had John de Taystek (a.k.a. Gaytrige), a monk of York, translate them into English verse. He titled it *The Lay Folks' Catechism*. The translation, as much to assist poorly educated clergy as to benefit the laity, expands the original Latin text by explaining each point in some detail. The text runs 576 lines.

Ironically *The Lay Folks' Catechism* was written primarily not for the laity, but for the clergy. Parish priests were to instruct the faithful who in turn were to teach their children "if thai any haue" (line 64).

*The Lay Folks' Catechism* begins with a summary of the creation story and the fall. Because of sin, no one any longer has knowledge of God by natural gift but must learn about salvation in the Church. Blaming the widespread ignorance of doctrine on the clergy, the catechism ordains that on Sundays every parish priest teach and preach to the faithful in English. Their teaching was to cover "six things":

1. the fourteen points of the Creed;
2. the Ten Commandments;
3. the seven sacraments;
4. the seven works of mercy;
5. the seven virtues;
6. the seven deadly sins.

The explanation of the Creed subdivides the fourteen articles, according a common medieval practice, into two groups of seven, the first dealing with the Godhead, the second with Christ's humanity ("manhede"). The Ten Commandments, divided according to the two tables, the first three describing our duty to God, the second seven our duty toward fellow Christians, correspond to the twofold command of love in the gospel (ll. 258–59). The seven sacraments are listed in the following sequence: baptism, confirmation, penance, the sacrament of the altar, the last anointing, order, and matrimony. After listing the seven corporal works of mercy, the catechism enumerates the seven spiritual works in rhyme. Of the seven virtues that Holy Writ teaches the first three (faith, hope, charity) teach how to relate to God, the other four (justice, prudence, strength of mind and purpose, temperance) teach us how to live with regard to ourselves and to fellow Christians.

The annual confession "in the lentyn tyme" offered an occasion to review the catechism. *The Lay Folks' Catechism* directed that "parsons and vikers and al paroche prestes" inquire of penitents whether they knew the "sex thinges" (ll. 67–68). The confessor was to impose an additional penance on individuals who did not know them. There was no excuse for ignorance because the archbishop had ordered that "thai be shewed openly on inglis o-monges the folk" (ll. 75–76). On the other hand, the archbishop offers forty days' indulgence to all who could recite the six things. Through them, the catechism concludes, one knows God, knowledge of whom (as John says) "is endeles life and lastand blisse" (l. 575).

In addition to Taystek's translation there is also a Lollard version of *The Lay Folks' Catechism* attributed to John Wyclif (d. 1384), the "Morning Star of the Protestant Reformation." Wyclif's teachings on jurisdiction and authority cut at the roots of medieval theocracy. His followers, known as Lollards and "Poor Preachers," stirred unrest by popularizing his attacks on monks and friars, pilgrimages, and indulgences, and his call for reform of clerical living. Like Wyclif the Lollards urged that the Bible, the only criterion for Christian life and belief, be read in English.

The translation attributed to Wyclif is almost three times as long (1429 lines) as Taystek's because it interpolates long sections, several that reflect Lollard teachings.[8] Wyclif is closer to medieval practice than Taystek in that he includes an explanation of the seven petitions of the Lord's Prayer and the Hail Mary. (Lollard influence can be seen in the commentary on the latter: it criticizes the insertion of the names of Mary and Jesus into the biblical texts: "sythe godis lawe seys [th]at men schulde nat vp-on gret peyne. adde to goddys word" [l. 205].)

*ABC's of Simple Folk*

The late medieval figure who had the most lasting influence in the history of catechesis was Jean Gerson (1363–1429), theologian, reknowned preacher, and mystic. Much of his career took place against the backdrop of the Western Schism when there were two, then three men who laid claim to the papacy. It was the Avignon pope, Benedict XIII, who named Gerson chancellor of the University of Paris in 1395. Gerson took a leading role in the reform movement of the time, and proposed a plan to restructure the theological curriculum in the university. He was prominent in 1415 at the Council of Constance when Wyclif's teachings were posthumously condemned and John Huss was sentenced to death for heresy. Gerson spent the last decade of his life in Lyons, continuing to write while revising some of his earlier works. His collected works include several catechetical and pastoral treatises.

Gerson's writings and sermons reflect the gradual change from the Latin of the schools to the use of the vernacular. The pastoral and catechetical works he wrote in Latin were for the use of the clergy. The most widely read, his *Opus tripertitum (Opus in Three Parts)*, written in 1395, was addressed to four groups: simple or illiterate priests who hear confessions; unlearned people who are unable to participate regularly in Church instruction; children and youth in need of basic instruction; and individuals who visit hospitals and show concern for the sick. As the title indicates it consists of three parts. The first part explains the Decalogue; it is prefaced by a summary of Christian beliefs concerning creation, the Holy Trinity, the goal of human life, original sin, the incarnation, and redemption. The second part deals with confession. It stresses the examination of conscience with a recommendation to make a table listing the seven deadly sins that will assist penitents in recalling the number and kind of their sins. The third part was written for individuals who were at the point of death and for everyone concerned about a happy death. Gerson proposed that the teaching be transcribed on placards and posted, whole or in part, in public places such as parish churches, schools, hospitals, and holy places.[9]

A French work, *ABC des simples gens (ABC's of Simple Folk)*, obviously addressed to the laity, is in the tradition of the medieval *septenaria*. Without explanation, it lists the things Christians should know:

> the five bodily senses;
> the seven mortal (deadly) sins;
> the contrary virtues (humility, love of neighbor, industry, patience, etc.);
> the seven petitions of the Our Father;
> the Hail Mary;
> the Creed (twelve articles);
> the Ten Commandments;
> the seven virtues (faith, hope, charity; the moral virtues);
> the seven gifts of the Holy Spirit;
> the seven Beatitudes;
> the seven spiritual works of mercy;
> the seven corporal works of mercy;
> the seven orders (porter, lector, exorcist, etc.)
> the seven sacraments;
> the seven offshoots of penance (fasting, almsgiving, prayer, etc.)
> the seven privileges of the glory of paradise (three of the soul, four of the body);
> the four counsels of Christ;
> the principal joys of paradise (e.g., day without night, wisdom without error);
> the pains of hell.[10]

Presumably the list was to be memorized. Gerson refers the reader who would know more to other treatises and specifically to his *Opus tripertitum*. A similar list for parish priests adds the liturgical formulas for the sacraments and a list of reserved sins. Gerson did prepare a fuller explanation of the same topics in his *Doctrinal aux simples gens*, which he meant to be read by parish priests to their congregations.[11]

Gerson was an early representative of the new attitude towards the education of children that began to appear in the fifteenth century. Even during his term as university chancellor, he took time out to catechize children—a practice which some said was beneath the dignity of a university chancellor. Gerson defended himself in a small treatise *De parvulis ad Christum trahendis (Drawing the Little Ones to Christ)* in which he said he knew of no more important duty than, "with the help of God, to tear the souls of children from the jaws of the hell-bound and the doors of the inferno." Among the ways in which the young are led to Christ he lists: "Public preaching. Private admonition. The disciplining power of teachers. Finally, and most characteristic of the Christian religion, confession." Each of the four reflections that make up the treatise ends with reference to Mark 10:14, "Let the little children come to me; do not stop them; for it is to such as these that the kingdom of God belongs."[12]

## The Humanist Tradition

*Erasmus*

The early decades of the 1400s gave rise to an endless series of educational treatises. Scholars taken up with the revival of humanistic learning saw themselves as educators. They championed learning for its own sake and were advocates of improved teaching methods for boys and girls. The invention of the printing press in the middle of the century provided a means for disseminating both religious and secular treatises. Books took on new importance with the rise of literacy among the laity and the spread of secular learning.

Many humanists such as Jakob Wimpheling, Johann Agricola, and Erasmus of Rotterdam were also reform-minded. For them ignorance was the mortal foe of true religion. They held that ideally a Christian combined simple faith in Christ, readiness to serve him, and a virtuous life.

Erasmus, who more than anyone spread the educational ideals of the "new learning," was born near Rotterdam in 1466. The Brothers of the Common Life at Deventer, imbued with the evangelical spirit of the *devotio moderna* (the new piety), greatly influenced his formative years. Later he joined the Canons of St. Augustine at Steyn where he was ordained a priest (1492), but after leaving the monastery to serve as secretary to the bishop of Cambrai, he travelled widely, gaining the friendship of the leading humanists and scholars of the day. Although he was an outstanding representative of the sixteenth-century Renaissance, Erasmus did not break entirely from the past. The two traditions, the *devotio moderna* with its emphasis on personal devotion and morality, and the humanist program with its emphasis on learning and return to ancient sources, run through most of Erasmus's writings.

These traditions converge in an early treatise, one of Erasmus's most famous and influential works, *Enchiridion militis christiani (The Handbook of the Christian Soldier).*[13] In 1499 he paid his first visit to England where he began a lasting friendship with John Colet and Thomas More. At the time Colet, one of the first scholars to be attracted to the humanist ideals in England, was lecturing on the Epistles of St. Paul at Oxford. Colet's piety and fresh approach to the Scriptures inspired Erasmus and modelled the way to use the new learning for the moral guidance and the cause of reform. Shortly after this visit, Erasmus undertook the *Enchiridion,* addressed to a layman, a soldier whose wife feared he might fall away from the faith. Erasmus describes at some length the weapons that Christians must use and the rules that must guide them in their relentless struggle against sin. The necessary weapons are prayer and knowledge of Holy Scripture. Criticizing religious practices that consist of outward signs and the multiplication of devotions, he calls his readers back to the simplicity of the gospel and the inward love of God and neighbor. In this work as in his later writings Erasmus emphasized Christianity as a way of life rather than a body of doctrines.

His commitment to the new learning notwithstanding, Erasmus followed the fixed canon of medieval catechesis. It is seen in the *Enchiridion* in the emphasis he puts on virtue and vice, particularly the theological virtues and the deadly sins. It is also seen in a catechism for adults that he wrote three years before his death in 1536. *Dilucida et pia explanatio symboli . . . decalogi praeceptorum, et dominicae praecationis,* as the title suggests, proposes to provide a clear and pious explanation of the Creed, the Commandments, and the Lord's Prayer.

### John Colet's Catechyzon

In 1509 John Colet became dean of St. Paul's Cathedral. With wealth inherited from his father who had twice been lord mayor of London, he built and endowed St. Paul's School in 1518. Colet explained that his main purpose in founding St. Paul's was "to increase knowledge and worshipping of god and our lorde Crist Jesu and good Cristen lyff and maners in the children." To this end he directs that the boys at the school begin by learning the *Catechyzon* in English.[14]

Colet's *Catechyzon* blends the traditional contents of medieval catechesis and devotion with the emphasis on moral virtue of Christian humanism. It contains the Apostles' Creed, the seven sacraments, a brief explanation of charity, and emphasizes the need for penance, Holy Communion, and extreme unction. Then follows fifty short precepts, such as

> Fear God.
> Love God.
> Bridle the affections of thy mind.
> Believe and trust in Christ Jesu; Worship him and his mother
>     Mary.
> Use ofttime Confession.
> Love all men in God.

"By this way," Colet says, "thou shalt come to grace and glory." The book ends with the Latin text of the Apostles' Creed, the Lord's Prayer, the Angel's

Salutation (the Hail Mary), and two other prayers. Erasmus's often printed *Christiani hominis institutum (Instruction of the Christian)* was a paraphrase of Colet's *Catechyzon* in 137 hexameter verses.

Other humanists besides Colet produced instructional texts characterized by ample references to the New Testament, emphasis on Christian moral virtue, and personal piety. One of the better-known examples in this tradition was by the Spaniard Juan de Valdes, *Diálogo de doctrina cristiana (Dialogue on Christian Doctrine)*. Although it was published anonymously in Alcalá, the negative reaction to its Erasmian tendencies caused Valdes in 1529 to move to Naples where he gathered a devoted group of followers. Shortly after his death there in 1549, his *Alfabeto cristiano*, a catechism for children, appeared.[15]


**Transition**

The hundred and seventy years between the publication of Archbishop Thoresby's *The Lay Folks' Catechism* and John Colet's *Catechyzon* was time of great change. The Italian Renaissance transformed culture and had a great impact on the lifestyle of Christians, including popes and bishops. The fall of Constantinople to the Turks and the continued threat of Islam in the Eastern Mediterranean led to the exploration of new routes to India and the discovery of the Americas. The printing press, much like today's microprocessor, was both a product and a sign of the times. It opened new means of communications, promoted literacy, and advanced learning.

Church councils and reform-minded prelates like Peckham, Thoresby, and Gerson recognized the responsibility that the Church had to instruct the faithful. Formal catechesis, as sporadic and occasional as it was in many places, followed the set pattern that had its roots in the ancient catechumenate. In one way or another formal instruction emphasized the "six things" of *The Lay Folks' Catechism,* beginning with the articles of the Creed.

Although Christianity permeated medieval culture, the Middle Ages produced no significant work on the theory and practice of catechesis. Adults and children (unless they were clerics) were for the most part catechized together. The principal difference between the medieval forerunners of the catechism and the early humanist catechisms was that the former were written for use by the clergy in instructing the faithful while the latter were used by the laity for their own instruction and edification. Both took baptism and Eucharist for granted, and had little to say about sacraments. Medieval reformers were not satisfied with the religious knowledge and practice of their co-religionists, but their solution was simply to insist on more frequent and more systematic instruction. Humanists like Erasmus and Colet also saw the need for reform and the eradication of ignorance. Their solution was to open the Scriptures to everyone who could read, and foster inward love of God and neighbor. Along with their criticism of abuses and formalism, they gave people a new vision of what it meant to be Christian, and thus willy-nilly prepared the ground for the Protestant Reformation.

NOTES

1. For more on medieval catechesis see the essays by Milton McC. Gatch, "Basic Christian Education from the Decline of Catechesis to the Rise of the Catechisms," in O. C. Edwards and John H. Westerhoff, eds., *A Faithful Church* (Wilton, Conn.: Morehouse-Barlow, 1981) 99–101; Gerard S. Sloyan, "Religious Education from Early Christianity to Medieval Times," and Josef A. Jungmann, "Religious Education in Late Medieval Times," in G. S. Sloyan, ed., *Shaping the Christian Message* (Glen Rock, N.J.: Paulist, 1958) 11–45, 46–69; and Mariko M. Isomura, "Religious Education in Late Medieval England. A Historical Perspective," in *Year of Liturgical Studies* 2 (1961) 33–75.

2. Augustine, *Our Lord's Sermon on the Mount* 2.11.38 (Nicene and Post-Nicene Fathers, first series, 6:46).

3. J.-P. Migne, *Patrologia Latina* 175: 406–14.

4. Nicholas Ayo, ed. and trans., *The Sermon-Conferences of St. Thomas Aquinas on the Apostle Creed* (Notre Dame: University of Notre Dame, 1988).

5. Geoffrey Chaucer, "The Prioress's Tale," in *The Canterbury Tales,* ed. A. C. Cawley (London: Deut, 1958) 376 (lines 516–17).

6. Herbert Thurston, s.v. "Primer," in the *Catholic Encyclopedia.* Charles C. Butterworth, *The English Primers (1529–1545)* (Philadelphia: University of Pennsylvania, 1953) 1–10.

7. The Latin text of the Lambeth canons is given in Thos. Frederick Simmons and Henry Edward Nolloth, eds., *The Lay Folks' Catechism or the English and Latin Version of Archbishop Thoresby's Instruction for the People,* Early English Tract Society, original series 118 (London: Kegan Paul, Trench, Trubner, 1901) 5, 7, 21ff.

8. The volume in the Early English Text series edited by Simmons and Nolloth prints the Lollard version side by side with Taystek's translation. The words, spellings, and inflections of the two versions are quite different because the former used the orthography of a southern dialect, the latter of a northern dialect. See ibid., xxvii–xxix.

9. For the French text of the three works that make up the *Opus tripertitum,* see P. Glorieux, ed., *Jean Gerson. Oeuvres Complètes,* vol. 7 (Paris: Desclée, 1966) 193–206, 393–400, 404–7. They appear together under the heading *Opusculum tripertitum* in Lud. Ellies du Pin, ed., *Joannis Gersonii opera omnia,* Tom. primus (Antwerp, 1706) 426–50. For a general introduction to Gerson and his works see, D. Catherine Brown, *Pastor and Laity in the Theology of Jean Gerson* (New York: Cambridge University, 1987).

10. Glorieux, *Jean Gerson,* 7: 154–57.

11. Ibid., 10:366–69, 295–321. See Brown, *Pastor and Laity,* 48–51.

12. An English translation of Gerson's fourth argument can be found in Robert Ulich, *Three Thousand Years of Educational Wisdom* (Cambridge: Harvard University, 1950) 181–90.

13. An English translation and introduction can be found in John P. Dolan, ed., *The Essential Erasmus* (New York: New American Library, 1964) 28–93. Another by Ford Lewis Battles is in Matthew Spinka, ed., *Advocates of Reform from Wyclif to Erasmus,* The Library of Christian Classics 14 (Philadelphia: Westminster, 1953) 281–379.

14. Peter Iver Kaufman, "John Colet and Erasmus' *Enchiridion,*" *Church History* 46 (September 1977) 296–312. For a general introduction to Colet's works and a reinterpretation of his relationship to Erasmus see John B. Gleanson, *John Colet* (Berkeley: University of California, 1989).

15. Jose C. Nieto, ed., *Juan de Valdes, Two Catechisms: "Dialogue on Christian Doctrine" and the "Christian Instruction for Children."* trans. William B. Jones and Carol D. Jones (Lawrence, Kans.: Coronado, 1981).

TWO

# The Genre Takes Shape:
# Reformation Catechisms

In the sixteenth century reforming zeal and the printing press combined to shape the catechism and make it an instrument of reform. Luther took a literary genre that was just beginning to take shape and put his own stamp on it. The popular acceptance of his catechetical works caused other reformers, Protestant and Catholic, to emulate him. As a result, the catechism, which had begun as a pastoral manual, became a medium that, while ostensibly reaffirming traditional beliefs, subtly and not so subtly stressed doctrinal differences. The catechism began to appear in two forms: "large catechisms" that served as theological resources for pastors, preachers, and teachers, and "small catechisms" that served as manuals of instruction in the hands of clergy, schoolmasters, and parents. Children were expected to commit them to memory. After the publication of the Heidelberg Catechism in 1563, some large catechisms also served as litmus tests of doctrinal orthodoxy.[1]

## Luther's Catechisms

In April 1529 Luther published his *Deutsch Catechismus* (German Catechism), and in May the *Enchiridion: Der kleine Catechismus* (Small Catechism). (In order to keep them distinct, the first came to be called the Large Catechism.) They were the fruit of the pastoral work Luther had begun before his break with Rome. Between 1516 and 1529 he preached and taught clergy and laity (adults and children), published a number of catechetical works distilled from his sermons, and encouraged his followers to do likewise.

In 1516 Luther preached a series of sermons on the Ten Commandments, and in Lent of the following year, a series on the Lord's Prayer. In 1518 he had a poster printed with the heading, "A Short Explanation of the Ten Commandments," as an aid to assist laity preparing for confession. The two series that Luther preached in 1516–17, first published in 1519 as a guide for other preachers, was reprinted several times, and eventually served as the basis for his "Short Form for Understanding the Decalogue, Creed, and Lord's Prayer." Later he incorporated this "Short Form" in his popular *Betbuchlein;* first published in 1522, this "Small Prayer Book" went through thirty-five German and two Latin editions in the next twenty-five years.

Luther recommended that the *Betbuchlein* be used as a basis of instruction, for he was realistic enough to know that "many a person listens to sermons for three or four years and never learns to give answer for even one essential article of faith, as I have discovered every day. Enough has been written in books, but it hasn't been written in the heart."[2] In the preface to the 1525 German Mass Luther urged a question-answer approach, but he was not satisfied with rote memorization. Children and servants, he said, must "be questioned point by point and give answer what each part means and how they understand it." Suggesting ways that the questioning might proceed, Luther recommended, "One may take these questions from our *Betbuchlein* where the three parts are briefly explained, or make others, until the heart may grasp the whole sum of Christian truth under two headings or, as it were, pouches, namely, faith and love."[3]

The immediate occasion that caused Luther to undertake the writing of the Large Catechism and the Small Catechism was a visitation he made in 1528 of the evangelical parishes in Saxony shortly after the disastrous Peasants' War. He used the visitation to deliver three series of sermons according to the medieval pattern of Commandments, Creed, and the seven petitions of the Lord's Prayer, to which he joined sermons on baptism and the Lord's Supper.

In his introductory sermon on the Creed, Luther explains the threefold division of the Creed that later appears in the Small Catechism:

> In former times you heard preaching on twelve articles of the Creed. If anybody wants to divide it up, he could find even more. You, however, should divide the Creed into the main parts indicated by the fact that there are three persons: God the Father, Son, and Holy Spirit. . . . The children and uneducated people should learn this in the simplest fashion: the Creed has three articles, the first concerning the Father, the second concerning the Son, the third concerning the Holy Spirit. What do you believe about the Father? Answer: He is the creator. About the Son? He is the redeemer. About the Holy Spirit? He is the sanctifier. For educated people one could divide the articles into as many parts as there are words in it. But now I want to teach the uneducated and the children.[4]

The first edition of the Large Catechism was published in mid-April and a second edition later in the year. Meanwhile Luther was at work on the Small Catechism. The latter had begun as a series of posters on the Decalogue, Creed, and Lord's Prayer. Posters four and five covered the morning and evening prayers, the *Benedictus* and *Gratias* (prayer of thanksgiving); posters six and seven focused on baptism and the Lord's Supper. When published in book form in May 1529, Luther added a preface and a table of duties patterned after Jean Gerson's "Concerning the Manner of Life for All Believers." (The printer added sections on baptism and marriage, incorporating two booklets written earlier by Luther.)[5] Twenty woodcuts by Cranach illustrated the text. The third edition, edited by Luther in 1529, contained a "Short Form for Confession" by way of introduction to the fifth part on the Lord's Supper,* and a litany of music and a series of appendices of a doctrinal or liturgical character: a collection of family prayers, a table of duties consisting of Scripture passages (1 Tim 3:2ff.; Rom 13:1ff.; Col 3:19ff.; Eph 6:1ff.), a marriage manual, and a baptismal manual. It ran to 120 pages.

Luther's preface to the Small Catechism clearly stated its purpose. Addressed to the lower clergy, he declared that in their hands the catechism would be an instrument to instruct the religiously uneducated laity. Luther wanted to reach the whole populace. In the patriarchal society of the time, the landed farmer was held responsible for the spiritual welfare of his household of servants and children. According to Luther, a person who did not know the fundamentals of the catechism had no right to be called a Christian nor to live in a principality that, through its clergy and government leaders, was committed to evangelical doctrine.

The popularity of the Small Catechism owed much to Luther's talent for going to the heart of the matter and explaining serious issues with the utmost simplicity. For example, he followed the canon of medieval catechesis, with three notable innovations. The first was to reorder the sequence, explaining the Commandments before the Creed and the Lord's Prayer; thus the catechism conformed to his law-gospel paradigm. The Commandments indict people, bringing them to know themselves as corrupt and guilty of sin. They teach people to recognize their illness and to come to grips with what they can and cannot do for themselves. The Creed presents God and the mercy God has offered in Christ. It teaches individuals where they can find the remedy, the grace

---

*Luther, unlike the Calvinists, valued private confession and absolution. In the Articles of Smalcald (1537) he wrote, "True absolution or the power of the keys, instituted in the Gospel by Christ, affords comfort and support against sin and an evil conscience. Confession or absolution shall by no means be abolished in the Church, but be retained on account of weak and timid consciences, *and also on account of untutored youth, in order that they may be examined and instructed in the Christian doctrine.* But the enumeration of sins should be free to every one, to enumerate or not to enumerate such as he wishes." Quoted in Schaff, *Creeds* 1:249 (emphasis added). After 1564 an enlarged section, "Confession and Absolution, or the Power of the Keys," was inserted either as part 5 between baptism and the Lord's Supper, as part 6, or as an appendix.

that justifies and heals them and helps them keep the Commandments. Finally, the Lord's Prayer teaches Christians how to ask for God's grace and to appropriate it.

The second innovation was to explain the Creed in three brief questions. Medieval writers customarily divided the Creed into twelve articles (according to the old legend that it was a joint composition of the Twelve Apostles) or, as did *The Lay Folks' Catechism,* into fourteen articles (two sets of seven, the first dealing with the Godhead and things eternal, the second, with Christ's humanity and his work in time). As he noted in the 1528 sermon quoted above, Luther wanted to simplify the message for the uneducated and children. His division of the Creed into three articles had the advantage of highlighting the Holy Trinity and the threefold theme of creation, redemption, and sanctification.

Although the third innovation had more to do with form than content, it was significant in the development of the catechism genre. Luther seems to have been influenced by the question-answer method of teaching used by the Bohemian Brethren—the *Unitas Fratrum.* German translations of an instructional book that dates from about 1500 in the original Czech were in circulation by 1522. The *Kinderfragen (Children's Questions)* had much in common with traditional medieval catechesis, but the style was different.

A number of his disciples composed catechetical works, but it was Luther's own Small Catechism that became the standard. Within a year of its appearance it was translated into Latin and Low German, and before the end of the century it had been translated into Bohemian, Danish, Dutch, Estonian, Finnish, French, Icelandic, Italian, Lettish, Greek, Polish, Old Prussian, Slovenish, Spanish, Swedish, and Wendish. Thomas Cranmer, the future archbishop of Canterbury, was the first to render it into English, adding it to his translation of Andreas Osiander's *Kinderpredigten (Children's Sermons)* in 1548.

Although Luther saw the Small Catechism chiefly as a beginning, he recognized that many would never progress much beyond it. He left it to pastors and preachers to offer further explanations of the gospel and to apply them to daily life, and it was for them that he compiled the Large Catechism. Based on Luther's own catechetical sermons, it directs the clergy on how they might address the needs of practical Christian living. Luther exhorted pastors to lifelong, daily study of the catechism because no one ever outgrows it. He substituted a new preface to the 1530 edition of the Large Catechism, in which he wrote that he recited the Lord's Prayer, the Ten Commandments, the Creed, and psalms every morning "and whenever else I have time." He added, "I cannot master it as I wish, but [I] remain a child and pupil of the Catechism" always. William Haugaard remarks that "Luther is not merely commending a salutary devotional practice; rather he is urging inadequately instructed and insufficiently motivated priests to use this and similar materials to inform their own grasp of theology and to guide them in teaching others."[6]

## John Calvin's *Geneva Catechism*

The Protestant Reformation was not a unified movement. Reformers in Switzerland and along the Rhine who followed Luther's lead in challenging medieval practices and Scholastic theology did not always agree with him with regard to doctrine. The "sacramentarians" (Luther's name for theologians who denied the real presence of Christ in the Eucharist), under the influence of Ulrich Zwingli, propagated their teachings in catechetical works that set them apart from Luther on the one hand and from Roman Catholics on the other. Two catechisms that gained international favor and exercised lasting influence were the Geneva Catechism of John Calvin (1541) and the Heidelberg Catechism (1563), which became the doctrinal standard of the Reformed Churches.

Among the reform ordinances that William Farel and John Calvin attempted to introduce in Geneva in January 1537 was one governing the instruction of children. It spoke of a practice "in ancient days," when "a definite catechism was used for initiating each one in the fundamentals of the Christian religion," which provided a formula that each child could use to declare his Christian beliefs. Thus the ordinance proposed

> that there be a brief and simple summary of the Christian faith, to be taught to all children, and that at certain seasons of the year they come before the ministers to be interrogated and examined, and to receive more ample explanation . . . until they have been proved sufficiently instructed. But may it be your pleasure to command parents to exercise pains and diligence that their children learn this summary. . . .[7]

To provide such a formula Calvin undertook to compose, at Farel's suggestion, a catechism in the French language. Based on the first edition of Calvin's *Christianae religionis institutio,* published the previous year, the work provided a constructive, non-polemical exposition of the reformed faith explained in thirty-three brief chapters.[8]

Geneva was not ready for reform, at least as Farel and Calvin conceived it, and in the spring of 1538 the city council voted them into exile. Calvin spent the next three years in Strasbourg, where his thought matured and he continued to write. By 1541 the political climate in Geneva had changed, and the people invited him back. He set immediately to work with the city's council to draft ecclesiastical ordinances that codified his plan of reform, and to compose an expanded catechism.

The new ordinances directed citizens and inhabitants of the city to bring "their children on Sundays at midday to Catechism." "The Order to be observed in the case of little Children" continued,

> A definite formulary be composed by which they will be instructed, and on this, with the teaching given them examined, they are to be interrogated about what has been said, to see if they have listened and remembered well.
>
> When a child has been well enough instructed to pass the Catechism, he is to recite solemnly the sum of what it contains, and also to make profession of his Christianity in the presence of the Church.
>
> Before this is done, no child is to be admitted to receive the Supper. . . .[9]

Calvin wrote the catechism in haste without a chance to revise the text because the printer set it in type as the pages came from his pen. The French text, *Le catéchisme de l'Église de Geneve,* was ready in 1541 or 1542, and a Latin edition in 1545.

It adapted and rearranged the material of the 1537 *Instruction,* and cast it in the form of questions and answers. The French text carried notes that distributed the contents of the catechism to fifty-five Sundays.

In the foreword to the Latin edition, "To the Reader," Calvin wrote,

> It has always been a practice and diligent care of the Church, that children be rightly brought up in Christian doctrine. To do this more conveniently, not only were schools formerly opened and individuals enjoined to teach their families properly, but also it was accepted public custom and practice to examine children in Churches concerning the specific points which should be common to all Christians. That this be done in order, a formula was written out, called Catechism or Institute. After this, the devil . . . subverted this sacred policy; nor did he leave surviving anything more than certain trivialities, which give rise only to superstitions, without any edifying fruit. Of this kind is that Confirmation, as they call it, made up of gesticulations which are more than ridiculous and suited rather to monkeys, and rest on no foundation. What we now bring forward, therefore, is nothing else than the use of a practice formerly observed by Christians and the true worshippers of God, and never neglected until the Church was wholly corrupted.[10]

When compared to Calvin's 1537 catechism the most obvious innovation in the 1541 edition is the question-answer format. Most often the minister draws information out of the child, but sometimes he uses the inquiry to make a statement and the child simply affirms the doctrine. The extended comment of the Minister concerning the prohibition of the second Commandment against graven images is an illustration:

> *M:* We are not then to understand that these words simply condemn every picture and sculpture whatever. Rather we are forbidden to make images for the purpose of seeking or worshipping God in them, or, what is the same thing, worshipping them in honor of God, or of abusing them at all for superstition or idolatry.
>
> *C:* Quite right. *[Verum.]*[11]

Calvin follows the medieval canon in identifying four parts in the catechism, concerning faith (the Creed), the Law (Commandments), prayer, and sacraments, but he also introduces subdivisions that differ from Luther's catechism and what had gone before. In the first part, for example, the child is asked to repeat the Apostles' Creed, and then before explaining each phrase the minister asks, "To understand the several points more thoroughly—into how many parts shall we divide this Confession?" The child responds, "Into four principal parts," and then is asked to name them: *"C:* The first refers to God the Father; the second concerns his Son Jesus Christ, and also includes the sum of man's redemption. The third part concerns the Holy Spirit; the fourth the Church and the divine benefits vouchsafed to it."[12] The catechism explains the Law by describing the obligations taught by each of the Ten Commandments, but here Calvin introduces an enumeration followed by the Greek Fathers that to this day differentiates the Protestant listing from that of Catholics who continue to follow the Latin tradition codified by St. Augustine.*

An underlying theme in the 1541 Geneva Catechism is divine worship. Each part of the catechism focuses on a different aspect. The first part, in speaking of the "whole doctrine of the Gospel," describes faith and repentance as a part of divine worship. A second part consists in service and obedience explained by the Law. The third part, the proper worship of God's divinity, is found in prayer, the most perfect expression of which is the Lord's Prayer. Here again Calvin innovates, abandoning the sevenfold petitions in favor of a divi-

---

*Two different pericopes in the Hebrew Scriptures list the "Ten Commandments," Exod 20:1-17 and Deut 5:6-21. They differ from each other in the motives they assign for Sabbath observance, and in their consideration of a man's wife. In Exodus a man's wife is classified with his possessions, whereas in Deuteronomy she is placed first, apart from the servants and property. The Jewish Rabbinic tradition, which follows Exodus, adopted by St. Jerome and the Greek Fathers, splits the prohibition against false worship into a ban against graven images and the vain use of the divine name. Thus the enumeration of the subsequent Commandments also differs, e.g., in the Protestant listing, observance of the Sabbath is regulated by the Fourth Commandment, in the Catholic listing and Luther's catechisms, by the Third.

sion into six "of which the first three refer to God's glory," and the remaining three "refer to ourselves and consider our interest."[13] The fourth part of divine worship consists of "the outward attestation of the divine benevolence towards us" that represents "spiritual grace symbolically, to seal the promises of God in our hearts, by which the truth of them is better confirmed." Calvin recognizes only the two sacraments of baptism and the Lord's Supper.[14]

Calvin's stated purpose in writing this catechism was to make the unity of faith shine forth. In the preface he justifies his writing in Latin, stating, "in this confused and divided state of Christendom, I judge it useful to have public testimonies by which Churches, that agree in Christian doctrine though widely separated in space, may mutually recognize each other." He goes on to say,

> There are other kinds of writing to show what are our views in all matters of religion; but what agreement in doctrine our Churches had among themselves cannot be observed with clearer evidence than from the Catechisms. For in them there appears not only what someone or another once taught, but what were the rudiments with which both the learned and unlearned among us were from youth constantly instructed, all the faithful holding them as the solemn symbol of Christian communion.[15]

Although Calvin's catechism never gained the popularity of Luther's, and was gradually displaced in the Reformed tradition by the Heidelberg and Westminster catechisms, it exercised pervasive influence in the early years of the Reformation.

## The Heidelberg Catechism

Luther saw the catechism, at least in its shorter form, as a pedagogical tool. Pastors and parents were to use it to instruct children and the uneducated. It offered a simple and direct introduction to the rudiments of Christian faith. Calvin saw it as something more, a symbol of unity and a means of testing the fitness of children who would participate in the Lord's Supper. In the hands of Frederick III, elector of the Palatinate, the catechism came to serve still another purpose. The Heidelberg Catechism commissioned by Frederick became the touchstone of orthodoxy and the centerpiece of religious instruction in the Reformed tradition.

About the time in 1559 when Frederick became the ruler of the Palatinate, the most influential of the German principalities, smoldering differences among the reformers broke into open flame. Frederick's predecessors had endorsed the Confession of Augsburg and had reorganized the Church according to a plan devised in consultation with Philip Melanchthon (himself a native of the Palatinate), but the reform leaders could not agree on the form of the liturgy and the doctrine of the Lord's Supper. Frederick, though attracted to the cause of the Protestant reformers, was by temperament an irenic ruler. He arranged a debate to air the issues. Lutheran theologians of various stripes disputed with theologians who were of the mind of John Calvin and Henry Bullinger, Zwingli's son-in-law and successor in Zürich. The latter group won Frederick to their views because, he said, their arguments were more biblical.

The Heidelberg Catechism was to be a principal instrument in Frederick's strategy to consolidate reformation efforts in the Palatinate. He appreciated the popular appeal of Luther's Small Catechism but regarded it as too general and too brief to serve as the doctrinal basis for a systematic program of religious instruction. Further, he wanted a standard of doctrine that, though basically Calvinist, would not alienate Lutherans. The one point, however, on which he was unwilling to compromise was the doctrine of the Lord's Supper.

The Heidelberg Catechism was the work of a number of hands, but the text is commonly associated with the names of Zacharias Ursinus and Caspar Olevianus, the former contributing the content, the latter the form. Ursinus had spent seven years under the tutelage of Philip Melanchthon and later toured the principal centers of Reformed theology, meeting Bullinger in Zürich and Calvin in Geneva. Although Ursinus was only twenty-eight at the time, he was already the author of two catechisms: *Summa theologiae,* containing 323 questions, and *Catechesis minor,* a condensation in 108 questions.[16]

The Heidelberg Catechism went through four editions in the first year. The first edition had a preface by Frederick in which he described it as "a fixed form and model" that ministers and schoolmasters were to use in instructing young and old, eschewing capricious changes and private opinion. Unlike most other catechisms of the time that used questions and answers, the Heidelberg Catechism numbered the questions. There were 129 questions in the later editions that added the notorious eightieth question, which condemned the Roman Mass and the doctrine of the Real Presence:

> Q.  What difference is there between the Lord's Supper and the Popish Mass?
>
> A.  The Lord's Supper testifies to us that we have full forgiveness of all our sins by the one sacrifice of Jesus Christ, which he himself has once accomplished on the cross. . . . But the Mass teaches that the living and the dead have not forgiveness of sins through the sufferings of Christ unless Christ is still daily offered for them by the priests; and that Christ is bodily under the form of bread and wine, and is therefore to be worshipped in them. And thus the Mass at bottom is nothing else than a denial of the one sacrifice and passion of Jesus Christ and an accursed idolatry.

It was added at Frederick's order, an obvious rejoinder to session 22 of the Council of Trent (1562) which affirmed the sacrificial character of the Mass and anathematized anyone who said otherwise.[17]

The fourth edition was published as an integral part of the Church ordinances, placed between the formularies for baptism and Holy Communion. This meant, writes Thomas Torrance, "that faith and order, doctrine and worship, were intentionally held together in unity, with the result that if the Catechism supplies the norm for the life and liturgy of the Church, it is no less true that its doctrinal instruction cannot be divorced from the daily worship of the Community."[18]

The Protestant Reformation had been underway more than forty years before Ursinus moved to Heidelberg. Unlike the first generation of reformers who willy-nilly had been formed in the tradition of late medieval Catholicism, Ursinus's challenge was to find a *via media* between Luther and Calvin. Hendrikus Berkhof says, "The real reformation of the catechetical tradition was reserved to Ursinus in his creation of the Heidelberg Catechism." The Heidelberg Catechism preserved the rudiments of the old catechesis—Creed, Commandments, and prayer—but made them serve a different purpose by situating them under the headings of "Misery," "Redemption," and "Gratitude." In Heidelberg's tripartite division the Law is treated at the beginning and the end in an evident effort to reconcile Lutheran and Calvinist views. Under "Misery" the Law is presented as a reminder of human wretchedness and an indictment for sin; under "Gratitude," it is presented as a teacher of righteous living. The Creed, together with an explanation of sacraments, is subsumed under "Redemption." The third part presents prayer as the principal expression of gratitude and explains the petitions of the Lord's Prayer. (Heidelberg follows Calvin in identifying six petitions.) "This tripartite composition," according to Berkhof, "transfers the whole content of faith from the sphere of objective credenda in which it had been located for centuries to the sphere of personal confession, decision, and action."[19]

Despite Elector Frederick's stated purpose, the catechism proved too difficult for children. In 1585 the then elector, John Casimir, published the Little Heidelberg Catechism. In the introduction Casimir declares that "various questions in the large catechism seem to be too long or too difficult for the common man and for the youth."[20]

The Heidelberg Catechism was translated into English early and often. A translation, based on the Latin text and accompanied by notes, was issued by the authority of the king for the use of the Church of Scotland in 1591; another translation was "appointed to be printed for use of the Kirk of Edinburgh" in 1615.[21] In the United States, where the Heidelberg Catechism is part of the tradition of the German Reformed Church and the Dutch Reformed Church, the English translations are based on the original German text.

## Test of Orthodoxy and Symbol of Discord

By endowing the Heidelberg Catechism with official status as the creedal norm of the Church in the Palatinate, Frederick III set a precedent. The Formula of Concord (1576), which became a part of the *Book of Concord* (1580), the standard of Lutheran orthodoxy, declared "we publicly profess that we also receive Dr. Luther's Smaller and Larger Catechisms as they are included in Luther's works, because we judge them to be, as it were, the Bible of the laity, in which all those things are briefly comprehended which in the Holy Scripture are treated more at length, and the knowledge of which is necessary to a Christian man for his eternal salvation." The Heidelberg Catechism was also a precedent for the Catechism of the Council of Trent (1566) and later for the Westminster Catechism, which became norms of orthodox teaching among Roman Catholics and Presbyterians respectively.

William Haugaard cites the dedication that Calvin composed for the Latin edition of the Geneva Catechism, quoted above. It may well be that no other writing witnesses to the doctrinal agreement of Churches more clearly than the catechism, but Haugaard comments, "Calvin might declare a catechism to be a symbol of Christian communion, and Lutherans might entitle their symbolic tome a *Book of Concord,* but the catechisms serve as well as symbols of Christian division and instruments of discord."[22] In that same dedication Calvin makes the success of Church reform rest on "the rightful return and use of Catechism, abolished centuries ago under the papacy." Whatever must be said of Calvin's allegation, the next chapters show that the papacy too looked to the catechism as a means of reform.

NOTES

1. For a bibliography and good survey of this period, see William P. Haugaard, "The Continental Reformation of the Sixteenth Century," in Edwards and Westerhoff, *A Faithful Church,* 109–73. Also, Ferdinand Cohrs, "Catechisms," in *The New Shaff-Herzog Encyclopedia of Religious Knowledge,* ed. Samuel Macauley Jackson.

2. Quoted by Gustav K. Wiencke, s.v. "Catechisms," in *The Encyclopedia of the Lutheran Church.*

3. Quoted by Haugaard, "Continental Reformation," 122.

4. Quoted in John Dillenberger, ed., *Martin Luther. Selections from His Writings* (Garden City, N.Y.: Anchor 1961) 208. The full text of the sermons can be found in *Luther's Works,* vol. 51 (Philadelphia: Muhlenberg, 1959) 162–93.

5. Heinrich Bornkamm, *Luther in Mid-Career 1521–1530* (Philadelphia: Fortress, 1983) 602–3.

6. Haugaard, "Continental Reformation," 123.

7. J. K. S. Reid, ed., *Calvin: Theological Treatises*, The Library of Christian Classics (Philadelphia: Westminster, 1954). An English translation of the "Articles concerning the Organization of the Church and Worship at Geneva proposed by the Ministers at the Council, January 16, 1537," are found on pp. 47–55. The text quoted appears on p. 54.

8. See John Calvin, *Instruction in Faith* (1537), trans. and ed. by Paul T. Fuhrmann, foreword by John H. Leith (Louisville: Westminster/John Knox, 1992). Calvin also published a "confession of faith," consisting of twenty-nine articles, which was to be binding on all the citizens of Geneva. Though it corresponds closely to the 1537 *Instruction,* the "confessio fidei" seems to have been compiled earlier. See Philip Schaff, ed., *The Creeds of Christendom,* sixth edition revised by David S. Schaff (Grand Rapids, Mich.: Baker, 1983 [reprint from the 1931 edition published by Harper & Row]); 1:468 n. 1.

9. Reid, *Calvin: Theological Treatises,* 69. Some modification of the ordinances was made for churches in villages outside the city. "The Ordinances for the Supervision of Church in the Country, February 3, 1547" stated, "Because each preacher has two parishes, Catechism is to take place each fortnight" (ibid., 77).

10. An English translation of the 1541 Geneva Catechism with an introduction can be found in ibid., 83–139. The above quote appears on p. 88.

11. Ibid., 109. See 84.

12. Ibid., 93.

13. Ibid., 123.

14. The older versions title the fourth part "De sacramentis." Theodore Beza, however, subdivides this section into "De Verbo Dei" and "De sacramentis." See ibid., 129 n. 5.

15. Ibid., 89, 90.

16. See Bard Thompson, in Bard Thompson et al., *Essays on the Heidelberg Catechism* (Philadelphia/Boston: United Church, 1963) 24–27.

17. The German text of the Heidelberg Catechism with an English translation can be found in Schaff, *The Creeds of Christendom,* 3: 307–55. See Schaff's note on the eightieth question, p. 336.

18. Thomas F. Torrance, *The School of Faith: The Catechisms of the Reformed Church* (London: James Clarke, 1959) 67.

19. Thompson et al., *Essays,* 86.

20. Quoted in ibid., 88.

21. Torrance, *The School of Faith,* 67.

22. Haugaard, "Continental Reformation," 131.

# THREE

# Four Pillars of Catechesis:
# The Catechism of the Council of Trent

As a whole, Catholics were slow in responding to Luther's demand for re-form. He had called for a general council as early as 1521, but it was not until December 1545, the year before he died, that the Council of Trent convened. Despite the initial reluctance of Rome to convoke a general council, Trent be-came the centerpiece of the Catholic reform effort.

The Council of Trent takes its name from the Alpine town where it met over a period of seventeen years, December 1545 to December 1563. Except for a brief interlude in 1547 when the council was transferred to Bologna because of an outbreak of typhus in Trent, all its twenty-five sessions were held there. In the course of the council, the question of a catechism surfaced several times, but there was little agreement as to the purpose it would serve or the audience to whom it would be directed. Historians identify three stages in the develop-ment of the Tridentine catechism: (1) in the early sessions of the council, when the catechism was proposed as a remedy for the widespread ignorance in the Church; (2) in the last period of the council, when a commission was formed to work on a catechism, though the council ended with the project being re-manded to the pope; and (3) the actual compilation of the catechism in the pe-riod following the close of council.[1]

### Antidote for Ignorance or Pastoral Guide?

The handful of bishops—thirty-four—who attended the beginning of the council spent the first weeks establishing procedures and apportioning work among various commissions. The first mention of a catechism surfaced in con-nection with the debate over the Bible and preaching. Participants at the coun-cil acknowledged that the faithful, clergy and laity, were woefully ignorant of the Sacred Scriptures. People avidly pursued secular studies while they neg-lected the study of Sacred Scripture. As a result, "children have no chance to learn, either from their parents or their teachers, what being a Christian means." In its report on 5 April 1546, the conciliar commission set up to examine the situation recommended two antidotes to remedy the widespread ignorance of clergy and laity. The first proposal called for the compilation of a short introduction to theology that would include a *methodus,* that is, "a comprehensive and coherent plan" to guide the pastoral clergy in studying and preaching the Scriptures. There was a great deal of debate as to the shape and contents of this compendium, but the underlying premise was that by raising the level of the theological formation of clergy, preaching and religious instruction of the people would improve.[2]

The second proposal recommended a catechism adapted to the needs of children and uneducated adults. Drawing on the Holy Scriptures and the writings of the Church Fathers, the catechism would be used as a guide to explain the profession of faith made at baptism and as an introduction to the Bible itself. The catechism would be written in Latin and translated into vernacular languages. Although there was a good deal of discussion, the council took no steps to implement either proposal.

In Bologna in 1547 the discussions turned to sacraments. The nature and number of sacraments was a divisive issue between Catholics and Protestants and among Protestants themselves. Catholic reformers for their part were concerned about abuses in the administration of the sacraments of baptism, confirmation, the Eucharist, and penance. It was in this context that support for the issuance of a catechism began to build. In November 1547, two months before the council suspended its deliberations, the bishops voted almost unanimously in favor of a *libellus catechismi* that would contain everything the clergy needed to know for celebrating the sacraments. The six-man commission appointed to compile it faded away without producing a text.

## Guarantee of Orthodoxy

Fifteen years passed before the topic was taken up again, but when the council reconvened at Trent in 1562, many influential voices urged the preparation of some kind of catechism. All agreed that the catechism should be an instrument for insuring orthodoxy, but they had different views as to what form it would take. Some prelates pictured it as a compendium of Catholic doctrine; some wanted a *postilla,* an official homilary that contained catechetical instructions and explanations of the Sunday gospel readings; and a third group spoke of an *agenda,* a directory for liturgical practice. In and out of the council there were many who advocated two catechisms, a large one for the use of teachers and pastors, and a small one that children and the illiterate could learn by heart.

Ferdinand I of Austria, the emperor's brother, instructed the imperial legates to insist that the council compile a *corpus doctrinae christianae*. Short or long, he saw it as a resource for doctors, pastors, and preachers, as well as teachers and headmasters of schools, an instrument that would help them refute heresy. The papal legates, not wanting to bring the matter before the entire assembly, gave the task to the commission that they had appointed to revise the *Index of Prohibited Books*—a prudential move because under Pope Paul IV the *Index* had censured a number of catechisms by Catholic authors.

Through the summer of 1563, as the council was winding down, a number of theologians were assigned to draft texts on articles of the Creed, sacraments, Commandments, and the Lord's Prayer. Their work was submitted to a new *deputatio* (committee) which was to edit it and submit a final draft to the council for formal approval. Meanwhile a series of reform decrees was being readied for discussion. In the form they were approved at the twenty-fourth session (11 November 1563), canon 7 charged bishops and parish priests with the responsibility of explaining the sacraments, "before they administer them to people . . . in the vernacular tongue . . . according to the form laid down by the holy council for each sacrament." Then it adds, "Similarly, during mass or the celebration of office on every feast or solemnity they should explain the divine commandments and precepts of salvation in the vernacular, and should be zealous to implant them in the hearts of all (leaving aside useless questions) and educate them in the law of the Lord."[3]

The *deputatio* working on the text of the catechism had not finished its task by the end of the council. In the final session, 4 December 1563, the council bishops handed the catechism project, along with proposals for the revision of the *Index of Prohibited Books,* missal and breviary, over to Pope Pius IV to complete and publish.[4]

## Compiling the Text

The third stage in the development of the Tridentine catechism was the actual writing of the text. Charles Borromeo, the cardinal nephew of Pius IV, is generally credited with coordinating the project, but the writing became the task of four men who had participated in the last sessions of the council. The group included three bishops, Muzio Calini, archbishop of Zara (Dalmatia), Egidio Foscarari, bishop of Modena, and Leonardo de Marini, bishop of Lanciano. Calini had been a member of the *deputatio* that worked on the catechism before the council ended. The fourth member of the team was the Portuguese theologian Francisco Foreiro, who had served as secretary of the conciliar commission of the *Index* at Trent. Foscarari, Marini, and Foreiro, Dominican friars all, were steeped in the Thomistic tradition.

A draft of the catechism, ready in the fall of 1564, was given over to the Latinist Julius Poggiano for editing and refinement of style. Some emendations, dealing mostly with revising biblical, patristic, and magisterial quotations, were added by Cardinal Guglielmo Sirleto and Bishop Mariano Vittori of the Vatican library. The death of Pius IV, on 10 December 1565, however, delayed the publication until September 1566. When it finally appeared under his successor, the title page read *Catechismus ex decreto Concilii Tridentini ad Parochos Pii V., Pontificis Max. Jussu Editus (A Catechism for Pastors by Decree of the Council of Trent Published by Order of Pius V, Supreme Pontiff)*. Because of its papal authorization and place of publication it became known simply as the "Roman Catechism." An Italian translation appeared that same year, and a short time later, Spanish, Portuguese, German, Polish, and French translations were in circulation. The first known English translation, by Jeremy Donovan, a professor at Maynooth, was printed in Dublin (1829).*

## The Four Pillars

The four-part catechism follows an outline based on directives of the Council of Trent: (1) faith and the Apostles' Creed, (2) sacraments, (3) Ten Commandments and divine law, and (4) the nature and necessity of prayer. Its structure is clear and orderly, but it does not attempt to offer a systematic theology. The authors acknowledged that it was not possible to include all the doctrines of the Catholic faith in one volume. The purpose of the catechism was simply "to instruct pastors, and others who have the care of souls, in those things that belong properly to pastoral care and are accommodated to the capacity of the faithful." It was intended as a handbook for clergy, and only included material calculated to assist them in instructing the faithful.

The preface lays down broad principles that ground catechetical content and method. The sum of Christian doctrine is knowledge and imitation of Christ. Christian education is to foster virtuous living, and "motivate the faithful to a love of God's infinite goodness towards us." The way one teaches is important; instruction must be accommodated to "the natural ability, cultural background and particular circumstances" of the hearers. Pastors must discern who needs milk and who is ready for more solid food. "The whole teaching of

---

*Another English translation (1923), by John A. McHugh, O.P., and Charles Callan, O.P., stayed closer to the letter of the Latin text than Donovan's. Despite its long periodic sentences and drab layout, it remained in print until the eve of Vatican II. The fifteenth printing is dated 1958. A more recent English edition, by Robert I. Bradley, S.J., and Eugene Kevane (Boston: St. Paul Editions, 1984) retrieves the subheading of the early Latin editions and is generally more readable than the McHugh-Callan version. The Bradley-Kevane translation is the one quoted in these pages.

Christianity which is to be handed on to the faithful is contained in the Word of God, which in turn is transmitted in Scripture and tradition."

Part 1, "Faith and the Creed," directs "the pastor to teach the people that the Apostles' Creed is a brief summary of the doctrine of this mystery regarding [the Triune] God." Although it acknowledges (perhaps a nod to Luther) that the Creed is divided into three principal parts, it falls back on the medieval division into twelve articles to organize its exposition of Christian doctrine.

The Roman Catechism never loses sight of its audience. In every section it gives directives to pastors on what to emphasize and suggests ways to motivate the faithful. Part 1 ends by stating that the pastor "will not only motivate the faithful to a desire of arriving at this [eternal] happiness: he will go further, frequently reminding them that to attain it without fail, they must practice the Christian life" (1. 12. 13). Similar directives appear in the catechism's explanation of almost every article of the Creed.

Part 2 is the longest and most distinctive part of the Roman Catechism. The contents recall the proposal made during the first years of the council for the compilation of a *libellus catechismi* that would guide pastors in the administration of the sacraments. The first section explains the nature, purpose, and constitutive parts of the sacraments in general, and sets their number at seven, "no more nor less." The second section explains each of the seven sacraments one by one.

In both sections the pastoral guidelines are frequent and specific. Pastors are instructed, for example, to seek out occasions to explain baptism to the people. Although the celebration of the rite itself is hardly the time to attempt a systematic catechesis, "the immediacy of the experience [presents an opportunity] to develop a point or two" (2. 1. 2). The baptismal instruction must always be *pastoral* in its orientation and the pastor must never fail to exhort "the faithful to persevere in the fulfillment of their baptismal promises, and so live as to be worthy of the name Christian" (2. 1. 77).

The lengthy treatment and pastoral directives with regard to baptism, Eucharist, and penance reflect the discussions in the council itself. The catechism further notes a neglect of confirmation. Tacitly acknowledging the attacks of Calvin and the sacramentarians, it states, "If there was ever a time when the Sacrament of Confirmation needed to be explained carefully, that time is now" (2. 2. 1). With regard to sacramental catechesis in general, "pastors should keep two objectives particularly in mind," one attitudinal and one practical. First, the faithful need to develop a deep sense of respect and reverence for the sacraments as gifts of God and means of salvation; second, they should understand the importance of using them.

Part 3, like part 2, is subdivided into two sections. The first, dictated by issues raised by the Protestant Reformers, describes the Catholic position regarding the nature and purpose of the Commandments. It introduces the Decalogue as a summary of the entire Law of God. In line with the catechetical tradition dating from Augustine, it explains that God gave the commandments to Moses on two tablets, "and indeed the Ten Commandments can be reduced to two: the love of God, and the love of neighbor" (3. intro. 1). Because the Decalogue summarizes the Law of God, the pastor should make it his study "night and day" (ibid., 2).

In the second section, the Commandments are explained one by one. The authors of the catechism adopted a certain pattern: they generally begin by explaining the importance of each Commandment and how it fits in with the entire Decalogue; they then move to describe its positive and negative aspects, what it commands and what it prohibits. (Commandments nine and ten are treated together because both deal with covetousness.) Part 3, like the preceding parts, singles out particular points that pastors should emphasize, suggests motives for observing the Commandments, and anticipates arguments of those who make excuses for not observing them.

Part 4, more so than the other parts, reads like a theological summa, a systematic treatise rather than a pastoral manual. Like the other parts, it is subdivided into two sections. The first addresses "the nature, necessity and practice of prayer." It begins by stating that a most important duty of the pastoral office is to instruct the faithful in Christian prayer. Pastors must help them "understand what they are to ask from God and how their prayer is to be done," but the advice it gives is stated in general terms. Even in the second section, where it expounds, at some length, the seven petitions of the Lord's Prayer, the explanation is theological and the tone exhortatory rather than pastoral and practical. It may be that the explication of the Our Father was planned as a fitting denouement for the entire work. It reviews many of the themes found in the other parts, but ends with an explanation of "Amen" that is anticlimactic, not to say pedestrian.

### The Catechism's Sources

The doctrinal presentation is ordered to pastoral concerns, chiefly to provide an antidote "against the heresies of our times." In some places, as for example in explaining the veneration and invocation of the saints, the catechism clearly manifests an apologetic purpose. To some extent the Reformers' objections dictated its emphasis on selected aspects of the seven sacraments. It explains papal primacy and limbo, doctrines questioned by Protestants but not discussed at Trent. On the other hand, it is silent on the doctrine of indulgences, which had been defined by the council.

The fact is, writes Robert I. Bradley, "the [Roman] Catechism is dependent on the council for relatively little of its overall content." Bradley's statement seems justified in light of the fact that the catechism has only four direct quotations from the council, and eighteen paraphrases or indirect quotations. All the quotations, direct and indirect, occur in part 2, the treatise on sacraments.[5] The catechism makes reference to the council in eight places; four of these citations occur in the part on the sacraments, one in the part on the Creed, and three in the part on the Commandments. (These are in addition to references to the council in the preface.)

If not the council documents, what sources did the compilers of the Roman Catechism draw on? This is a complex question that is not easily solved because no outlines or preliminary drafts of the text are known to exist. The principal source for part 2 seems to have been the *Commentary on the IV Books of the Sentences* by the Dominican Domingo de Soto (d. 1560) who attended the earlier sessions of the Council of Trent as the imperial theologian of Charles V. Another Dominican active in the early sessions of the council was Bartolomé de Carranza (d. 1576), the author of *Comentarios sobre el catechismo christiano.* (He compiled this work in England during the restoration under Mary Tudor and Philip II when he was theological advisor to Cardinal Pole.) Although Carranza was regarded as suspect by the Inquisition, his catechism seems to have been known to the redactors who compiled the text of the Roman Catechism. Its influence is seen in all four parts, most notably in part 1.[6]

If this is true, Carranza's work is the link that connects the Roman Catechism to the catechetical tradition of the sixteenth century. Carranza seems to have drawn on two early efforts by Catholics to respond to Luther's Large Catechism: the *Enchiridion Christianae institutionis* of Johannes Gropper (1538) and the *Catholicus catechismus* of Frederick Nausea (1543). Nausea and Gropper follow the late medieval pattern that focused on the Creed, Decalogue, and prayer. Both inserted an explanation of the seven sacraments between the Creed and the Decalogue, thus giving them more prominence than Luther, who put them at the end. Gropper saw the sacraments as part of the Creed, "for they are the most certain symbols or signs of our faith."[7] (It might also be noted that Erasmus's catechism of 1533 explained the sacraments in the context of the Creed under the article *communio sanctorum.*) Although Carranza placed his treatise on the sacraments in third place, after the Creed and Commandments, it is evident that Catholic catechisms of the time saw the sacraments as a principal pillar of catechesis.

### The Test of Time

The original edition did not have chapter or paragraph headings (a fact that was noted and deplored by Pope Pius V in authorizing a new edition in 1571),[8] but printed in the margins were references to the Scriptures and

Church Fathers, as well as brief notes indicating the gist of the argument in each section. From the sixteenth century on, many editions and translations (Donovan's included) appended a "Praxis catechismi" that correlates the catechism text to the Sunday lectionary in the *Missal of Pius V*. The idea was suggested, no doubt, by the catechism's preface (and perhaps Calvin's distribution of catechism lessons over the Sundays of the year). It urges pastors and "all who have the responsibility of this teaching," to connect their explanation of the Scriptures to one of the catechism's four headings. By way of example, the preface illustrates how a homily on the gospel reading for the first Sunday of Advent (Luke 21:25) could be linked to the article of the Creed, "He shall come to judge the living and the dead." (No less an orator than Cardinal Newman wrote, "I rarely preach a Sermon, but I go to this beautiful and complete Catechism to get both my matter and my doctrine.")[9]

The Catechism of the Council of Trent has stood the test of time rather well. The 1992 *Catechism of the Catholic Church* describes it as "a work of the first rank as a summary of Christian teaching." The success of the Tridentine reform did not, however, rest on the intrinsic worth of the catechism alone. The catechism was only one piece in the broad strategy of raising the level of education of pastors and clergy who had the responsibility for preaching and catechizing the faithful. It went hand in hand with Trent's reform of seminaries and the seminary curriculum, including a call for more and better Bible study. Trent also undertook the reform of the liturgy, bringing a uniformity to the Latin Rite that had not previously existed. The common expression of faith owed as much to the Roman Missal (perhaps more) as to the Roman Catechism, both of which played major roles in shaping the spirit, language, and theology of the Tridentine Church.

The Catechism of the Council of Trent reflects the times in which it was written. Without being polemical it relies on authority—proof-texts from Scripture and the Church Fathers—to expound and defend Catholic doctrine. As a handbook of Catholic teaching it managed to be relatively complete without confusing basic doctrine with theological conclusions, substance with details. Later chapters will show that the Catechism of the Council of Trent was more open and, at times, inspirational than many of the abridgments and adaptations that attempted to popularize it.

NOTES

1. The best study in English of the Catechism of the Council of Trent is by Robert I. Bradley, *The Roman Catechism in the Catechetical Tradition of the Church* (Lanham, Md.: University of America, 1990). Bradley draws extensively on the comprehensive

study by Pedro Rodriguez and Raul Lanzetti, *El catecismo romano: Fuentes e historia del texto y de la redaccion* (Pamplona: Ediciones Universidad de Navarra, 1982). See also Gerhard Bellinger, *Der Catechismus Romanus und die Reformation: Die katechetische Antwort des Trienter Konzils auf die Haupt-Katechismen der Reformation* (Paderborn: Bonifacius, 1970).

2. Bradley gives an English translation, *The Roman Catechism,* 113–14.

3. Norman P. Turner, ed., *Decrees of the Ecumenical Councils,* vol. 2 (Washington, D.C.: Georgetown University, 1990) 764. Also quoted in Bradley, *The Roman Catechism,* 118.

4. Turner, *Decrees,* 2:797; Bradley, *The Roman Catechism,* 118.

5. Bradley lists the places where these quotations are found in the catechism along with the places where they are found in the *acta* of the council, *The Roman Catechism,* 134–35 nn. 31–33.

6. For references to these works and a general study of the sources, see Rodriguez and Lanzetti, *El catecismo romano,* 135–201. Also, Bradley, *The Roman Catechism,* 95–96.

7. Quoted in Bradley, *The Roman Catechism,* 96.

8. Rodriguez and Lanzetti, *El catecismo romano,* 213 n. 12; Bradley, *The Roman Catechism,* 139. The discovery of the original *manuscript* of the *Roman Catechism* in April 1985 has thrown new light on the way it was prepared for publication. See Pedro Rodriquez and Raul Lanzetti, *El manuscrito original del catechismo romano* (Pamplona: Ediciones Universidad de Navarra, 1985).

9. John Henry Newman, *Apologia pro vita sua* (New York: Modern Library, 1950) 272.

FOUR

# Catechisms of the Counter-Reformation: Canisius, Auger, and Bellarmine

Although the Catechism of the Council of Trent was translated into most European languages, it remained the preserve of the clergy. The ordinary faithful learned the rudiments of doctrine from short catechisms compiled by individuals, usually priests and bishops. Catholic reformers made the catechism their major concern. The authors of many of the early catechisms were members of the newly established Society of Jesus. Peter Canisius, a Dutch Jesuit from Nijmegen, was the author of several catechisms that had lasting influence in countries north of the Alps. In France, Edmund Auger, S.J., published large and small catechisms as a Catholic response to John Calvin's Geneva Catechism of 1541. The catechism of Jesuit Robert Bellarmine was translated from Italian into more than sixty languages to become the mostly widely used catechism in the Catholic world. Jesuits Gaspar Astete and Jerome Ripalda published catechisms in Spain that made their way to the New World. These early catechisms presented the Christian message and Church teaching and also served an apologetic purpose. Few catechisms were openly argumentative or polemical, but most were to some degree shaped by Catholic-Protestant controversies. Issues that divided the Churches were often given more emphasis than the faith they held in common.[1]

## The Jesuits' Approach

About the time that John Calvin was writing the *Institutes* and the Geneva Catechism, Ignatius of Loyola was laying the foundation of the Jesuits (or, more properly, the Society of Jesus). In 1540 Ignatius and a small group of friends met in Rome to outline the basic elements of the organization they hoped to establish. Their deliberations resulted in a statement of purpose known in Jesuit circles as the *Formula of the Institute*. It described the mission of the society as "the propagation of the faith and progress of souls in Christian life and doctrine." Ten years later it was expanded to read *"the defense and propagation of the faith."*[2]

The *Formula* identifies "the instruction of young and uneducated persons in Christianity" as a specific goal. In practice this meant teaching the catechism. Although they varied their methods, even using song to teach the lessons, Ignatius and his early companions concentrated on the traditional elements: the Creed, the Our Father and Hail Mary, the Decalogue, and the works of mercy. A number of early Jesuits compiled and published catechisms for use in their ministry.

In Jesuit schools, students studied the catechism for an hour or so each week. In areas where the Reformation had taken root, the newly established society recognized the school as the arena in which Catholic and Protestant ideologies would compete for the allegiance of young minds and hearts. In the tradition of Erasmus and the humanists, the Jesuits used Latin grammars and other school texts to promote religious and moral instruction. The introduction of the catechism had an unexpected outcome. According to John W. O'Malley, it "helped promote a subtle—and for the Jesuits generally unintended—shift from 'learning one's religion' (in order to practice it) to 'learning truths about one's religion' (in order to have them in one's arsenal of information)."[3]

## The Catechisms of Peter Canisius

The intellectual climate of German universities and the natural curiosity of youth afforded rich soil for the seeds of Lutheran ideas. On the Catholic side the Jesuits came to see themselves as a bulwark against the Protestant Reformation and assumed the mission of teaching Christian doctrine to boys and young men. In 1549 Claude Lejay and Alfonso Salmeron, two of Ignatius's original companions, and Peter Canisius, a young Dutchman who had joined the society six years earlier, began preaching and teaching in the university city of Ingolstadt in Bavaria, a stronghold of traditional Catholicism. Concentrating as they did on religious instruction, these early Jesuits petitioned the Society's headquarters in Rome for a catechism adapted to the German situation. They were not clear as to what they had in mind: they asked that the task be assigned to theologians, but they were not looking for a scholarly opus; they wanted a work that could serve both as a textbook in schools and as a manual for the instruction of children and simple folk.[4]

King Ferdinand I of Austria, however, had his own agenda that was as much political as it was pastoral. He summoned Lejay to Vienna and arranged for the university senate to charge him with the task of drafting a *Summa quaedam*—some sort of compendium of Christian doctrine to be used by teachers, pastors, and preachers. Reporting to his Jesuit superiors in Rome, Lejay complained that he was not up to the enterprise. He tried to get out of it by pointing to works by Peter Soto, Johannes Gropper, and other German authors that could serve the purpose. Ferdinand was not to be put off. He wanted something more extensive, a work that both expounded Christian doctrines and defended them against prevailing errors. He wanted a work composed by his own theologians and published in Vienna under his own direction for use in all the schools throughout his domains.

Peter Canisius was brought from Ingolstadt to assist Lejay in the project, and after the latter's death in August 1552 he carried on alone. His correspondence speaks of a trilogy that would eventually include an *Enchiridion* for pastors, a *Summa theologica* for theological students, and a basic textbook for use in schools. Although Ferdinand's priority lay with the *Summa*, Canisius was more interested in the instruction of children and youths. He saw the basic textbook as a kind of foundation that would be expanded and elaborated in the other works.

When, in the spring of 1554, the king saw the first part of Canisius's *Summa*, he seemed satisfied. In order to speed publication Ferdinand directed that a German translation be undertaken even before Canisius completed the second part. A year later the completed work was published under the descriptive title, *Summa doctrinae christianae, per quaestiones tradita et in usum christianae pueritiae nunc primum edita (A Compendium of Christian Doctrine, Developed by Means of Questions, for Use by Christian Children, Now Published for the First Time)*. The German translation, published in Vienna, appeared in mid-1556; meanwhile the Latin text was reprinted three times in Vienna and at Louvain. The edict of King Ferdinand that serves as a preface to the work does not mention Peter Canisius (though it does name the printer!), creating the impression that it was the work of several hands. Canisius felt that the king would be better safeguarded, the people better served, and the work itself would have wider influence if it did not seem to represent the teachings of one man. The royal edict concluded with the command, "this Catechism alone and no other is [to be] propounded, explained and taught to school-children, whether publicly or privately, by school-masters, tutors and instructors," in all the territories under Ferdinand's jurisdiction.[5]

The first edition of Canisius's *Summa* presented 211 questions. The definitive edition of 1566 (Cologne) was expanded to 222 questions, with about 2,000 biblical citations and 1,200 references to the Church Fathers inscribed in the margins. This latter edition shows the influence of the Council of Trent in a number of places, most notably in the lengthy appendix on original sin and justification. The *Summa* was clearly intended as a study text, for while the questions are short, some answers run to three or four pages.

It was also clearly intended to address the issue of faith and works contested by Luther's doctrine of *sola fides* (faith alone). Inspired by a verse from Ecclesiasticus found in the Latin Vulgate (1:33), "Son, if thou desirest wisdom, keep justice and God will show her to thee," Canisius divided the work into two parts. Under the heading of "Wisdom," he ordered the first part according to the medieval pattern. In this pattern, based on Augustine's *Enchiridion,* wisdom has for its object the theological virtues of faith, hope, and charity. What we believe is taught by the Apostles' Creed; what we hope and pray for by the Lord's Prayer; and what and how we must love by the Commandments. A short chapter explaining that the sacraments are a necessary means both for coming to wisdom and the "keeping" of justice serves as a transition from the first to the second part. Under the heading of "Justice," Canisius described sins that are destructive of justice, and the good works that are the fruit of faith and hope.

In the foreword to the 1560 German edition, Canisius explained:

> During this time of sin and temptation, of disagreement and disappointment, we Christians are challenged to be especially mindful of the wellbeing of our souls. Faith and devotion are diminishing more and more, love is growing cold, and malice is gaining prominence. At the same time, it is possible to find a great number of books and booklets, which claim to point to the true Christian path and save us from our godlessness. Upon thorough examination, however, we will find that while they contain a varnish of truth, they are laced with false and destructive teaching. The average person will not be aware of this. Therefore, everyone is advised and admonished to be careful of what he chooses to read, most especially such books as catechisms and prayer books.... Here [in this book] you will find the concrete basic teachings of the true Christian, Catholic, and saving religion. To remain children of God and gain everlasting life in Christ, we need faith, hope, love, the sacraments, and a desire for justice. Without faith, we will not recognize God, without hope we will despair in spite of grace. Without love we remain in darkness, even in death, though we may have faith and hope.... Without the proper reception of the sacraments, the grace of the Holy Spirit remains unavailable. Whenever justice is absent, Christ is absent and we are in the presence of the evil one...[6]

Canisius's *Summa* is important for a number of reasons, not the least of which is that it shaped the syllabi of post-Reformation catechisms and textbooks along the lines of late medieval catechesis. Its table of contents resonates in many a contemporary curriculum:

I.

1. Faith—the Creed.
2. Hope—Lord's Prayer and Hail Mary.

3. Charity: The Decalogue and Precepts of the Church.
4. Sacraments.

IIa.

1. The Seven Capital Sins.
2. Complicity in the Sins of Others.
3. Sins against the Holy Spirit.
4. Sins Crying out to Heaven for Vengeance.

IIb.

1. Three Kinds of Good Works.
2. Works of Mercy.
3. Cardinal Virtues.
4. Gifts and Fruits of the Holy Spirit.
5. Eight Beatitudes.
6. Evangelical Counsels.
7. Four Last Things.

The *Summa* became the basis for two other catechetical works from Canisius's hand: In 1556–57 he published an abbreviated version that is hardly more than a synopsis for the use of small children and the uneducated, and a *Catechismus minimus* (Short Catechism) for the lower and middle grades. The abbreviated version appeared first as an appendix to a Latin grammar (Ingolstadt, 1556), and then was translated into German a few months later. It consisted of 59 questions and answers for memorization and included prayer texts for all occasions—morning and evening prayers, prayers before and after Mass, prayers to be said when the clock strikes, prayers when someone lights a candle, and a prayer for all the needs of Christendom, to be recited daily. A year or so before he died (1597) Canisius prepared an edition of the abbreviated version that divided the words into syllables to enable children to learn it more easily.

The *Parvus catechismus* or *Catechismus minor* is known variously in English as Canisius's Small Catechism and also as his Intermediate Catechism. It is the work that most authors have in mind when they refer simply to "Canisius's catechism." He intended it for school children who had progressed beyond the primer but who had not reached the level of the college or university. Like Canisius's other catechetical texts, this one appeared first in a Latin edition (Cologne, 1558). In 1564 he published expanded editions in both Latin and German. The Latin edition (Cologne) included an "Horarium of the Eternal Wisdom of God, Jesus Christ Our Lord, together with Some Exercises of Christian Piety." The "Horarium" was based on the writings of Blessed Henry Suso, the noted Dominican mystic. The works of piety center on virtues modelled by

Jesus in his life on earth. Each day of the week highlights a specific virtue (humility on Sunday, meekness on Monday, patience on Tuesday, etc.).

Canisius does not expound at great length the fundamental doctrines of the Christian faith that were not at issue between Catholics and Protestants, but he does treat topics on which there was conflict: the sacraments, the Church, holy orders, the Mass, the obligation of fasting, the veneration of the saints, Communion under one species. He lists but does not explain the individual precepts of the Church, and offers an apologetic for their legitimacy by defending ecclesiastical usage and the Church's pastoral authority.* Although the catechism was adapted to the needs of the day, it has none of the polemic and acrimony found in many sixteenth-century works. "This book," writes Canisius in his Confessions, "strives, in a charitable manner, to raise up those that have fallen, and to bring back, with the help of divine grace, those who have gone astray."

The third German edition (Dilligen, 1564) did not contain questions and answers. It was published as a "Catechism and Prayerbook." The prayerbook mixes psalms with prayers authored by Augustine, John Chrysostom, Bede, John Damascene, Francis of Assisi, and Thomas Aquinas. Another fifty short prayers focus on events in the life of Christ; they are followed by a kind of "rosary" meditation on his passion. The prayerbook provides, among other things, instructions for morning and evening prayer, an examination of conscience at the end of the day, and prayers for the assistance of the souls in purgatory. Canisius also included a liturgical calendar with notes and recommendations for the proper observance of feasts and saints' days. The text was enhanced with 105 woodcuts depicting scenes from the life of Christ and Mary as well as Old and New Testament figures.[7]

### Canisius in Translation

Shortly after Canisius published his catechisms, one of the architects of the educational program for Jesuit schools, Diego de Ledesma (d. 1575) published two catechisms in Italy, the one for the "very ignorant," the other for the

---

*All ecclesiastical laws are "precepts or commandments of the Church," but in the catechetical tradition they refer to a handful of obligations binding on all the faithful. Ninth-century penitentials and prayer books list obligations that should be a matter for examination of conscience. They included such duties as attending Mass on Sunday and holy days, fasting and abstaining at designated times, and receiving the Eucharist at Eastertime. Ignatius of Loyola made the precepts a part of his catechesis (O'Malley, *The First Jesuits,* 119). Peter Canisius listed five precepts (celebrating feasts of the Church, hearing Mass, fasting and abstaining at designated seasons and days, confessing to a priest once a year, and receiving the Eucharist during the Easter season). Robert Bellarmine listed six in his *Summa doctrinae christianae* (1589). See the *New Catholic Encyclopedia* 4:8.

"less ignorant." They seem to have been influenced by Canisius's works. In 1565 the General of the Jesuits reported that the society had three thousand copies of the Small Catechism and two thousand copies of the *Dottrina cristiana* available for distribution to the catechetical centers in Rome. The first probably referred to Canisius's work, the second to Ledesma's.[8]

Before Canisius died in 1597 his catechisms were being read in fifteen different languages, including Japanese and Hindustani, and had been reprinted more than two hundred times. Laurence Vaux (1519–85), the recusant Lancaster priest, published an English adaptation under the title *A Catechisme or a Christian Doctrine, necessarie for children and ignorant people* (Louvain, 1567). The Latin text of Canisius's *Summa* was in circulation in England as early as the 1570s. It was translated into English towards the end of the century under the direction of Henry Garnett, the priest hanged (1606) for his alleged role in the Gunpowder Plot. Garnett added some material on pilgrimages, the invocation of saints, and indulgences.

One of the most zealous promoters of Canisius's catechisms was the Italian Jesuit Antonio Possevino, who gained fame as a preacher and papal diplomat. It is said that he drew as many as fourteen thousand to his Lenten sermons in Rouen (France) in 1570. Possevino himself relates that he devoted three afternoons a week to the instruction of those in prison. "It was necessary for me," he wrote, "to send to Paris six times that Lent for supplies of the Catechism of Canisius in French. It was reprinted six times and brought to Rouen, where the booksellers' assistants paraded in the street crying, 'Here is the Catholic Catechism which the preacher teaches.'"

J. Brodrick, the biographer of Canisius, quotes a memo written by Possevino sometime between 1573 and 1577:

> [I recommend] that the Smaller Catechism of Peter Canisius be taught in the Schools at least twice a week and that the pupils learn it by heart. In explaining its text masters can use the *Summa* of Peter Canisius, which has long been approved by the Apostolic See and is expounded in Rome and practically everywhere else in Europe. . . . Further, it would be better that this Catechism, which, with the exception of the Catechism of the Council of Trent, written for parish priests, is by far the most popular in all parts of Europe and the Indies, should be employed as a text-book rather than any pagan treatise on ethics, so that Christian faith may be safeguarded and the poison which the heretics are now spreading everywhere with their pestilential catechisms be checked by its flow.[9]

## Edmund Auger, S.J.

Edmund Auger (1530–91) was received into the Jesuit novitiate by Ignatius of Loyola in Rome in 1550. After ordination to the priesthood in 1559 he was sent to Pamiers, where Calvinism was making deep inroads. Much of his active ministry took place during the period of upheaval described by historians as the "wars of religion" that rent France (1547–98). Auger proposed to block the spread of Protestantism in the south of France by launching a vigorous counterattack.

A majority of the students at the college in Pamiers were attracted by the new doctrines, and were said even to bring Calvin's catechism to class. Auger set about to write a catechism of his own. The manuscript received the approval of the theology faculty of the University of Paris in 1563 and was published in autumn of the same year. Entitled *Catéchisme et sommaire de la doctrine chrétienne,* it was a direct response to Calvin's 1541 Geneva Catechism. Written in French and addressed primarily to youths, it nonetheless included "the text of selected prayers and several admonitions for all manner of people." In the course of numerous editions it would encompass several forms: a large catechism in the form of questions and answers for adolescents and adults that included detailed formulas for confession according to one's state of life (clergy, nobility, jurists, literati, merchants, artisans, married persons, children and servants); a *Bref recueil* for the uneducated and illiterate; a small catechism for children in the lower grades; and finally, for the upper grades and educated clergy, a catechism in Latin and even in Greek.[10]

Since his strategy was to respond to the Calvinists point by point, Auger organized his material under the four headings of the Geneva Catechism: faith, Law, prayer, and the sacraments. Points of contention between Catholics and Protestants received more attention than the doctrines on which they agreed. Thus Auger devoted nineteen questions to the Church, with emphasis on its visibility and on the cult and invocation of the saints. Two-thirds of the work was given to the sacraments, with eight lessons on the Eucharist, including lengthy explanations of the reality of the sacrifice of the Mass, the doctrine of the real presence, Communion under one species, suffrages for the dead, and indulgences.

Auger recognized the urgency of responding to the Protestants by clarifying Catholic teaching. His catechism was an immediate success. Between 1563 and 1582 more than twenty editions were printed, with translations in Spanish, Italian, and Dutch. But the defects of the work were not slow in surfacing. In his effort to challenge Protestant doctrines and answer their criticisms of the Church, Auger did not distinguish the essential from the secondary. In explaining the articles of the Creed, the Commandments, and the sacraments, he put everything on the same plane. The lessons emphasized instruction and offered very little by way of formation in the Christian life.

Before the century was out Canisius's catechism completely supplanted Auger's work in France. The former was more discrete in the presentation of Catholic doctrine and the refutation of Protestant criticisms. Further, as the tide of Protestant expansion began to ebb in France, Auger's catechism fell more and more into disuse. Nonetheless, the change of method and of objective introduced by Auger (and Calvin) and the importance attributed to the cognitive and didactic elements of catechesis continued to characterize the history of the catechism.

## Bellarmine's *Dottrina Cristiana*

The popularity of the catechisms of Canisius and Auger seems to have been limited to regions north of the Alps. In the Mediterranean countries, especially Italy, the catechetical works of Robert Bellarmine held sway.

Bellarmine entered the Society of Jesus at the age of eighteen. He studied philosophy in Rome and theology in Padua and Louvain, where he taught for a period (1570–76) before returning to Rome as professor of apologetics. The Jesuit authorities relied on his advice, as did Pope Clement VIII (1592–1605), who nominated him to the college of cardinals in 1599. It was at the urging of Clement that Bellarmine composed two small manuals of Christian doctrine based on catechetical instructions that he had given to the lay brothers in the Jesuit community. The first, a Short Catechism *(Dottrina Cristiana breve)*, published in 1597, was intended for children and illiterates.

By way of introduction Bellarmine provided a preface filled with pastoral insights and an explanation of his method. In selecting the contents, he says he was guided by two principles, namely, the necessity of knowing basic truths, and the learner's capacity to assimilate them. He takes his cue from the Catechism of the Council of Trent which, he says, "doubtless is the most authentic of all," and focuses on the Creed, the Lord's Prayer with the Hail Mary, the Ten Commandments and precepts of the Church, and the sacraments with the forgiveness of sins. It also seemed "useful to add some things but few and easy," namely, "the principle virtues which are the fountains of good actions; and the seven capital vices which are the sources of all sins; the works of mercy, very agreeable to God, the sins which displease him greatly of which the Scripture says, that they cry to Heaven for vengeance; the evangelical counsels, the four last ends and the mysteries of the Holy Rosary."

The text itself consisted of ninety-six questions and answers. Bellarmine reduces the presentation of doctrine to barest essentials. The catechism begins with the teacher asking the question, "Are you a Christian?" and the pupil responding, "I am, by the grace of God." And before beginning to explain the Creed and other prayers, Bellarmine introduces a series of questions on the Sign of the Cross that becomes, in later catechisms, a standard way of introducing simple folk and children to the mysteries of the Trinity and the incarnation.

*Master.* How then is the mystery of the most Holy Trinity shown in the sign of the cross?

*Disciple.* Because this word, "in the name" signifies the Unity; the other words [Father, Son, and Holy Ghost] show the Trinity.

*M.* Show now the second [mystery of the incarnation and death of our Savior]?

*D.* The figure of the cross represents the Death of the Savior, who after having become man, and having taught the way of salvation by his doctrine, his examples and miracles, died on the wood of the cross.

The brevity of the questions and answers was designed to make it easy for the learners to memorize them. By the same token Bellarmine omitted the twelve gifts of the Holy Spirit and the Beatitudes because, as he says in his introductory note, "knowing them by heart is of little use to anybody and, besides, even learned men would be puzzled to repeat them in their right order."[11]

The following year Bellarmine published a companion work for teachers, a *Longer Declaration of Christian Doctrine (Dichiarazione piu copiosa della dottrina Cristiana)*, which contained 273 questions and answers. In the *Longer Declaration* the order is reversed, with the learner asking the questions and the teacher responding. The questions, anticipating pupils' inquiries, draw forth illustrations and examples that catechists might use in answering them. It begins,

*Pupil:* What are the chief and most necessary parts of Christian doctrine?

*Teacher:* They are four, the Apostles' Creed, the Our Father, the Ten Commandments, and the Seven Sacraments.

*Pupil:* Can you give me an illustration which will make clearer the necessity of these four parts of Christian doctrine?

*Teacher:* St. Augustine draws a comparison from the building of a house. The first thing to do is to lay the foundations; then to erect the walls and finally to cover it with the roof, for all of which work tools are necessary. So it is in building up the edifice of salvation in our own souls. We must lay the foundations of faith, erect the walls of hope and roof them over with charity, our tools being the most holy sacraments.[12]

Pope Clement had the catechism examined by the cardinals of the Congregation of the Reform, and then warmly authorized its publication and mandated its use. Clement's brief, dated 15 July 1598, alluded to "the several Catechisms, written by various persons and according to different methods," that were "giving rise to no little difficulty and confusion in both teaching and learning." It was "to remedy this evil," he said, that he had ordered Bellarmine "to write a new catechism divided into two parts." In the same brief, the pope then conceded to the Confraternity of Christian Doctrine in Rome "all rights over this work for a period of ten years, insomuch that no one in the Holy City or in any part of our ecclesiastical dominions may print or sell this or any other Catechism without leave from the officers of the same Confraternity, under pain of our displeasure and a fine of five hundred gold ducats." Clement ordered the use of the text in papal territories so that "henceforth there may be but one method in teaching and learning the catechism." He also "exhorted" patriarchs, archbishops, bishops, and parish priests to adopt and use Bellarmine's catechism in their respective Churches, dioceses, and parishes.[13] Pope Urban VIII in 1633 strongly recommended its use in mission countries, and in 1742 Pope Benedict XIV urged its adoption as the official catechism in every diocese.

Much changed in the generation that separated Canisius and Bellarmine. The Council of Trent was a watershed. Canisius, incorporating the contents and, to some extent, the structure of medieval catechesis in his texts, continued to have a strong following in German-speaking lands, but it was Bellarmine's catechism that became the archetype of Counter-Reformation catechisms. Bellarmine's ordering of the material differed somewhat from the structure of the Roman Catechism, but his theological framework and general orientation were inspired by the Council of Trent. The definitions in his catechism are more concise and the number of references to Scripture are fewer than in Canisius's work. The kind of institutional ecclesiology associated with Bellarmine's name is evident throughout; it is oriented toward the visible, hierarchical Church. The authority of Rome is held up as a sure guide. Although Bellarmine's theological works engage Protestant authors, he avoids open controversy in his catechisms.

In the popular mind the Bellarmine catechism became the symbol of the Counter-Reformation and loyalty to the pope. The people of Lombardy, for example, protested in 1768 when Joseph II's minister tried to bowdlerize the text, excising or modifying passages contrary to the Jansenist tenets and anti-papal nationalism promoted by the government in the Austrian dominions. By then generations had learned from Bellarmine that they were Catholics not because they were born Italian or French, nor because they were baptized, nor because they confessed Christ, but because they were obedient to the pope, the vicar of Christ.[14]

The Bellarmine catechism soon became the most widely used text in the Catholic world. Missionaries used it themselves and put it in the hands of catechists. When the Seminary of the Propagation of the Faith, established in Rome to train missionaries, set up its own printing press in 1626, Bellarmine's catechism was translated into dozens of languages and dialects of Asia and Africa. The next chapter describes how missionaries employed catechisms as instruments of evangelization and inculturation.

NOTES

1. For a bibliography and brief survey of these developments see John W. O'Malley, *The First Jesuits* (Cambridge: Harvard University, 1993) 87–90, 115–26, and passim. See also Mary Charles Bryce, "Evolution of Catechesis from the Catholic Reformation to the Present," in Westerhoff and Edwards, *A Faithful Church,* 204–16.

2. O'Malley, *The First Jesuits,* 5.

3. Ibid., 125.

4. J. Brodrick, *Saint Peter Canisius, S.J., 1521–1597* (Baltimore: Carroll, 1950) 204–52.

5. Fridericus Streicher, ed., *S. Petri Canisii catechismi Latini et Germanici* (Rome: Pontificia Universitas Gregoriana, 1933) pars prima, p. 5.

6. Ibid., pars secunda, pp. 3–4.

7. The pictures are reproduced in Streicher's edition: ibid., pars secunda, pp. 3–87.

8. O'Malley, *The First Jesuits,* 125.

9. Brodrick, *Canisius,* 249–50.

10. Jean-Claude Dhotel, *Les origines du catéchisme moderne* (Paris: Aubier, 1967) 50–64 and passim.

11. Robert Bellarmine, *Summary of the Christian Doctrine,* translated from the Italian by Rev. N. Simon (New Orleans, 1875).

12. J. Brodrick, *The Life and Works of Blessed Robert Francis Bellarmine, S.J. 1542–1621* (London: Burns, Oates, and Washbourne, 1928) 1:390–91.

13. The text of Clement's brief is found in ibid., 1:395.

14. Ibid., 1:397–98.

FIVE

# Evangelization, Inculturation, and Latin American Catechisms

The development of the catechism coincided with missionary expansion among the peoples of the Far East and the discovery of the New World. The history of evangelization and catechesis in these regions cannot be told without reference to the competitive interests of the great Catholic powers, notably Portugal and Spain, the spread of the Tridentine reforms, and the activity of the Congregation for the Propagation of the Faith. This chapter does not attempt a comprehensive account of these and related developments. The scope of the work permits mentioning only a few significant catechisms produced for use in the Orient in order to allow for a more detailed survey of the evolution of the catechism in Central and South America.

### Early Attempts at Adaptation

The Society of Jesus was only a few years old when Francis Xavier (1505–52) journeyed to India. Almost as soon as he arrived in Goa in 1542, he introduced a little catechism based on the catechism of Juan de Barros, which had been published shortly before Xavier departed Lisbon. He used it to instruct children and adults who could speak Portuguese. For two years he instructed the poor pearl fishers, enlisting native-born lay catechists to teach in Tamil. He reduced the catechism to its most basic elements, which children memorized by repeating the text of the catechism and the standard prayers in a singsong voice. In 1545 Xavier published a set of directives to guide the catechists' work, and the following year he prepared *Symboli Catholicae fidei declaratio,* a catechism for their use based on the Creed.[1]

Jesuit missionaries in other countries too adapted the catechism genre as a means of evangelizing native peoples. In Japan in 1570, A. Valignano, S.J., published an explanation of Christian doctrine in Japanese that was designed to appeal to Buddhists. In China the first Jesuit missionaries, with the help of native writers, published a catechism in Chinese (1584) that was sensitive to native religious practices and the value that Confucians put on discipline and order. French-born Alexandre de Rhodes (1591–1660) established a network of lay catechists in Vietnam to assist him in his work of evangelization. In 1629 he produced a bilingual catechism in Latin and Vietnamese, *Catechismus pro iis qui volunt suscipere baptismum in octo dies divisus* (a catechism intended for persons seeking baptism with the lessons being divided over eight sessions [days]). De Rhodes directed it towards Buddhists. This catechism, the oldest example of Vietnamese prose, was later translated into Thai and French.

These early attempts at inculturation, despite initial successes, divided the missionaries and ultimately were casualties of the polemics of the "Chinese rites" controversy. It was in part to settle disputes among the missionaries that the newly reorganized (1622) Sacred Congregation for the Propagation of the Faith mandated the use of the Roman Catechism by the clergy in the missions. As noted in the previous chapter, the congregation in 1626 set up a printery to provide Christian books and catechetical texts for missionary countries. The congregation printed innumerable small catechisms and, by a directive of Pope Urban VIII, the catechisms of Robert Bellarmine in over sixty languages, thus making it the most widely disseminated catechetical text in the Catholic world.[2] In 1651 the congregation published de Rhodes's catechism which up to that point had been circulating in manuscript form.

### Juan de Zumárraga in Mexico

Three more or less discrete moments illustrate different approaches to missionary activity in Central and South America.[3] The first embraces the early years of evangelization in the vast territory of Mexico, a period that corresponds to the episcopate of Juan de Zumárraga (1527–1548). Zumárraga had entered the Order of Friars Minor at an early age and ended a term as provincial superior shortly before being appointed archbishop of Mexico City. The art of printing was just coming into its own when Zumárraga went to Mexico in 1528, and he recognized the potential of the press as a means of evangelization and catechesis.

It was at the insistence of Zumárraga that a printing press was sent to Mexico. Although some Aztecs were quick to learn Spanish, he saw the need to present Catholic doctrine in their native Nahuatl if the gospel message were to appeal to them. The difficulties he had met with in attempting to print a short compendium convinced him of the importance of having a printing press close to hand. The manuscript had been forwarded to Juan Cromberger of Seville, the leading printer of the time in Spain. After typesetters began work on it, no one could be found in Seville sufficiently conversant with Nahuatl to proof the text, and the post was such that it required many months for proofs to be sent across the Atlantic from Spain to Mexico and back again. The solution was to have Cromberger establish a branch of his publishing house in Mexico. He dispatched Juan Pablos with a press, type, ink, and paper to set up shop near the residence of Zumárraga in what is now Mexico City.

Cromberger intended to maintain tight control of the Mexico operation. All books were to carry the notice that they were printed "in the House of Juan Cromberger." No work was to be printed without a license from the bishop of Mexico, and Pablos's name was not to appear on the imprint. Cromberger further stipulated that when type became worn, Pablos was to melt it down so that no one else could use it. These restrictions would seem to have frustrated one of Zumárraga's goals in bringing the printing press to Mexico, namely, to teach the art of printing to the Indians.

In 1539, fifteen years before Canisius completed his catechism and a hundred years before the first book was published in the English colonies (the celebrated *Bay State Psalm Book*), Juan Cromberger printed *Breve y mas compendiosa doctrina cristiana en lengua mexicana y castellana* in Mexico. It is said that the small booklet of twelve pages contained the most necessary points of faith for the advancement of the Indians and the salvation of their souls. As the title suggests, it was probably written in Spanish with a translation into Nahuatl.

Very few examples have survived from Juan Pablos's earliest effort. There are no surviving copies of the bilingual compendium just described. There are, however, three pages extant of a pastoral manual, printed in 1540, that provided guidance in instructing and baptizing indigenous adults. By 1544 the House of Cromberger was able to publish a number of titles in such quantity that copies have survived. One such text, a work bearing Zumárraga's name and first published in 1544, was entitled *Doctrina cristiana: más cierta y verdadera para gente sin erudicion y letras*. It came to be cited simply as *Doctrina breve*.[4] In the 1546 edition it appears as a two-part work: the first part consists of a seventy-six folio section that explains "the fourteen articles of the Catholic faith," the sacraments, and the Commandments, and the second part, a twenty-four folio supplement, is a moving exhortation that encourages all Christians to learn of Jesus Christ by reading Scripture.

Zumárraga was more a compiler-editor than the author of *Doctrina breve*. The source of the first part is a *Summa de doctrina cristiana*, by Constantino Ponce de la Fuente, published a few years before in Seville. Zumárraga made no significant changes in the text except to convert the dialogue style of the original into a continuous narrative, and he mentions Indians *(los naturales)* and the New World *(las Indias)*.[5] He does not acknowledge his source, which was just as well because a few years later Constantino ran afoul of the archbishop of Seville, who was also the inquisitor general at the time. Charged with heresy, Constantino's books were condemned to be burned, and he ended his days in prison. (By 1552 Jesuits in India were also using Constantino's catechism, and Francis Xavier wanted to take it with him to China.)[6]

Given the religious climate of Spain in the middle of the sixteenth century, Erasmus, Zumárraga's other principal source, could have met the same fate had he been alive at the time. Although Erasmus's name does not appear in it, the *Doctrina breve* owes much to the Renaissance scholar. Its exposition of the seven deadly sins follows Erasmus's *Enchiridion,* and the final exhortation is little more than a paraphrase of his *Paraclesis* (the inspiring introduction to his Greek edition of the New Testament).

Another work by Zumárraga was a Spanish translation of Gerson's *Opus tripertitum,* which he proposed for use in conjunction with the *Doctrina breve.* The resulting *Tripartito* consists, as the title suggests, of three parts: (1) the Commandments, (2) confession, and (3) the art of a happy death. Although Zumárraga seems to have intended both these works for the use of the missionaries, at the end of the *Tripartito* he encourages religious orders to translate this and similar works into local languages as a means of evangelizing native peoples.

### Pedro de Cordoba and Pedro de Gantes

The *Doctrina breve* and the *Tripartito* were important in that they kept the medieval catechetical tradition of the Old World alive in the New World. But it was another work, the *Doctrina cristiana* by the Dominican Pedro de Cordoba (1482–1521), printed by the House of Cromberger and edited and paid for by Zumárraga, that made an inchoate effort to bridge the two cultures. Cordoba arrived in Hispaniola, now the Dominican Republic, in 1510. His *Doctrina cristiana* has the distinction of being the first catechetical text and perhaps the first book actually composed in the New World.[7] (Cordoba has the added distinction of being instrumental in persuading Bartolomé de las Casas to free his slave and join the Order of Preachers. Las Casas became celebrated as "defender of the Indians.")

Cordoba's work was in use for some twenty years before it was printed. Although the extent of Zumárraga's editing can only be guessed at because none of the manuscript versions is extant, it probably consisted in adapting the text so that it would be more relevant in Mexico. The customs and beliefs of the Nahuatl-speaking Aztecs differed from those of the indigenous peoples of the Caribbean for whom Cordoba had originally written. Such changes likely included the allusion to the idolatries, rituals, and names of the gods of the

Aztecs. Zumárraga's hand can also be seen in the closing section, where Christians more advanced in the faith are encouraged to study the *Tripartito.*

Within a few years, anonymous Dominican friars translated Cordoba's text into Nahuatl and edited it extensively. The 1548 and 1550 editions were bilingual, and the text, arranged according to themes, was shaped into ready-made sermons that a preacher could use for catechetical instruction.

Five years before Zumárraga arrived in Mexico, another Franciscan, Pedro de Gantes (1486–1572), had founded a school where boys were taught Christian doctrine, reading, writing, singing, and such skills as carpentry and stone-cutting. Later he established a hospital for training boys in European medical practices, and in 1532, with the support of Zumárraga, he organized a school for girls. At some point in his long career he wrote a textbook designed to teach reading and language skills. The printed edition of 1569 was trilingual—Spanish, Latin, and Nahuatl—an indication that Gantes was trying to introduce the indigenous population to the languages of the conquistadors and the Church.

Gantes also wrote two catechetical works. The one written in Nahuatl, *Doctrina christiana en lengua mexicana,* was first published in Amberes, Belgium, in 1528, but was later reprinted in Mexico in 1547 and 1553. Like other works of this period, the text was in narrative form. It was prefaced by a calendar that listed feasts and fast-days. The title page and the first page of each chapter were illustrated with woodcuts.

More interesting, however, is Gantes's pictographic catechism. Exploiting the Aztec familiarity with hieroglyphics, he introduced Christian symbols and concepts. He invented pictographs to represent God, the Father, the Son, and the Holy Spirit. Other symbols represented heaven and earth, life and death, sin, a saint, the Church, Amen, and other Christian terms. Gantes used these symbols to teach prayers and to explain the Creed, the Commandments, the sacraments, and the works of mercy. In content it followed the order of other works of Christian doctrine, but the idiom was adapted to the culture. It was a technique that other missionaries in Central and South America were to adopt in order to overcome language barriers.

### Toribio de Mogrovejo in Peru

The second moment in the history of evangelization and catechesis in Latin America began in 1581 with the arrival of a new archbishop, Toribio de Mogrovejo (1538–1606), in Lima, Peru. At the time the ecclesiastical province of Lima included most of South America and parts of Central America. The ten bishops who ministered in the territory had to cope with vast distances, mountainous terrain, extremes of climate, and a variety of cultures among the native peoples. Mogrovejo quickly learned Quechua, one of the dominant languages of the region, travelled to various parts of his diocese, and fostered contacts with the native peoples. In 1583, at the orders of the king, he called the Third Council of Lima.[8]

From the beginning the provincial councils had expressed concern about the methods and means of evangelization and catechesis. The council of 1567 warned against hasty baptism and insisted on the systematic instruction of catechumens and neophytes. It mandated the study of native languages, strictly prohibited reliance on an interpreter in the hearing of confessions, and closed ordination to the native peoples.

Almost twenty years passed between the close of the Council of Trent and the convocation of the Third Council of Lima, enough time for the Tridentine decrees and spirit to travel overseas to the New World. Among the principal acts of Lima III was an order to prepare a Spanish catechism that would incorporate the teachings of the Tridentine catechism in a question-answer format. The catechism was to be translated into Quechua and Aymara, the two major languages of the Andean region, and was to be adopted as the sole instrument for instruction throughout the ecclesiastical province.

A letter on translations accompanying the catechism and supplementary texts stressed the need to communicate effectively. It acknowledged that not all priests were fluent in the native languages and that even those who were experienced difficulties in finding words to express Christian concepts. This emphasis on the importance of native languages represented a change in policy from that of the previous archbishop, Jeronimo de Loaysa, who had insisted on using only Spanish or Latin in catechisms. Despite Loaysa's instructions, however, missionaries were known to use local languages in instructing the people. A provincial meeting of the Jesuits in 1576, for example, ordered the creation of a large and a small catechism in both Quechua and Aymara.

Although it is known as the "catechism of St. Toribio de Mogrovejo," the catechism mandated by Lima III was a collaborative effort. A *Christian Doctrine*, based on the Catechism of the Council of Trent, was first prepared in Spanish. It was likely the work of the Jesuit Jose de Acosta, and it served as the basis for the catechism that was translated into Quechua and Aymara by another group of scholars. The catechism appeared in two versions: a short catechism for the uneducated and day laborers; and the *catecismo mayo* for extended instruction. The former had three parts: (1) seventeen short questions and answers (the first two questions are: Does God exist? and, How many gods are there?); (2) a short exhortatory sermon (less than two pages) summarizing what Christians should know; and (3) a one-page syllabary containing an alphabet and pronunciation guide. The longer version follows the Tridentine outline: Creed, sacraments, Commandments, and an exposition of the Lord's Prayer. An introduction outlines the genesis of the catechism at the

Third Provincial Council of Lima, and explains that it is intended to help priests in determining what should be emphasized. In time the catechism of Toribio was translated into other Indian languages. It continued to be the official catechism in South and Central America until 1901.

Another work, a pastoral manual for hearing confessions, was commissioned by Lima III to be used in conjunction with the catechism. This *confessionario* turned the sacrament of penance into a catechetical moment and may have had a greater impact on the indigenous culture than did the catechism itself.* After leading the penitent in the recitation of the Lord's Prayer, the Hail Mary, and the Apostles' Creed, the priest examined him or her as to what it means to be a Christian. When it came to confession itself, the priest was to go through the commandments, applying them to the penitent according to social status (tribal chief, mayor, government treasurer, etc.). The rite of confession was supplemented by a pastoral instruction that included, among other things, an exposition of common superstitions and idolatrous practices. Although the instruction provides extensive information about the beliefs and practices of the indigenous peoples, it says nothing about how these beliefs and practices might be used to give a deeper insight into the Christian mysteries.

### The Catechisms of Ripalda and Astete

The third moment that demands attention in this overview of the evolution of the catechism in Latin America did not occur in the New World but rather in Burgos, Spain, in 1591. That was the year in which Jeronimo Martinez de Ripalda, S.J. (1536–1618), published *Doctrina cristiana con una exposicion breve*. This was to become the principal catechism of Mexico into the twentieth century.

The structure of Ripalda's catechism follows that of Peter Canisius: what Christians should believe (Creed), how they should pray (Lord's Prayer; Hail Mary), what they should do (Commandments), and what they should receive (sacraments). This last section includes questions on indulgences, the works of mercy, sin, and virtue, and instructions for assisting at Mass, saying the rosary, and making a nightly examination of conscience. Each section contains a brief explanation of some doctrine followed by very specific questions and answers.

---

*The *confessionarios*, a popular genre in Latin America in the sixteenth and seventeenth centuries, served much the same purpose as the Irish Penitentials in the early Middle Ages. The *Confessionario mayor, en la lengua mexicana y castellana* and a short version, the *Confessionario breve* (1565), by Fray Alonso de Molina were the only confessional manuals in the language of the Aztecs until the end of the century. Though born in Spain, Molina was reared in Mexico and had leaned Nahuatl as a child from his Indian playmates. Burkhart calls him "the Franciscans' star linguist" (*The Slippery Earth*, 198).

Another catechism of the same period, Gaspar Astete's *Doctrina cristiana y documentos de crianza* (1599), very similar to Ripalda's in structure and style, became popular elsewhere in Latin America (and the Philippines). Its appeal was probably due to the brevity of its questions and answers.

Although it did not take into consideration the circumstances of the New World, the Ripalda catechism was extremely popular in Mexico. It was translated into Nahuatl, Mixteca, Guarani, and Maya. Local councils, bishops, and even civil authorities promoted its use. The 1758 Nahuatl translation follows Ripalda in method, order, and style, but the translator, Ignacio de Paredes, S.J., admits that it does not follow the original text word for word; he defends this by noting that each language has its own rhythm and cadence and what is elegant and appropriate in one language can be barbaric in another. In explaining the observance of feasts and holy days of obligation, the Nahuatl translation acknowledges the particular circumstances of Church life in eighteenth-century Mexico, but there is nothing in the catechism that suggests an awareness of the indigenous culture.

The three moments described here are just that: brief time-bytes in a long history of evangelization and catechesis in Latin America. Missionaries in the New World, like the Jesuit missionaries in the Far East, were constrained not only by the alien culture in which they worked but also by the Tridentine reforms that put a high premium on uniformity. The Roman ritual that guided the administration of the sacraments, for example, focused on infant baptism and gave little emphasis to adults either in regard to sacramental preparation or the reception of baptism itself. Catechisms represented only one facet of the catechetical enterprise. They were used in a variety of settings from finishing schools to adobe huts to open-air campsites, but the songs, pictures, and games that the missionaries and catechists used to supplement them were not thought of as integral to the rites of initiation. The survey of developments in Central and Latin America illustrates how the catechism was used as an instrument of inculturation, and it raises the perennial questions about how language and ritual—symbols, idioms, and figures of speech—must be adapted if the gospel message is to take root in people's lives. The issue of language is a challenge that catechists face everywhere, not only in mission lands. The next chapter tells the story of Claude Fleury, one author who recognized that it was also a problem in seventeenth-century Europe.

NOTES

1. John Hofinger, "Saint Francis Xavier, Catechist," *Lumen Vitae* 8 (1953) 537–44.

2. For further information on these early missionary catechisms see André Seumois, s.v. "Missionaria (Catechesi): Storia" in *Dizionario di Catechetica*, ed. J. Gevaert (Turin: Editrice Elle Di Ci, 1986).

3. The bibliography of primary sources and modern interpretations of evangelization in Mexico and Peru is extensive. The more recent works reflect a renewed interest as the quincentennial commemoration of Columbus's discovery of the "New World" approached. For Mexico see the discussion of sources and the bibliography in Louise M. Burkhart, *The Slippery Earth: Nahua-Christian Dialogue in Sixteenth Century Mexico* (Tucson: The University of Arizona Press, 1989) 195–202, 215–33. For Peru, see Sabine MacCormack, *Religion in the Andes: Vision and Imagination in Early Colonial Peru* (Princeton: Princeton University, 1991); and E. Garcia Ahumada, *Comienzos de la Cateqesis en América y particularmente en Chile* (Santiago de Chile: Seminario Pontificio Mayor de los Santos Angeles Custodios, 1991). For a survey of early catechisms used in Latin America, see Pietro Braido, *Lineamenti di storia della catechesi e dei catechismi dal "tempo delle riforme" all'età degli imperialismi (1450–1850)* (Rome: Università Pontificia Salesiana, 1989) 86–102.

4. Thomas F. Meehan ed., *The Doctrina Breve in Facsimile* (New York: The United States Catholic Historical Society, 1928). I must acknowledge the work of Annamaria Diaz, former student and sometime research assistant, that is incorporated into this section on Zumárraga.

5. William B. Jones, "Evangelical Catholicism in Early Colonial Mexico. An Analysis of Bishop Juan de Zumárraga's *Doctrina Christiana*," *Americas* 23:4 (April 1967) 423–32.

6. O'Malley, *The First Jesuits*, 118.

7. For an English translation of Cordoba's work, see Sterling A. Stoudemire, ed., *Christian Doctrine for the Instruction and Information of the Indians* (Coral Gables, Fla.: University of Miami, 1970).

8. James Riley, "Who is St. Toribio of Mogrovejo?" *The Living Light* 26:3 (1990) 238–42. Nicolas de Jesus Rodriguez, "From Trent to Puebla: Evangelization in Latin America," ibid., 243–56.

SIX

# The Use and Misuse of Catechisms:
# An Early Critique

By the end of the sixteenth century, Catholics had published dozens, perhaps hundreds, of catechisms, but it was in the seventeenth century that the modern catechism began to take definitive shape in content and approach. While the earlier works emphasized Church doctrine, the newer texts were more sensitive to pastoral issues and, in some cases, to pedagogy. In France the reforms of the Council of Trent were taking root. Vincent de Paul, an innovator in pastoral ministry, was one of many clerics to write a catechism and inspired others to do the same. Jean Jacques Olier, the founder of the Society of Saint Sulpice in Paris, developed catechetical programs and methods that were copied into the twentieth century.[1]

## Jacques Benigne Bossuet

Trent's emphasis on episcopal responsibility for preaching and teaching led many bishops either to commission catechisms or to compose their own texts. Intended primarily for local use in their place of origin, some of these catechisms, either by merit of the works themselves or by reason of the prestige of their authors, were reprinted and sometimes translated for use in other regions. One such catechism that gained a wide audience was the *Catéchisme du diocèse de Meaux* by the great orator and Churchman Jacques Benigne Bossuet (1627–1704).

Bossuet spent the first years of his public ministry in and around Metz, where he gained a reputation as a preacher. Between 1670 and 1681 he served as preceptor to the dauphin, that is to say, he was the private tutor to the heir-apparent to King Louis XIV. It was during this period that Bossuet wrote several theological treatises, including the "Discourse on Universal History," which rivaled Augustine's *City of God* in vision and scope. In 1681 Bossuet turned his attention to pastoral ministry in the diocese of Meaux, where he engaged in polemics against Protestant doctrine and in theological debate with his fellow Catholics. He took issue with Fénelon, the archbishop of Cambrai, in the Quietism controversy and denounced the works of Catholic biblical scholar Richard Simon.

It was during this third period of his life that Bossuet wrote his celebrated *Catéchisme* (1686). It was actually three catechisms in one with a strong emphasis on sacraments and liturgy. The first, for small children preparing for confirmation and the sacrament of penance, is a brief summary of basic doctrines and prayers. The second prepares older children for first Communion; it is prefaced with a brief survey ("Abrégé de l'histoire sainte") and concludes with a series of questions and answers that review the main points of Bible history. The third, structured around Church feasts and rituals, is for all the faithful. The entire catechism is laced with practical advice on how to link biblical texts to doctrine, and it suggests ways of presenting the material to the learners according to their age and ability.

### Claude Fleury

Bossuet acknowledged his indebtedness to Claude Fleury's *Catéchisme historique,* the most original of the new generations of catechisms. Fleury (1640–1723) is best remembered as a Church historian because of his monumental twenty-volume work on ecclesiastical history. He began his career as a lawyer but earned a lasting reputation as an educator.[2] He studied at the Jesuit College of Clermont, was admitted to the bar at the age of eighteen, and practiced law in Paris for about ten years. During that time he read widely in civil and canon law, history, literature, and archeology.

Although Fleury lamented the widespread ignorance and lack of appreciation for the Christian tradition, he lived at a time when Catholicism was a major force in French society. The first half of the seventeenth century witnessed a remarkable renewal of Christian life and practice under the leadership of Francis de Sales, Vincent de Paul, the Oratorians, and the Sulpicians. Cornelius Jansen laid the foundation of Jansenism with the publication of *Augustinus* (1640), and Abbé Saint-Cyran began to exercise an insidious influence over the Arnaulds and Port-Royal, the mainspring of the movement. The second half of the century, dominated by the "Sun King," Louis XIV (1643–1715), was a period of brilliant Church leaders, preachers, spiritual counselors, writers, and exemplary Christians. Fleury was a protégé of the great Bossuet and a friend of the almost equally famous Fénelon. Other luminaries among Fleury's contemporaries were the renowned Jean Baptiste de La Salle, Louis-Marie de Montfort, and Margaret Mary Alacoque. The popularity of religious writings is further evidence of interest in the spiritual life at the time. Sermons, works on mental prayer, lives of saints, and devotional works of every description commanded a wide audience of clergy, religious, and laity alike.

A meeting with Vincent de Paul inspired Fleury to become a priest. Bossuet introduced him to the French court, where he held appointed positions for much of his adult life. In 1672, at the time when Bossuet was tutor for the dauphin, Fleury became the tutor for Louis XIV's daughter, the princess of Conti. From 1680 to 1684 he served as a tutor for another of the king's sons. In 1689 Fénelon had him recalled to court to tutor Louis XIV's grandsons, a post he held for sixteen years. He wrote a number of works that connect him with the educational methods of Port-Royal and the Oratory. In 1683 he published the *Catéchisme historique,* which is the focus of this chapter.

## The Design and Use of the *Catéchisme historique*

The *Catéchisme historique* incorporates two catechisms in a single book. The first, the Short Catechism *(Petit catéchisme historique),* was intended for catechists and parents to use in teaching illiterate peasants and children. The second, the Great Catechism, was for the instruction and edification of adults. Both are subdivided into two parts. The Short Catechism presents "a summary of the sacred history" and "a summary of the Christian Doctrine." The Great Catechism follows much the same outline but treats the sacred history at greater length and in the second part presents "the principles of religion."

Fleury introduced the work with a long preface, "A Discourse concerning the Design and Use of this Catechism." As the title suggests, it provides a rationale that explains Fleury's aim and purpose, but it is, in fact, also a critique of existing catechisms. He begins by describing widespread "want of instruction" on the Christian mysteries and rules of morality, not simply among peasants, but among men and women of letters and devout people. He acknowledges that the cause of this ignorance and the resistance to study is original sin, but he refuses to accept this as an excuse. When it comes to business and trade, even the illiterate manage to learn whatever is necessary to safeguard their own interests.

Ignorance of the Christian religion is in large part, says Fleury, "the fault of us priests, and of all who are deputed to instruct." We give books to the educated, but even the well disposed find them unintelligible and uninteresting because they are written in Latin, "full of curious questions," and tedious. Lives of the saints are more inspirational, but they have the same shortcoming that renders most sermons ineffective: sermons, taking their inspiration from the feast, the readings, or the purpose of the preacher, treat of particulars without situating them in the overall framework of Christian doctrine. And biblical texts are cited as if everyone in the world was acquainted with their context and meaning.

Fleury held up the new catechisms as a beacon of hope. They present the essentials of Christian doctrine in a brief but ordered way, using questions and answers as an effective means of instruction. In a tribute both to catechisms and to the Jesuits, he writes, ". . . these catechisms have produced most wonderful fruits: for whatever ignorance be remaining amongst the Christians, it is not comparable to that which reigned amongst them two hundred years ago, before St. Ignatius and his disciples had revived the custom of catechizing children."[3]

This accolade notwithstanding, Fleury found the catechisms then in circulation off-putting. "The style of catechisms," he says, "is commonly very dry," and children have great difficulty in comprehending and retaining the lessons. He has a plan for improving the catechisms, but first he asks why they are so dry. He traces the cause to the authors: theologians trained in Scholasticism. They abridge the contents of learned tomes and translate the text into the vernacular without adapting the language and style for the ordinary reader. They rely on philosophical definitions, subtle distinctions, and logical divisions that are beyond the reach of peasants, housekeepers, and children.

## The Language of Catechisms

Fleury draws on his own experience as a catechist in the royal household. "The best method of teaching," he writes, "is not that which appears the most natural, when truths are to be considered, abstractly, and in themselves; but that which is experienced to be the most proper for carrying these truths into the minds of the hearers." It is at this point that he begins to argue his case for a catechesis centered on "a narration and a bare recital of facts *[faits]** on which were built the dogmas and precepts of morality."

According to Fleury's reading of events, the true religion was preserved by oral tradition alone for the first two thousand years of human history. Even after "Moses, inspired by God, collected all these ancient traditions, and wrote them in the Book of Genesis and the following books," knowledge of the events was passed on orally from generation to generation. "For the whole times of the Old Testament, religion was preserved by narrations, and by histories." And the same method was used to promulgate the new covenant. Even before the accounts of Jesus' life, his discourses, miracles, resurrection, and establishment of the Church were written down, Stephen's sermon and the preaching of the apostles recorded in Acts make it clear that their instructions "were always grounded on a deduction of facts." Their words ". . . were to remind the Jews of what God had done for their fathers, and of what he had promised to them. . . .

*The 1753 English translation renders *faits* as facts. In today's idiom, "deeds" or "events" better capture Fleury's thought.

And to inform the infidels that God had created the world, that he governed it by his providence, and that he has sent an extraordinary man to judge it."[4]

Similarly, examples of catechesis in the writings of the Church Fathers show that they too relied on narrative. They instructed catechumens by recounting all that God has done for humanity from the foundation of the world to the promulgation of the gospel. The *First Catechetical Instruction* of Augustine illustrates how the narration was accommodated to the capacity of the listeners and the time available.

Fleury states that "there are reasons to believe" that this manner of instruction continued as long as the ancient discipline of the catechumenate endured. Beginning in the ninth century, however, when "few besides infants were baptized, these public instructions degenerated into formalities; and the misery of the times, having ushered in a profound ignorance, even among the clergy, the effectual instruction was much neglected." When children memorized the Creed and the Lord's Prayer, they were considered to have learned the entire catechism. It was thought that if Christians had "a moderate knowledge of the creed, they might generally spare themselves the trouble" of becoming acquainted with the narratives on which the ancients laid such great importance.

When addressing the educated, the Church Fathers sometimes used rational arguments to convince their audience that "there is a God, the creator of all things, who preserves them, and governs them by his providence; that human nature is corrupt, that the soul is immortal and cannot find happiness in this life." But children and adults of limited ability and short attention span are not capable of following this line of reasoning. Therefore, God

> . . . has built the doctrine of his religion on proofs well fitted to every capacity, which is to say, on facts; on evident, illustrious, sensible facts, such as the creation of the world, the sin of the first man, the deluge, the calling of Abraham, the going out of Egypt.
>
> That the truth of these facts might never be called in question, by such who had not seen them, God has . . . borne witness to those who related them, by other extraordinary facts, that is to say, by miracles, such as those of Moses, and of the prophets, and in fine, of Jesus Christ, and his disciples.[5]

There is no better way to teach than by storytelling. Everyone can understand and enjoy a good story. Facts essential to the narrative, because they engage the senses and excite the imagination, are easily remembered. Fleury warns, however, against fanciful stories from "ill-written lives of saints" that are at best uncertain and most often simply improbable. Children may be captivated by them, but as they grow older and discover that the tales are untrue, they develop a contempt for everything they learned in childhood "without distinguishing what was solidly good." The catechism "is the word of God," and should not contain anything that cannot stand public scrutiny and is unbecoming "the majesty of religion."

Another way of helping the catechism arouse the imagination of children is by illustrating the biblical stories with pictures. Yet Fleury criticizes the woodcuts in most catechisms he has seen on a number of counts. First, the illustrations give more attention to the Book of Genesis than to the historical books and, consequently, obscure incidents like the punishment of Adonibezec and Agag and the revolt of Zamri are highlighted, while more significant events, like the promise of a messiah made to David and the lives of the prophets, are ignored. Second, the pictures are episodic and the catechisms do not explain how the events they depict relate to one another. Third, books full of illustrations are more expensive and become out of the reach of the poor, "who have the greatest want of instructions." The problem is further compounded when, to cut costs, publishers omit the woodcuts. When the cuts are removed the text is not easily understood, because the text is designed to explain the pictures. These reservations notwithstanding, Fleury thought pictures too important to omit and, in fact, his own catechism was first published with pictures that he himself drew.

The polemic character of Fleury's prologue, generally subdued, bursts into the open when he describes catechisms that use Scholastic terms. He berates authors who find it acceptable that Christians are "strangers to the names of the patriarchs and prophets, to the captivity of Egypt, and of Babylon, provided they know, that in God there are three persons, that the second was made man, and that there are seven sacraments." He does not accept the excuse that the small catechisms are too short to include narratives of this kind because, he notes, their authors make room for topics that are not matters of faith. Time and again he hammers at this theme, citing, by way of example, such terms as *infused* and *theological virtues, dulia* and *hyperdulia,* and a long list of philosophical distinctions such as *matter and form* and *act and potency.* Terms of this kind, difficult enough for the educated to understand, have no meaning for ordinary people and do nothing to enhance their understanding of the faith.

The language of catechisms, Fleury insists, should imitate as much as possible the manner and style of Jesus, the apostles, and the prophets. Their expressions were the kind that fire the imagination—familiar, plain, and concrete. He contends that few people are capable of thinking and remembering without reliance on the imagination. "We can never be too careful," he says, of preserving a certain uniformity in our speech. Catechisms should incorporate the language of the liturgy, the ancient Creeds, and prayers found in the breviary and missal. Fleury, writing at the time when the cult of the Sacred

Heart and other popular devotions were being introduced, disapproves of the "itching desire for new and singular devotions." He does make allowance for the rosary as a concession to those who cannot read.

Despite themselves, the authors of whom Fleury complains do make mention of certain events. There is no way to account for the Decalogue without reference to Moses, or to explain the Creed without referring to the sin of our first parents and the historical circumstances surrounding the birth of Jesus, his miracles, and his passion, death, and resurrection. These facts are far more intelligible and memorable when they are described at a reasonable length and related to one another in some kind of chronological sequence than when only passing reference is made to them in connection with some point of doctrine.

It is not simply a question of becoming acquainted with the stories because they are the basis of doctrine and beliefs; indeed, familiarity with the patriarchs, kings, and prophets is the basis of Christian literacy. Without some knowledge of the stories and principal actors in the Bible, Fleury asks, how can one profit from books of piety and sermons that make frequent allusion to biblical figures, places, and events? It is simply not possible to grasp the significance of the Sunday readings, the hymns, and the sacramental rites celebrated in and by the Church without an acquaintance with the Old and New Testaments.

In criticizing the contemporary situation, Fleury romanticizes the past. "If all Christians were now as capable as they were in primitive times, of reading the Scripture, and of understanding it, they would need no other instruction." Most ordinary people come to a standstill when they confront the sacred text. The length of the Bible, the diversity of its books, the divide between ancient and modern cultures, obscure expressions, and imperfect translations contribute to the difficulty. Nor are all the books of equal importance; the historical books are more necessary "than Job, the Canticle [of Canticles] and the prophets [!], and the New Testament more than the Old." Before confronting the faithful with each book and passage, Fleury proposes to present an overview, a kind of study guide, that marks a point of departure and highlights texts that deserve greatest attention.

Fleury offers his critique of the catechisms in use at the time as a justification for his own catechism. The *Catéchisme historique* is designed, he says, to ground the explication of the Creed and Christian doctrine in the biblical narrative. He used the method in his own teaching, and found that it yielded positive results. The outline follows a chronological development "insomuch that the order of the Scriptures includes the whole economy of God's designs." Fleury was not the first to use sacred history as a means for teaching doctrine. Luther and Calvin had presented doctrine as "salvation history," that is, as the story of sin and redemption. Several Jansenist catechisms then in circulation adopted a similar framework. Fleury, however, had a broader vision of history. He saw the Church as the people of God, whose roots were deep in the Old Testament and whose growth and development were intertwined with cultural developments and political institutions.

As noted above, the Short Catechism is subdivided into two parts, "a summary of the sacred history" and "a summary of the Christian Doctrine." The first part consists of twenty-nine lessons that, beginning with the story of creation, survey highlights of the Old and New Testaments up through Constantine's emancipation of the Church to the development of monastic life. The summary of Christian doctrine, also consisting of twenty-nine lessons, is more traditional. It presents the four pillars: the Creed, the Lord's Prayer and other prayers, the Decalogue and the (six) precepts of the Church, and the seven sacraments. The Great Catechism expands on these two summaries. Its explanation of the Eucharist is noteworthy because it includes an extensive instruction on the sacrifice of the Mass and its parts.

Both catechisms use a narrative style to expound their lessons, but they are significantly different from previous catechisms in several respects. The Short Catechism appends a list of questions and answers to each lesson. Some questions highlight points made in the body of the lesson, but others extend it, making inquiry into points that are only treated in the Great Catechism.

> Some perhaps will wonder at the connected discourse [the narrative], which I have joined to all the lessons of the short catechism, before the questions and answers. The historical method obliged me so to do. For a history is much better understood when presented at one view, than when divided into questions. Besides, that it might seem strange to interrogate a child before we have taught him anything . . .[6]

Fleury did not intend the questions and answers to be memorized; ideally, they were to serve as points for discussion. In any case, "I desire," he wrote, that "the catechist would give himself all the necessary liberty, as to the enlarging or shortening the questions as well as the discourse."

Notwithstanding that it was placed on the *Index of Prohibited Books* "*donec corrigatur*" ("until corrected") in 1728, the influence of the *Catéchisme historique* was widespread. Outside of France, German Pietists and English Methodists, including John Wesley, borrowed from and even recommended Fleury's catechetical approach. The earliest English translation, "printed for Ignatius Kelly, at the Stationers-Arms in St. Mary's Lane (Dublin)," is dated 1753. In 1813, French-born Jean Lefebvre de Cheverus, Boston's first bishop, authorized an English translation of the *Petit catéchisme* for use in the newly formed New England diocese.[7] An 1859 survey of fifty-seven Catholic schools in Australia showed thirty-one of them using Fleury's catechism.[8] His voice echoed in repeated pleas in England and the United States for catechesis through sacred history.[9] Henry Formby, a strong advocate for such an approach, published an edition of Fleury's Short Catechism, "continued down to the recent Vatican Council" (1871).

Fleury's criticisms of the common run of catechisms apply also to English-language works, with one exception. The catechism in the Book of Common Prayer, as will be seen in the next chapter, was unique. It differed from other classic catechisms as much as the Reformation in England differed from the Reformation on the Continent. It had a different history, served a different purpose, and never gained the prominence of other Reformation classics.

### NOTES

1. The classic work for this period is Jean-Claude Dhotel, *Les origines du catéchisme moderne* (Paris: Éditions Montaigne, 1977). See Joseph Colombo, "The Catechetical Method of Saint Sulpice," in Gerard S. Sloyan, ed., *Shaping the Christian Message* (Glen Rock, N.J.: Deus Books/Paulist, 1958) 98–118.

2. Raymond F. Wanner, *Claude Fleury (1640–1723) as an Educational Historiographer and Thinker* (The Hague: Martinus Nijhoff, 1975).

3. Claude Fleury, *An Historical Catechism Containing a Summary of the Sacred History and Christian Doctrine* (Dublin: Ignatius Kelly, 1853) vii. All English quotations in the text are taken from this translation.

4. Ibid., xii.

5. Ibid., xvi.

6. Ibid., xxxiii.

7. Reference is made to Fleury's *Catechismus historicus minor* in a public controversy, sometime about 1806, between the faculty of St. Mary's University, Baltimore, and a group of Protestant ministers. See Charles Carmody, *The Roman Catholic Catechesis in the United States 1784–1930: A Study of Its Theory, Development, and Materials* (Ph.D. diss., University of Loyola of Chicago, 1975) (facsimile edition: Ann Arbor: Xerox University Microfilms) 51 n. 24.

8. Cited by Edmund Campion, "With an Eye to the Past," in Andrew Murray, ed., *The New Catechism: Analysis and Commentary* (Manly, N.S.W.: Catholic Institute of Sidney, 1994) 8.

9. See Carmody, *The Roman Catholic Catechesis,* 97–99, 108–10, and passim.

SEVEN

# English Catechisms I:
# Primers and the Book of Common Prayer

Reformers, Protestant and Catholic alike, saw the printed word as central to their cause. Books, becoming ever more accessible to ordinary folk, nurtured Christians, individually and corporately, in knowledge and practice of their faith. They provided a ready means to communicate ideas and attitudes and to advance the cause of reform. Furthermore, printed texts begot standardization and insured uniformity to a degree that manuscripts, produced piecemeal, could not. All over Europe authorities "sought to control the book trade and to use it for their own political and religious purposes."[1] Early in the sixteenth century the Fifth Lateran Council (1512–17), for example, recognized the great potential for good of the printing press and at the same time instituted procedures of censorship.[2]

In no country was the cause of Protestant reform more closely tied to the printed word than in England. The Book of Common Prayer, made obligatory throughout the realm in 1549, became the bellwether of its progress, a witness to unity in the Church of England and ultimately in the worldwide Anglican communion. From the beginning the Book of Common Prayer included a catechism, the vicissitudes of which were also a measure of the fortunes of Protestantism in the realm.[3]

From the time it first appeared in print, the Book of Common Prayer was intended to be the exclusive liturgical text of the Church of England. Its use was made obligatory beginning Whitsunday (June 9), 1549. It was revised in 1552, 1559, and again in 1604, and a special edition was prepared for use in Scotland in 1637. During the time of the Commonwealth (1649–60) its public use was prohibited, but with the restoration of the monarchy it came back into fashion. With the new Act of Uniformity in the time of Charles II, the 1662 edition was made obligatory. Over the years revisions were proposed, but none was authorized by the Church of England until 1962, when a revised text was approved for trial use.[4]

Before the development of the catechism is traced, however, the Book of Common Prayer must be placed in the context of Tudor political and religious strategies initiated under Henry VIII (1509–47).

## Uniformity in Doctrine and Expression: Primers

The centerpiece in the program of the English reformers from John Wyclif (d. 1384) to Thomas Cranmer and the Puritans was the vernacular Bible.[5] They held that Holy Writ, at least the Gospels and the Epistles of St. Paul, ought to be accessible to all. In 1547 Cranmer, archbishop of Canterbury (1533–56), published under royal authority a set of injunctions that required every parish church to have copies of the Great Bible, Erasmus's *Paraphrases* on the Gospels and Acts, and the *Book of Homilies,* a collection of twelve sermons, and to use them for public reading, Bible study, and preaching.[6] Inspired by Erasmian ideals of education and reform, Cranmer and his collaborators challenged Rome and sought to transform the Church in England into an independent, national model of the Christian commonwealth. Their goal was to impose uniformity in doctrine and expression on the faithful in England and Ireland.

In 1545, two years before his death, Henry VIII had published a primer "to be taught, learned, and read: and none other [is] to be used throughout all his dominions."[7] The first edition in English was followed by a bilingual printing in English and Latin, and finally by one in Latin alone. An injunction at the beginning of this Authorized Primer explained its purpose and design. It was intended as a means to counteract "the diversity of primer books that are now abroad, whereof are almost innumerable sorts which minister occasion of contentions and vain disputations, rather than to edify, and to have one uniform order of all such books throughout all our dominions, both to be taught unto children, and also to be used for ordinary prayers of all our people not learned in the Latin tongue."[8] Although considerably revised, the Authorized Primer followed the outline of similar works of the time. There were first the preliminary features—liturgical calendar, Lord's Prayer, Ave Maria, Creed, Commandments, grace for meals; second, the offices and psalms that were the core of the genre; and finally, the Passion according to St. John, followed by "a large and unusual collection of prayers."[9]

Henry's primer, clearly a part of the national campaign to impose religious uniformity, was nonetheless an offspring of earlier primers that had begun more and more to introduce English content into the Latin manuals. London printer Wynkyn de Worde, for example, published a Latin primer in 1513 that contained an English paraphrase of the Ten Commandments in rhyme. In 1523 Worde published another primer that contained "englysshe" translations of the Creed and the Pater noster as well as a form of confession in English.[10]

The translation of select prayers was one thing; English primers were quite another. The reputation of their authors, generally associated with the reform movement, and the rendering of extensive passages of Scripture (including the psalms) in the vernacular made them suspect of heresy. An English primer was outlawed by an ecclesiastical commission in 1530, in part because it contained an English text of the psalms for matins and vespers and translations of the entire psalter, and in part because of what it omitted. Thomas More, then Lord Chancellor, faulted it for suppressing the litany "lest folk should pray to saints," and the dirge (i.e., office of the dead) "lest a man might happen to pray thereon for his father's soul."[11] It also embodied an English version of a *hortulus animae* (garden of the soul), a common genre that described a collection of prayers and often included a short catechism. Like many outlawed texts, this primer was printed abroad, probably in Antwerp.

Thomas More attributes this 1530 primer, including the *hortulus,* to the priest George Joye "that is wedded now." Although Joye did not intend the work primarily for the young, he included "a fruitful and a very Christian instruction for children," consisting chiefly of prayers to be said morning and evening, and of graces before and after meals. The prayers are derived from Lutheran sources—either Luther's *Betbuchlein* (1522) or his Small Catechism (1529), probably the latter. The "fruitful instruction" is followed by a catechism expounding the Creed and the Ten Commandments. Joye's title for this latter section is "a dialogue wherein the Child, asked certain questions, answers to the same." It starts out:

> The question.
> Speak my dear child, what art thou?
> The answer.
> As concerning my first birth, I am a creature of God endowed with wit and reason, the son of Adam; and as touching my new and second birth I [ac]knowledge myself to be a Christian.[12]

In 1534 William Marshall, an ardent Protestant, published in London *A goodly prymer in englyshe.* Although it does not credit the source and alters the order, Marshall's work reproduces virtually the entire contents of Joye's *hortulus,* including the catechism, supplemented by material from Luther's works. Marshall's exposition of the Commandments, Creed, Pater noster, and Ave Maria is derived from Luther's *Betbuchlein.* In Marshall's primer the catechism, consisting of twenty-two questions and answers, follows the Liturgy of the Hours and the psalms. The first edition follows Joye in having the father ask the questions with the child answering. In the second edition, however, the roles are reversed; the child asks the questions and the father replies.

In the hands of the reformers the primers became more and more manuals of instruction, but not every primer contained a catechism. In 1539 John Hilsey, who had succeeded John Fisher as bishop of Rochester, compiled a *Manual of Prayers* that he hoped would replace versions of the primer that had become focal points of controversy. Hilsey collected the contents into three sections dealing with faith, prayer, and works. The first centered on the Creed and the passion, the second on the psalms for matins and the hours, and the third on the Commandments and scriptural admonitions suitable for the various "estates" of society. It did not, however, embody a catechism.

Hardly a year had passed when a London printer, Nicholas Bourman, adopted Hilsey's *Manual* as the basis for his own primer. He included a catechism that borrowed from the "dialogue" in Marshall's primer. He described it as, "A Catechismus, or childish instruction which all parents are bound to see their children to know by rote, set forth question and answer wise."

Henry VIII's is another primer that did not contain a catechism. Maintaining the traditional forms, it introduced prayers adapted from works of the continental reformers and used biblical translations of the English reformers. Implicit throughout was the effort to gain for the English language a status equal to that of Latin in prayer and worship.

### English Catechisms

Thomas Cranmer (1489–1556), named archbishop of Canterbury in 1532, was a principal strategist behind the Protestant reform in England. In the time of Henry VIII, Cranmer, among his many projects, promoted the dissemination of the Bible in English and took a personal interest in shaping and promulgating the Authorized Primer. During the reign of Edward VI Cranmer lent his hand to compiling a number of catechisms, the most famous of which was incorporated into the Book of Common Prayer of 1549 and 1552.

The first "Church catechism," as it is called in England, was based on a 1543 document of Henry VIII, "A Necessary Doctrine and Erudition for Any Christian Man," popularly known as the "King's Book." It included questions on the baptismal promises, the Creed, the Ten Commandments, one's "duties" toward God and neighbor, the Lord's Prayer, and "desire," that is, what is to be hoped for in praying the Pater noster. Published with a preface by the king, it was Henry's aim to instruct the faithful in what it was necessary for them to know: faith, the Creed, the sacraments, the Commandments, the Lord's Prayer, the Ave Maria, free will, justification, good works, and prayer for the souls departed. (This emphasis on prayer for the departed souls was one of the marks that distinguished moderate English reformers from the more radical "protestant" wing. Confirmation was another.)

After King Henry's death, Cranmer's Protestant views came more and more into the open. In 1548 he published a catechism based on Justas Jonas's Latin version of the Brandenburg-Nürnberg catechism. Although the preface states that it is intended "for the behove of yong children, whiche muste be brought up with playne and shorte lessons," the catechism consists of a series of twenty-three sermons. They include an explanation of the Commandments, the Creed, the Lord's Prayer, instructions on baptism, the power of the keys, and the Lord's Supper. Cranmer lamented the ignorance of youth and the neglect of confirmation (which Henry had considered desirable but not mandatory for salvation).

The most enduring monument to Cranmer's pastoral genius, however, is the Book of Common Prayer. As its title suggests, it was to serve as a convenient and comprehensive volume for clergy and laity alike. In doctrine and ritual the original version (1549) represented a compromise between the old and the new, and it pleased partisans of neither side. The Act of Uniformity of 1549 imposed it throughout the realm and at the same time proscribed the possession of all other prayer books whether for public or private use. Parliament decreed "That all books called Antiphoners, Missals, Grailes, Processionals, Manuals, Legends, Pies, Portuasses, Primers in Latin or English . . . other than such as are or shall be set for by the King's majesty, shall be by authority of this present Act clearly and utterly abolished, extinguished, and forbidden for ever to be used or kept."[13]

The catechism in the Book of Common Prayer of 1549 was unlike other catechisms of the period. Since its immediate purpose was to prepare children for confirmation, it did cover all the basics of Christian doctrine. Cranmer copied the arrangement of Herman von Wied's *Simplex ac pia deliberatio.*\*

---

\*Although Scottish catechisms do not figure directly into this development, it should be noted that the catechism published by Archbishop John Hamilton of St. Andrews in 1552 was influenced by Wied's *Enchiridion Christianae institutionis.* Hamilton's catechism, intended to be a moderate statement of the traditional faith, followed the standard pattern except that it changed the order: Commandments, Creed, sacraments and "the maner how Christin men and wemen suld mak thair prayer to God." The last included a section on prayer for the departed souls. Written in the Scottish dialect, the catechism was to be placed in the hands of rectors, vicars, and curates, for their own instruction as well as that of the Christian people. The clergy were directed to read and recite it from the pulpit on Sundays and feast days, but under severe penalty were not to give copies to secular persons. Archbishop Hamilton was hanged by Protestants in 1571. See *The Catechism set forth by Archbishop Hamilton together with The Two-Penny Faith,* preface by Alex F. Mitchell, facsimile edition (Edinburgh: William Patterson, 1882).

(Wied had been archbishop of Cologne until he was deposed for his Lutheran leanings in 1546.)[14]

Cranmer intended this catechism to be a review of the syllabus outlined in the charge given to the godparents at the end of the baptismal service. It was the duty of godparents to teach their godchildren the Creed, the Lord's Prayer, and the Ten Commandments. The catechism was designed to find out whether children knew these prayers, for by ancient custom they could not be confirmed until they could repeat them. The wording of the Ten Commandments are shortened as in the "King's Book," and the explanation of the Lord's Prayer goes back to the exhortation before the 1544 litany. The catechism of the 1549 Book of Common Prayer is exceptional in that it does not contain anything on the sacraments.

When Queen Mary succeeded Edward VI on the throne, she restored the ancient services (1553), only to have Queen Elizabeth reissue the Book of Common Prayer with some slight alterations in 1559. The Acts of Uniformity of 1549, 1552, and 1559 which imposed the Book of Common Prayer to the exclusion of all other forms of worship seem, however, to have allowed exceptions in the case of catechisms.

John Ponet, sometime lecturer in Greek and a leading member of Cranmer's group of reformers, produced a *Catechismus brevis* (1552). An English translation, *A Short Catechisme*, gained some kind of official recognition when it was published together with the Forty-Two Articles in 1553. The title page of the Latin edition indicates that it was recommended for use in schools—"omnibus Ludimagistris authoritate Regia commendatus." A modern translator describes it as "a typical piece of Renaissance-Reformation writing . . . with its dual purpose of serving education as well as religion."[15] Its studied style is further indication that it was deliberately intended as a schoolbook. Written in classical Latin, the author takes pains to vary the words and phrases so as to build a broad vocabulary and provide diverse examples of syntax. The introduction defends the question-answer form by citing Socrates' use of dialogue in philosophy and that of Apollinarius in theology.

Ponet's catechism orders the material according to the general pattern of Reformation catechisms: the Commandments, Creed, and Lord's Prayer. The most noteworthy element in its exposition of the Creed is the emphasis given to the ascension and session of Christ. (This doctrine had special significance for the Reformed theology of the Eucharist—the body of Christ is in heaven, not on earth.) The article on the Holy Spirit leads into a discussion of the sacraments.

During the reign of Queen Mary, Ponet fled to exile in Strasbourg, where he died in 1566. In the time of Elizabeth, his catechism was superseded by a work of Alexander Nowell (c. 1507–1602), *Catechismus, siue prima institutio, disciplinaque pietatis Christianae* (1570). Thomas Norton, who translated it into English as *A Catechisme, or first Instruction and Learning of Christian Religion* (1570), added a preface that suggests Nowell's work was also intended for school use: ". . . in which Catechism there hath also great labor and diligence been bestowed about the purity of the Latin tongue, that such as were studious of that language . . . might at once with one labor learn the truth of religion and the pureness of the Latin tongue together."[16]

Like that of the Catholic Peter Canisius, a contemporary, Nowell's catechism appeared in three sizes—large, middle, and little. Although the Large Catechism, probably approved by Convocation in 1563, was not printed until 1572, the Middle Catechism, the one described here, was printed in 1570.[17]

With the ascent of James I to the English throne as successor to Queen Elizabeth, the disgruntled Puritan party presented the Millenary Petition with its list of grievances. One of the complaints was that the catechism in the 1559 Book of Common Prayer was too brief, while Nowell's Middle Catechism which had been authorized in 1570 was too long to be learned by heart. Further, it was suggested that one uniform catechism was needed.[18] Thus the catechism in the 1604 *Book of Common Prayer* incorporated some changes in the rites of baptism and confirmation, and an instruction on baptism and the Lord's Supper was added based on Nowell's catechisms. The canons then required that the 1604 catechism be learned as a precondition for confirmation and Holy Communion.[19] (The Puritans were not satisfied with the 1604 revision of the Book of Common Prayer, including the catechism.)

Just as the changes in the prayer book and catechism in 1604 were the result of demands by Puritans, changes in the 1662 edition came at the insistence of Presbyterians. The catechism was separated from the confirmation service and replaced by a series of questions and answers in conjunction with the renewal of the baptismal vows. A change in the rubrics allowed the bishop greater latitude in judging readiness for confirmation. Previously, the ability to recite the Creed, Lord's Prayer, and Ten Commandments and knowledge of the catechism were requirements for confirmation, but in 1662 the rubrics were more general. They allowed the curate to bring forward the names of those whom he deemed "fit." Further, the rubric for Communion directed only that one be confirmed "or be ready and desirous to be confirmed."[20]

## Modern Revisions

Revisions to the 1662 catechism were suggested over the years, but none was authorized until the 1962 Book of Common Prayer appeared. The archbishops' commission, charged with revising the catechism, incorporated material from previous unauthorized editions, including that of 1887, as well as from other Churches of the Anglican communion and non-Anglican Churches.[21] The commission sought to enlarge the content, adding material on the Church, grace, the Bible, Christian duty, and Christian hope. For reason of intelligibility, it also moved to make the language more contemporary and reflective of today's social conditions. The "Revised Catechism" of 1962, "after reinstatement of the devil," was authorized for a seven-year period.[22] The period was extended in 1969 by the Convocations of Canterbury and York, and again in 1973, 1980, and 1985 by the General Synod of the Church of England.

The 1962 catechism follows a question-answer format because it "emphasizes the moral responsibility of each person for his actions." The archbishops' commission cautions against insisting that the catechism be learned by heart because "it would place a heavy strain even on retentive memories, and it is not intended as a burden grievous to be borne." How the catechism is to be used depends on the catechist who is instructed "to select from the Catechism, or to enlarge and amplify it."[23]

From 1662 onward the catechism was placed in the Book of Common Prayer between the section on baptism and the order of confirmation. Nonetheless, the 1928 version "according to the use of The Protestant Episcopal Church in the United States of America" moved the catechism to the back of the book. In its usual place were substituted "The Offices of Instruction" in an apparent effort to continue to associate catechesis with the liturgical setting. Each of the two rites begins with a collect and a series of versicles and responses, followed by questions and answers based on the catechism. Prayers are introduced to separate one topic from another, and each office closes with a prayer. Material on Church and ministry from the unauthorized text of 1887 is introduced (though in the "Offices of Instruction" rather than in the catechism itself).

In 1973, the standing liturgical commission drafted a catechism to be considered for inclusion in the Book of Common Prayer used in the United States. This new catechism owed much to both the "Offices of Instruction" of 1928 and the 1962 revised catechism of the Church of England. The catechism in the 1979 Book of Common Prayer incorporated many texts from the 1973 draft, at the same time expanding and altering them. One significant difference is the shift in pronouns from the first person singular to the first person plural. This change seems to reflect the new emphasis on a covenant community evident elsewhere in the catechism (notably in the sections on the Church [pp. 854–55] and baptism [pp. 858–59]).

The 1979 catechism is in question-answer format "for ease of reference." Described as a "point of departure for the teacher," "an outline for instruction," and "a brief summary of the church's teaching for an inquiring stranger," it is clearly not a prerequisite for confirmation. Nor is the order of confirmation specific as to the type of instruction to be given in preparation. Nonetheless, canon 21, governing instruction of the faithful, mandates that the catechism be taught: "It shall be the duty of ministers of this Church who have charge of Parishes or Cures to be diligent in instructing the children in the Catechism, and from time to time to examine them in the same publicly before the Congregation."[24]

Until the recent changes, the prayer book catechism continued the practice of situating religious instruction in a devotional and liturgical context. This tradition, enshrined in the primers of the fifteenth century, was further advanced by the educational ideals and methods of Erasmian humanists, who saw knowledge of faith and morals as a means of nurturing devotion and piety. After the Acts of Uniformity imposed the Book of Common Prayer, itself a descendant of the medieval primers, and it became a manual for private use as well as public worship, it subsumed the primer's chief function. The spirit of the medieval primer, however, did not die, but went underground. Recusant works in England and Ireland continued the tradition in devotional works that supplement the texts used in the official liturgy. The next chapter will show how Roman Catholic prayer books, especially Richard Challoner's *Garden of the Soul* (1740), served as manuals that instructed generations in knowledge of the faith and Christian living as well as resources for personal piety.

NOTES

1. John E. Booty, ed., *The Godly Kingdom of Tudor England: Great Books of the English Reformation* (Wilton, Conn.: Morehouse-Barlow, 1981) 6.

2. Norman P. Tanner, ed., *Decrees of the Ecumenical Councils* (Washington, Georgetown University, 1990) 632–33.

3. See Fredrica Harris Thompsett, "Godly Instruction in Reformation England: The Challenge of Religious Education in the Tudor Commonwealth," Westerhoff and Edwards, *A Faithful Church*, 174–203.

4. The 1662 edition was the basis for the American *Book of Common Prayer* issued by the first General Convention in 1789. In the course of time, changes and additions were introduced in the American prayer book, major revisions taking place in 1892, 1928, and, most recently, 1979.

5. In the wake of the stir caused by Wyclif's insistence that a vernacular translation of the Bible be given to English readers, Church authorities imposed severe restrictions. A convocation at Oxford in 1408 decreed that "no one shall in future translate on his own authority any text of holy scripture into the English tongue" under penalty of excommunication. See Charles C. Butterworth, *The English Primers (1529–1545)* (Philadelphia: University of Pennsylvania, 1953) 5.

6. John N. Wall, Jr., "Godly and Fruitful Lessons: The English Bible, Erasmus' Paraphrases and the Book of Homilies," in Booty, *Godly Kingdom*, 47–48.

7. Butterworth, *The English Primers*, 256.

8. Quoted in ibid., 257. Spelling modernized.

9. Ibid., 259.

10. Ibid., 6, 8.

11. Ibid., 23.

12. Ibid., 35.

13. Edmund Bishop, ed., *Introduction to Henry Littlehales, the Prymer or Lay Folks' Prayer Book* (London: Early English Text Society, 1897) no. 109, part 2, p. ix.

14. G. J. Cuming, *A History of Anglican Liturgy* (New York: St. Martin's, 1969) 45, 87.

15. T. H. L. Parker, ed., *English Reformers*, The Library of Christian Classics 26 (Philadelphia: Westminster, 1966) 150.

16. Alexander Nowell, *A Catechism*, ed. G. D. Corrie, Parker Society (Cambridge: Cambridge University, 1953) 107. Quoted by David Siegenthaler in Booty, *Godly Kingdom*, 242.

17. It is on the basis of the close resemblance of Dean Nowell's Little Catechism and the catechism in the 1549 Book of Common Prayer that the argument is made for his authorship of the latter. See Edwin B. Redlich, *The Church Catechism: Its History and Meaning* (London: Macmillan, 1924) 145–46.

18. For a list of grievances, see Cuming, *Anglican Liturgy*, 136–37.

19. This dates back to the so-called Peckham's Constitutions issued by the Council of Lambeth in 1281. To suppress abuses concerning the Eucharist and to combat the neglect of confirmation, Archbishop Peckham ordered that "none be admitted to the Sacrament of Lord's Body and Blood that is not confirmed, except on the point of death, unless he have a reasonable impediment." This prohibition continues to the present in the Church of England. It was the practice in the Episcopal Church in the United States until the ratification of the 1979 Book of Common Prayer.

20. Redlich, *The Church Catechism*, 156.

21. *A Revised Catechism: Being the Report of the Archbishops Commission to Revise the Church Catechism* (London: SPCK, 1961) viii.

22. Cuming, *Anglican Liturgy*, 255.

23. *Report*, vi–vii.

24. *Constitution and Canons of the Episcopal Church*, title 3, canon 21.2(a) (New York: Seabury Professional Services, 1979) 93. The *Alternative Service Book 1980* of the Church of England neither contains nor makes specific reference to a catechism. David W. Lankshear and Leslie J. Francis write, "While the catechism remains an important touchstone of Anglican identity according to the formal canons of the church, its referencing in catechetical material has significantly diminished during the past four decades." See "The Use of the Revised Catechism in Anglican Churches," in *British Journal of Religious Education*, vol. 13, no.2 (Spring 1991) 96.

EIGHT

# English Catechisms II:
# The Penny Catechism and Its Predecessors

Catholics, failed in their attempt at restoration of the old order under Mary Tudor, became more and more isolated and driven underground. With the new Act of Supremacy and the promulgation of the Thirty-Nine Articles in the early years of Elizabeth's reign (1559–1603), the direction of the Reformation was set and its future assured. Positions hardened. The decrees of the Council of Trent, then in its last sessions, removed any remaining ambiguity about Catholic doctrine and sacramental practice. With the excommunication of Queen Elizabeth in 1570 all hope of compromise or accommodation vanished. The next two centuries saw the number of Catholics in England shrink precipitously and their position in society become perilous. Paradoxically, it was also the period in which the seeds of a Catholic revival were sown.

That the Catholic faith in England survived at all was due in large measure to the work of the English College at Douai, then in the Spanish Netherlands. The college began its life as a center of studies for exiled Catholic scholars under the aegis of the newly founded University of Douai, but soon began to train secular priests for the English mission. Its alumni took the lead in preparing the ground and sowing the seeds that later blossomed in the Catholic revival. The town also became an influential publishing center, disseminating books and pamphlets that defended the faith and nourished the piety of generations of Catholics. The most famous publication was the Douai Old Testament (1609–10), but it was also the source of the less well-known "Doway Catechism," the distant ancestor of *A Catechism of Christian Doctrine*, popularly known as the "Penny Catechism," that was in common use in Great Britain and many countries in the Commonwealth up to the eve of the Second Vatican Council.[1]

## Vaux's Catechism

Early in Queen Elizabeth's reign—some seventy-five years before the Doway Catechism appeared—a Lancashire priest, Lawrence Vaux (b. 1519), published *A Catechism, or Christian Doctrine necessarie for children and ignorante people* (Louvain, 1567).[2] In his preface Vaux wrote, "I have compiled this little booke for young scolers and the unlearned, and what I have set furth, the grounde and substance I have collected and translated out the Scripture and generall Councells, out of the bookes of D. Petrus de Soto and D. Canisius, adding here and there some sentences of the anncient Fathers."[3]

Vaux follows Augustine's outline, dividing the material under the three-fold heading of faith, hope, and charity and centering them on the Creed, the Our Father, and the Commandments. He is like Canisius and the medievals before him in that he presents what is to be believed and done more by way of commentary on the classic texts than by the emphasis on fixed definitions characteristic of later catechisms. Another vestige of medieval influence, not found in later works, is an examination of conscience on the proper use of the five senses. Even though Vaux wrote at the time when Elizabethan reforms were being debated, the main body of his catechism is singularly devoid of polemics. He did add, however, an appendix directed against the new "heresies." The work went through a number of printings, but it was eventually eclipsed by an English translation of Robert Bellarmine's small catechism, one edition "with images," which began circulating in an English translation early in the seventeenth century.

## The Doway Catechism

Whereas Vaux drew on Canisius's catechism, Henry Turberville seems to have followed Bellarmine's outline in compiling *An Abridgement of Christian Doctrine with proofs of Scripture for Points controverted: Catechistically explained by way of Question and Answer*. Turberville's work came to be known as the Doway Catechism because it was first printed there in 1649. As a youth of nineteen, Turberville left his native Staffordshire for Douai where he was ordained. It was after he returned to the English mission, around 1640, that he wrote this work. He also wrote a *Manual of Controversies* that was likewise published in Douai. He died in prison in 1678 at about 69 years of age.

Like Bellarmine, Turberville begins with the question, "Child! What religion are you of?" Under the headings of faith, hope, and charity, he expounds the twelve articles of the Creed, the Pater noster and Hail Mary, the Commandments, the precepts of the Church, the seven sacraments, the fruits and gifts of the Holy Ghost, the works of mercy, the eight Beatitudes, sin, and the four last things. Turberville reflects, especially in the sections on Church, worship, and Eucharist, the controversies of the time. He is particularly direct in addressing the teachings of the Puritans. In the rare book collection of the Mullen Library at The Catholic University of America in Washington, D.C., there is a 1680 edition, printed in Basel, that begins with a note "To the Reader." It states,

> The principal part of this Catechism is an Abridgment of Christian Doctrine; defended and cleared by proofes of Scripture, in points controverted between Catholiques and Sectaries, an explained by the familiar way of Question and Answer.
>
> To this in the former Impressions was only adjoyned a necessary exposition of the Masse, our Ladies Office, and the Festival daies of the yeere: But to this last Edition is added an Explication of certain Ceremonies of the Church, which now renders it capable of instructing the ignorant in the whole Doctrine, and Discipline of the Catholique Church. Besides, I have here corrected some fals citationes, and other Errata's, which, by the Printer's negligence, occurred in the former Impressions.
>
> Peruse (good Reader) with such Charity as I have penn'd it, and by its perusal, thou shalt become moreknowing in the Law of Christ and in practice more dutiful to God and they Neighbour, it wil abundantly recompence of the labour of Thy wel wishing friend and servant in Christ, H.T.

"Shortened, rewritten, and then lengthened again," writes Charles Carmody, "the Doway contains the core developed by the major catechisms of English-speaking Catholics for the next three hundred years." The descriptive titles of the various transmutations (*Abridgement, Abstract, Revision,* etc.) confirm Carmody's observation, and at the same time make it difficult to keep them distinct one from the other. (See chart on page 81.)

Turberville's *Abridgement of Christian Doctrine* was large (352 pages in the 1680 edition) and more suitable for advanced students than for young children. Very shortly after his death, there appeared a much shorter version, which may have been by Turberville himself. No author is named. The edition at the Catholic University of America, printed in Basel in 1681, carries the title *An Abstarct [sic] of the Catechism.* It has 185 very small (8½ x 6 cm) pages. Later impressions carry the title *An Abstract of the Doway Catechism, for the use of children and ignorant people* (London, 1688), to which was added a new chapter called "A Short Daily Exercise."[4] The editor of this Doway Abstract may well have been John Gother, a member of the English mission, who is said to have added a series of "Instructions on the Sacraments." (Gother was chaplain at the Catholic manor where young Richard Challoner, raised a Presbyterian, lived with his mother. Gother instructed Challoner in the Catholic faith, and thus is the link between Turberville and Challoner, about whom more will be said below.)

Another effort to provide a more basic text was made by the anonymous compiler of *A Short Abridgement of Christian Doctrine, for the instruction of*

## The Doway Catechism and Its Offshoots

| Official Title | Author | Date | Popular Title |
|---|---|---|---|
| 1. *An Abridgement of Christian Doctrine with proofs of Scripture for points controverted* | Turberville | 1649 | Doway Catechism |
| 2. *An Abstract of the Doway Catechism for the use of children and ignorant people* | John Gother (?) | 1681 | Doway Abstract |
| 3. *A Short Abridgement of Christian Doctrine, for the instruction of beginners* | Anonymous Compiler | 1729 | *Short Abridgement* (of Doway) |
| 4. *An Abridgement of Christian Doctrine* | Challoner | 1759 | Challoner Catechism (in the U.S., a.k.a. Carroll Catechism) |
| 5. *An Abstract of the Doway Catechism: Revised, Improved and Recommended by authority for the use of the Faithful in the Four Districts of England.* | | 1826 | Revised Challoner |
| 6. *A Catechism of Christian Doctrine* | | 1859 | Penny Catechism |

*beginners* (1729). It further abridged and simplified the Doway Abstract; whereas the latter had over four hundred questions, the *Short Abridgement* had only a few more than a hundred. The Doway Abstract and its predecessors opened with the question, "What religion are you of?" The *Short Abridgement* is the first of the English catechisms to start off with the question that was to become standard in the Penny Catechism used in Great Britain and the Abridged Baltimore Catechism used in the United States: "Who made you?" This new opening echoes the starting point of Fleury's catechism which began in much the same way.

After examining printers' lists from the mid-eighteenth century, Dom Marron concluded

> that the three recognized catechisms of Christian doctrine among English Catholics at that time were Turberville's *Doway Catechism,* the *Doway Abstract* and the *Short Abridgement;* that the first two were in use at the [Standon Lordship] school for the older and the young students respectively; that the Short Abridgement was not used at the school because it was meant only for very young children; and finally that this *Short Abridgement* had now superseded Bellarmine's little catechism as the catechism for beginners.[5]

Standon Lordship was founded by Bishop Challoner near London (it later became St. Edmund's, Ware). The *Rules and Customs* of the Standon school go into detail and further emphasize that there were different catechisms for the various age levels:

> Breakfast being ended, one Notice given by ye Bell, which it were to be wish'd could always be at 8 o'clock, all repair to School, on school days, to say their Lesson in some Catechism suitable to their Age & Capacity, as lst ye Doway Abstract, with Mr. Gother's Instructions for Children, 2ndly, Fleury's Historical Catechism, 3rdly, Tuberville's etc., with Chief Master's Approbation. The short Abridgement of ye Christian Doctrine is indeed ye Catechism in use for Children very young.[6]

### Richard Challoner

Although Catholic priests were fugitives and the penal laws remained on the books until the Catholic Relief Act of 1778, the Church was able to reorganize and survive underground. In 1688 England was divided into four ecclesiastic districts, each headed by a vicar apostolic. The London district, which included ten counties, the Channel Islands, and British colonies in North America (chiefly Pennsylvania and Maryland), was headed for forty years by Richard Challoner (1691–1781), first as coadjutor (1741) and then as vicar apostolic in his own right (1758). Before returning to England as a missionary,

Challoner, a convert to Catholicism at the age of thirteen, spent twenty-five years at the English College in Douai as student, teacher, and administrator.

During the short reign of King James II (1685–88), the jurisdiction of the bishops was reestablished, but Catholics continued to be isolated and scattered. The main centers of the old religion were the great manors in the north where Catholic families like the Holmans, for whom Challoner's mother worked, sustained the Church. The usual site for Sunday Mass was not a parish church but a rented room in an inn, a barn, or a cock-pit where small groups could gather without attracting undue attention. The handing-on of the faith depended chiefly on the printed word. Books, collections of prayers, and pamphlets of all kinds kept the tradition alive.

Although much of his literary output was by way of editing and translating, Challoner is the prime example of a cleric who extended a formative influence well beyond the territory of his pastoral charge by means of his pen. For almost two centuries his revised translation of the Douai-Rheims Bible, to which he added almost two thousand explanatory notes, was the standard version of Scripture used by Catholics in the English-speaking world. He published *The Following of Christ,* an English translation of the *Imitatio Christi,* and translations of Augustine's *Confessions* and the *Introduction to the Devout Life* by Francis de Sales. He composed several collections of meditations, the best known of which were *Think Well On't* (1728) and *Meditations for Every Day in the Year* (1753), and compiled several collections of prayers.

In 1737 Challoner published *The Catholik Christian Instructed in the Sacraments, Sacrifice, Ceremonies and Observances of the Church by Way of Question and Answer,* said to be his "most original catechismal work."[7] His most popular work, however, *The Garden of the Soul* (1740), harkened back to the earlier primers. Published about the time that he took up his duties as vicar apostolic, it was at once a prayer book, a manual of devotions, and a practical guide to the spiritual life for Catholics living in the world. At the beginning there is a synopsis of Christian doctrine under three headings. "What Every Christian Must Believe" expands on the Creed. "What Every Christian Must Do To Obtain Life Everlasting" follows the outline of the Ten Commandments. Under the first Commandment it explains the virtues of faith, hope, charity, and the virtue of religion "the chief acts of which are adoration, praise, thanksgiving, oblation of ourselves to God, sacrifice and prayer"—all in a brief paragraph! (A surprising feature is that Challoner follows the "Protestant" breakdown of the Commandments so that the fourth covers observance of holy days (he does not mention Sunday as such), the fifth, the love, reverence, and obedience due to parents, etc. Under the third heading he presents a selection of New Testament verses, mostly from the Gospels, that serve as moral maxims for Christian living. The prayers include popular texts from the medieval primers, an assortment of psalms, and a short series of meditations. The heart of the book centers on the Mass, the reception of Holy Communion and preparation for confession. Challoner presents a series of prayers that attempt to capture the action of the Mass because, in those days, it was forbidden to translate the Eucharistic canon.

*The Garden of the Soul* continued to be reprinted into the nineteenth century and, according to J. D. Crichton, gave rise to the sobriquet "Garden of the Soul Catholic," which described someone "solid in the Faith, steady in devotion and regular in the practice of religion."[8] The first of several American printings, based on the seventh edition, was issued by Joseph Crukshank in Philadelphia about 1773. Challoner's work served as a model for the popular prayer books by Father Lasance and similar devotional works that shaped American Catholicism up to the Second Vatican Council.

### "The Challoner Catechism"

Another work attributed to Challoner, *An Abridgement of Christian Doctrine,* eventually evolved into the Penny Catechism. The title page of the copy in the Oscott College Library states it was "Revised and Enlarged/By R.C./At St. Omer:/Printed by H.F. Boubers/M.DCC.LXXII." "R.C.," by all accounts is Richard Challoner.[9] The "abridgement" seems to be a reference to the *Short Abridgement* of the Doway Catechism for beginners, but R.C.'s revisions and enlargement were such as to turn it into a new catechism. In terms of size it increased the number of questions from 109 (in the *Short Abridgement)* to 290.

The revised *Abridgement* owed a great deal to Canisius, Bellarmine, and the various editions of the Doway Catechism. It incorporated the contents that by this time had become traditional. It began with questions about creation, and then moved on to the Creed, the Our Father, and the Commandments, to which were appended the medieval lists of virtues and vices, and the Beatitudes. It concluded with chapters titled "The Christian's Rule of Life" and "The Christian's Daily Exercises." The former, Challoner's own contribution, is both inspirational and practical in the emphasis it gives to love of God and neighbor. The latter describes how Christians should begin their day with morning prayer, sanctify their actions throughout the day, including meals, and end it with an examination of conscience and night prayers.

### The Penny Catechism

For some reason, probably because of Challoner's name, the Abridgement gradually displaced other catechisms in England. It was revised four times in the nineteenth century, and with each revision the emphasis on doctrinal matters became more pronounced and the phraseology more Scholastic. The rules for Christian living and the devotional features were less accented than in the original edition.

The first revision of the *Abridgement of Christian Doctrine,* made in 1826, was published a year later with the approval of the vicars apostolic and coadjutors under the title *An Abstract of the Doway Catechism. Revised, Improved and Recommended by Authority for the use of the Faithful in the Four Districts of England.* Apart from recasting a few questions and even more answers in the section explaining the Godhead and Christology in the language of Scholastic theology, it was mainly Challoner's book. Bernard Pickering, commenting on the greater theological emphasis in the answers, says the changes "would be justified" by a new purpose of the catechism "for now, instead of being a book for children" it was recommended for all the faithful.

The changes in the second revision extended to the other parts of the *Abridgement* as well. In 1850 the Holy See had reestablished the diocesan hierarchy in England, and appointed Nicholas Wiseman, vicar apostolic of the London district since 1849, the first cardinal archbishop of Westminster. The newly constituted hierarchy held a series of provincial synods at which there was discussion of further changes in the catechism. At the end of the Third Provincial Synod in 1859, the bishops published *A Catechism of Christian Doctrine* with the approbation of Cardinal Wiseman who wrote: "We hereby approve of this edition of the Catechism, in our own name and that of the other bishops, *and prescribe its exclusive use.*"

There were two more revisions after the recess of the First Vatican Council. The first made extensive changes, the second (1883) only minor ones. Vatican I's definition of papal infallibility necessitated a new explanation of the pope's office. In Challoner's *Abridgement* there was only one question, "Has the Church any visible Head on Earth?" (Answer: "Yes; the Bishop of *Rome,* who is the Successor of *St. Peter,* and commonly called the Pope.") The Penny Catechism provides a series of questions that, in the words of J. D. Crichton, "gives a mini-treatise on the papacy, the succession, primacy and of course, infallibility."[10] The reasons for the other changes are not so clear.

In the end the Penny Catechism is very different from the *Abridgement* in content and tone. If it can be said that "R.C." revisions turned the *Short Abridgement* of Doway into a new catechism, it is even truer that the nineteenth-century revisions of the *Abridgement* made it a very different book from the one that bears Challoner's name. The *Short Abridgement* had 109 questions, the revised 1772 edition had 290, and the Penny Catechism 360. Even the fact that the number of questions was increased by one-fourth does not tell the whole story. Many questions in the *Abridgement* were conflated to make room for new questions, even more answers were changed, and numerous phrases were modified from one revision to another. Furthermore, in seeking to make the answers more theologically precise, the later redactors made the text less conversational, more wooden.

In the twentieth century the Penny Catechism came under harsh criticism from many quarters. It was revised twice more, in 1936 by F. H. Drinkwater, and again in 1958 with the title *Experimental Revised Catechism of Christian Doctrine.* Canon Drinkwater, the founder of *The Sower,* the popular catechetical journal in which he propagated his ideas for a half-century, criticized the Penny Catechism (and all catechisms) chiefly for pedagogical reasons. As a military chaplain in World War I he found that few troops, despite the fact that they had been forced to commit the Penny Catechism to rote memory, either understood or even remembered what they had learned as small lads. Later as parish priest in Birmingham he concluded that the way the catechism was taught abused children's sensibilities and engendered boredom in adolescents.[11]

Canon Crichton, another critic of the Penny Catechism, reproached it for its forced-feeding of the meat of Scholastic theology to youngsters who needed to be nurtured on milk. Citing his own experience in being taught the catechism, Crichton describes how the chapters "The Christian Rule of Life" and "The Christian's Daily Exercise" never received the same attention that the doctrinal chapters did. Crichton lamented that while Challoner's name was linked to the Penny Catechism, those who taught it forgot that the venerable bishop saw Christianity as a way of life, not a string of theological assertions. Whether or not all these criticisms were valid, the Penny Catechism had lost considerable ground in the years before the Second Vatican Council.

Although there are notable differences, the history of the catechism in England in many ways parallels the story of the catechism in Ireland. In Tudor England the interaction between religion and politics fueled a contest between Latin and English for hegemony. In Ireland the contest was between Gaelic and English. And in both countries, in the nineteenth century, there was a push on the part of bishops for a uniform catechism text. Irish catechisms are the subject of the next chapter.

NOTES

1. The standard essay on the subject is J. S. Marron, "On the History of the Penny Catechism," *The Sower* 125 (October–December 1937) 197–203. Subsequently Charles J. Carmody uncovered earlier editions of some of the works quoted by Marron and others (*Roman Catholic Catechesis,* 27–37, 439). Unless otherwise noted, I have adopted Carmody's dates. For background on this period, see J. D. Crichton, "Religious Education in England in the Penal Days (1559–1778)," in Sloyan, *Shaping,* 70–97.

2. Because of his opposition to the new Acts of Supremacy and Uniformity, Vaux took flight to Louvain. When he later returned to England, he was imprisoned in Clink prison where he died in 1585. According to Philip Hughes, there is "an excellent account of his career" in T. G. Law's edition of Vaux's Catechism, Chetham Society, n.s. 4 (1885) 96. See Hughes, *The Reformation in England*, vol. 3. (London: Hollis & Carter, 1954) 248 n. 4.

3. Quoted in Brodrick, *Canisius*, 243.

4. Bernard Pickering, "Bishop Challoner and Teaching the Faith," *Clergy Review* 65 (January 1980) 7.

5. Quoted in Marron, "History of the Penny Catechism," 201.

6. Bernard Ward, *History of St. Edmund's College* (London: Kegan Paul, French, Trubner, 1893) appendix A, 300–301. Quoted in Carmody, *Roman Catholic Catechesis*, 34.

7. Carmody, *Roman Catholic Catechesis*, 35.

8. In Sloyan, *Shaping*, 91.

9. Until recently no one disputed that Challoner compiled the *Abridgement* bearing the 1772 date. Marron raised the question but concluded that Challoner was the author. Later J. D. Crichton, on the basis of some rudimentary textual criticism, expressed some doubt, but upon further investigation, confirmed Challoner's authorship. See J. D. Crichton, "Challoner's Catechism," *Clergy Review* 63:4 (April 1978) 146. Carmody does not challenge the authorship, but the date. He examined a microfilm of a 1759 edition in the British Museum (B.M. 1490 bb 17. [1]); see Carmody, *Roman Catholic Catechesis*, 36 n. 94.

10. Crichton, "Challoner's Catechism," 141.

11. F. H. Drinkwater, *The Secret Name* (Leominster: Fowler Wright, 1986). The biographical data reported here is taken from a "memoir" by J. D. Crichton that prefaces this collection of Drinkwater's essays and reflections, few of which deal with catechetics (11–45).

# NINE

# Irish Catechisms:
# Compilations in Gaelic and English

The story of the catechism in Ireland further illustrates a phenomenon, already latent in the publication of the Heidelberg Catechism, that became more and more apparent in the eighteenth century. Compendia and manuals published in the first instance to safeguard doctrinal orthodoxy become vehicles of inculturation and instruments of political policy.

The first book printed in Ireland in the Irish language was a catechism by the Protestant Sean O'Kearney in 1571. Tudor policy under Henry VIII had been to tie Ireland closely to England and simultaneously to undermine Irish allegiance to Rome by imposing the English language on Eire. Queen Elizabeth, in effect, acknowledged the failure of Henry's program. She recognized that if she was to advance her political goals and promote the Church of Ireland, she would have to use the language of the people. To implement the new policy, Elizabeth founded Trinity College in Dublin in 1571 and commissioned Irish translations of the Bible and Book of Common Prayer.[1] From Elizabethan times to the decline of Irish as a spoken language in the nineteenth century, a number of Protestant catechisms were printed and circulated in the Irish language.[2]

## Early Catholic Catechisms

It was forty years after the publication of O'Kearney's catechism before Catholics responded in kind. In 1611 the Irish Franciscans in Louvain published *Teagasg Criosdaidhe* by Bonaventure O'Heoghusa (in English, "O'Hosey" or "O'Hussey") to frustrate Protestants in their efforts to use the Irish tongue for political purposes. The use of the Gaelic script and verse forms show that O'Heoghusa was steeped in the tradition of the classic Bardic schools, but for the summary of Christian doctrine he relied on the catechisms of Peter Canisius and Robert Bellarmine.

Other Catholic catechisms followed, some in Irish for the people, some in Latin and English for use by priests. In 1625 the Franciscan Florence O'Conry published an Irish catechism at Louvain, "Mirror of a Christian Life." According to one report, O'Conry, like O'Heoghusa before him and Theobald Stapleton later, wrote his catechism for the benefit of the Irish troops serving in the Netherlands.[3] These catechisms, produced on the continent in the early penal days, reflected in various degrees the influence of Canisius, Bellarmine, and the Council of Trent. A catechism by Stapleton printed in Brussels in 1639 seems to have been almost totally dependent on Bellarmine's *Copiosa explicatio.*[4] The catechism was intended for priests, who, in turn, were to explain the doctrine to the people, children included, in language that could easily be understood. The text was in both Latin and Irish. Stapleton thought he would reach a wider audience by simplifying the Irish spelling and printing the catechism in Roman characters. After publishing the catechism Stapleton returned to Ireland, where he was one of the victims slaughtered by Cromwell's army in Cashel on 14 September 1647.

It was characteristic of O'Heoghusa's catechism and, to a lesser extent, of Stapleton's that they included frequent exhortations to virtuous living, helps toward pious exercises and, like the catechism of Peter Canisius, aids to devotion. Doctrine was presented as the basis and nutriment of the spiritual life. Anthony Gearnon's *Parrthas an Anma* (1645) was likewise "a Catholic prayer book which enshrines a Catechism." Gearnon structured his work in seventeen sections, one for each letter of the Irish alphabet. Although this use of the alphabet as a mnemonic device was common in Irish oral tradition, Gearnon was the first to use it in a printed work.

Dr. Joannes Dowley, sometime vicar general of Tuam, compiled an Irish catechism published in Louvain (1663). The lengthy title (in Gaelic) described it as an essential compendium of Christian doctrine containing devotional prayers before and after confession and Communion and a serviceable table of sins for preparation for confession. In the preface Dowley disavowed any intention of supplanting "the clear and concise manuals" of O'Heoghusa and Gearnon, but explained that he saw a need for a shorter catechism that would be cheaper and more suitable to troubled times and the needs of ordinary people.

These first Irish catechisms published in Louvain and Brussels were positive presentations of Catholic doctrine supplemented with prayers and devotional practices. The catechism by Francis O'Molloy, O.F.M. (Gaelic: Froinsias Ó'Maolmhuaidh), which was commissioned, published, and disseminated by the Congregation for the Propagation of the Faith in Rome (1676), struck a different tone. Following the usual custom, O'Molloy, in his foreword, described his catechism *(Lucerna fidelium)* as a handbook of Christian doctrine in which every form of heresy was refuted and by which all Catholics were confirmed in the true faith. He compiled *Lucerna fidelium* from existing works. The first part was taken directly from Gearnon's *Parrthas an Anma*, the second was a translation of Bishop Bossuet's *Exposition de la doctrine catholique sur les matières de controverses* (1671). The third part borrowed from two other recent works, Francis Porter's *Securis Evangelica* (1674) and Francis Veron's *Methode de traiter des controverses de Religion per la secule Escriture saincte* (1675).[5] O'Molloy's apologetic, even polemical, tone may be due to the influence of Veron.[6]

## Irish Catechisms in English

The English language came to be used more and more in Ireland through the eighteenth century, and by 1800 it was the dominant language. The policies of Elizabeth and her successors to Anglicize Ireland both as to language and to religion had limited success. The penal laws remained on the books, but they were not vigorously enforced. By 1731 Ireland had a resident Catholic hierarchy and only two hundred fewer priests than before the penal legislation was enacted. In a change of policy, the government inaugurated a system of charter schools in 1733. The charter schools, endowed to train poor children for the emerging industrial society, instructed them in the English language and "the fundamental principles of true religion." Irish Catholics responded by publishing catechisms in English.

The Congregation for the Propagation of the Faith recognized the increasing use of English when, in sending priests to Ireland, it equipped them with copies of both O'Molloy's *Lucerna fidelium* and the Doway Catechism of Henry Turberville. Sometime about 1727 Michael O'Reilly, later archbishop of Armagh, published a catechism in English and Irish that remained in use in some parts for two centuries. It contained 189 questions and answers, grouped under "the four things necessary for salvation": faith, Commandments, sacraments, and prayer. The "Galway Catechism" (1725) by F. O'Kenny, a professor in the Royal College of Navarre, was written in English.[7] Little more than an adaptation of Henry Turberville's work, it was reprinted in a bilingual edition by Bishop Sylvester Lloyd for the diocese of Killaloe, *The Doway Catechism in English and Irish for the Use of Children and Ignorant People* (1738).

The catechisms of O'Kenny, Lloyd, and O'Reilly, intended primarily for children and the poorly educated, provoked a reaction. Andrew Donlevy, provisor of the Irish College in Paris, professed shock at the scarcity of those "large Irish Catechisms published upwards of a hundred years ago by the laborious and learned Franciscans of Louvain."[8] Donlevy thought it right for "children whose minds are weak as their bodies" as well as beginners to learn the short catechisms by heart, even though they do not understand them. But grownups, he felt, should be provided with more explanation. To meet this need Donlevy compiled a catechism that incorporated most of O'Reilly's questions and answers, supplemented with material from Gearnon's *Parrthas an Anma* and Turberville's Doway Catechism. The text was bilingual "for the sake of those who understand only the English, or who may be inclined to learn the Irish by means of this translation." Toward the end of the century a critic judged Donlevy's work "on the whole a very flimsy production."[9]

The recurring pattern in the Irish catechisms of one author borrowing and adapting material from earlier works is further exemplified by a work published by Thomas Burke in Lisbon in 1752, *A Catechism Moral and Controversial Proper for such as are already advanced to some Knowledge of the Christian Doctrine. To which is annexed by way of an Appendix a Practical Method of Preparing for Sacramental Confession.* The author acknowledged in the preface that "in this work I pretend to no other merit than that of a compiler from other works of a much greater bulk."

## The Butler Catechism

The work that was to exert a dominant influence in Ireland (and to some extent in the United States) for close to two centuries was the manual compiled by James Butler II, archbishop of Cashel (1774–91). It came upon the scene when Anglo-Irish nationalism was emerging and political concerns began to overshadow religious differences. The Butler catechism was both a reflection and an instrument of the new political movement.

Throughout the seventeenth century the Tridentine reforms gradually took root. Diocesan and parish ministry replaced the ancient monastic structures that had been swept away by the Protestant Reformation. At the beginning of the century only two or three Irish bishops resided in their sees; most were living in exile. By 1731, however, twenty-two Catholic bishops were in residence in their dioceses. They encouraged priests to be conscientious about the administration of the sacraments, preaching, and catechesis. Catholic schoolmasters, operating under severe restrictions, were expected to teach the catechism to the boys in their charge. Parish priests were admonished to preach and teach the catechism to adults on Sundays and holy days. Despite the penal laws that remained on the books, many priests developed programs to enlist and educate candidates for ordination to the priesthood.

By the last quarter of the eighteenth century, when James Butler II had succeeded his namesake and kinsman, James Butler I (1757–74), as archbishop of Cashel, a Catholic middle class had begun to emerge. Many families that had lost their property turned to trades and commerce, wool and linen manufacturing, glass-making, and import-export. Although most Catholics were mired in poverty, they began to exercise a good deal of political influence. Because of the perennial struggle for title to the English throne and competition with other European powers, the government was vulnerable to economic and political pressures. Reverberations from the American and French Revolutions were felt in Ireland.

A descendant of the Catholic gentry, James Butler II was born in Dublin in 1742. Orphaned at the age of seven, he received his early schooling in Ireland before going to France in 1760 to complete his education. He began his studies in philosophy and theology at San Sulpice in Paris and was ordained to the priesthood at St. Omer in 1771, where his kinsman and patron, Alban Butler, famed for his compilation of the *Lives of the Saints,* was college president. Ordained coadjutor bishop to James Butler I in 1772, he nonetheless remained at St. Omer until the latter's death in 1774.

James Butler II returned to Ireland at a time when efforts on the part of the Catholic community to work out a new relationship to the British crown had divided the hierarchy. Butler became a leader in the party that was willing to take an Oath of Allegiance to the English king George III in exchange for the passage of the Catholic Relief Bill of 1778. Not all the bishops, however, agreed with the distinction he made between the obedience owed the civil authority and the religious allegiance due the pope as head of the Church. To allay their opposition Butler got the theological faculties in Paris, Louvain, and Douai to state that according to Catholic doctrine no one, not a cardinal, not a pope, could absolve and free a citizen from oaths of fidelity to the king.

The change in policy also provoked opposition and suspicion in Protestant circles. The Protestant bishop of Cloyne, Richard Woodward, published a pamphlet entitled *The Present State of the Church in Ireland* (1787), which brought up the old question "Can Catholics be loyal subjects?" Butler replied with a pamphlet of his own in which he carefully documented Catholic teaching and traced the history of his own actions and those of his fellow bishops with the government.[10] He cited the catechism that he had written several years before to show that the tenets of the Catholic religion firmly support civil and social rights and duties.

Although it came to be spoken of simply as the "Butler Catechism," its proper title was *A Catechism for the Instruction of Children.* It was first published in 1777, but the oldest copy extant is a Gaelic translation printed in Dublin in 1784. The text reflects French influence, evidence of the time Butler spent at St. Omer, first as a student and then in his last years there as vicar general of the diocese. St. Omer, like most French dioceses in the eighteenth century, had its own catechism, in large and small editions, which Butler seems to have drawn on for his own work.

The most striking feature of Butler's work, however, is the way he organized the material. He incorporated most of O'Reilly's questions and the customary pillars of catechesis—Creed, Commandments (including "the six Commandments of the Church"), prayer, and sacraments—but his presentation seems dictated more by logic than by tradition. Bellarmine's small catechism began by asking, "Are you a Christian?" and followed with an explanation of the Sign of the Cross. Butler's catechism began with questions about the creation of the world and the immortality of the soul, and ended rather abruptly after an explanation of the sacraments of extreme unction, holy orders, and matrimony, with a series of questions on eternal rewards and punishments. The questions are not numbered, and one can only wonder whether the division of the work into thirty-nine lessons was intended as a Catholic rejoinder to Queen Elizabeth's Thirty-nine Articles.

Butler's presentation reflects the concerns of the Enlightenment—the Age of Reason—when the center of religious controversy shifted from disputes among Catholics and Protestants to issues of faith and reason. Evidence of this is seen throughout the work but nowhere more clearly than in Butler's definition of mysteries as "truths we cannot comprehend." The reason, according to Butler, for us to believe what we cannot comprehend is "that we submit our reason as well as our will to his holy law." The strength of the Butler catechism was its logical progression from theme to theme and question to question.

The emphasis was on knowing the Church's doctrine. In a letter of 18 June 1780 to his friend Dr. Plunket, Archbishop Butler described his manner of conducting formal visitation in parishes: "I announced to them [the pastors] that I'd confirm no children under seven and none past seven who were not well instructed in the principal mysteries, the commandments, and the seven Sacraments particularly Confirmation, and the disposition for a good confession, and who did not know the acts of Contrition, Faith, Hope and Charity. . . ." The children were examined by the clergy while the archbishop met with the grownups to "inveigh against the abuses" the pastor had told him about and to instruct them on the dispositions "requisite for a good confession as outlined in my catechism."[11] Dr. Plunket himself conducted similar visitations in the diocese of Meath. He demanded that pastors take care "that the children understand the Christian doctrine as contained in their catechism." Children who "rattle it off like parrots" were corrected.

## The "Butler-General"

Butler's catechism was an immediate success. Prelates throughout Ireland adopted it for their own dioceses. With the rise of a new national consciousness, Butler's catechism became a rallying point in the delicate area of

Church-state relations. The French Revolution was the catalyst that, in the words of Patrick Wallace, "transformed the relationship of the Catholic hierarchy to the Protestant government from that of timid acceptance into an attempt at an open marriage." The Irish hierarchy made common cause with British conservatives in denouncing the revolution and the political philosophy that spawned it. When the Irish colleges in France were destroyed in the wake of the revolution, the British government subsidized the establishment of a national seminary at Maynooth to educate students for the priesthood. When Napoleon's armies sacked Rome, England became the champion of the pope.

One step in reassuring the English Parliament was to add to the catechism questions explaining the civil and social responsibilities of a good subject. It was an idea suggested by Sir John Hippisley, the unofficial British agent at the Vatican, and, he claimed, unanimously accepted by the Roman Catholic hierarchy at their meeting in Dublin in 1800. They ordered that five questions be inserted into the Butler text and that it be declared "a General Catechism for the Kingdom." In 1802 there appeared *The Most Reverend Dr. James Butler's Catechism, Revised, Approved and Recommended by the Four R.C. Archbishops of Ireland as a General Catechism for the Kingdom.*

The Catechism of the Four Archbishops, or, as it came to be known popularly, the "Butler-General," while maintaining the overall plan of the original, made extensive changes. Twenty questions in the original were omitted, eighty-three new questions were added, and forty-four others were changed. The changes, including an increased number of questions dealing with the sacraments, seem to serve an apologetic purpose and are more detailed regarding pastoral practice. The questions that deal specifically with civic responsibility are the following:

Q.   What are the duties of subjects to the temporal powers?

A.   To be subject to them, and to honour and obey them, not only for wrath, but also for conscience sake, for so is the will of God. 1 Peter. Romans XIII.

Q.   Does the Scripture require any other duty of subjects?

A.   Yes; to pray for kings, and for all who are in high station, that we may lead a quiet and peaceful life. 1 Tim. II.

Q.   Is it sinful to resist or combine against the established authorities, or to speak with contempt or disrespect of those who rule over us?

A.   Yes; St. Paul says, "Let every soul be subject to the higher powers; he that resisteth the power resisteth the ordinance of God; and they that resist purchase to themselves damnation." Rom. XII.2.

These are followed by three more questions that outline the chief duties of masters towards servants and others under their care, and the duties of servants towards masters. Throughout the Butler-General there is an emphasis on obedience that is not found in the Butler original. This is exemplified by the answer to the question "What was the end for which God made us?" The Butler original responds: "To know and *love* him here on earth and after to see and enjoy him in heaven." The Butler-General answers: "To know and *serve* him here on earth and after to see and enjoy him in heaven."

## Maynooth Catechism

In 1882, eighty years after the publication of the Butler-General, the Irish hierarchy, meeting in a national synod, commissioned a new edition. The title page, with no reference to Butler, describes it as *The Catechism Ordered by the National Synod of Maynooth and Approved by the Cardinal, the Archbishops, and the Bishops of Ireland.* The revision was dictated in part by the need to make mention of the doctrine of the immaculate conception, promulgated in 1854, and papal infallibility, promulgated by the First Vatican Council (1871).[12]

A few questions were dropped (including the one about resisting, combining against, and speaking with disrespect of "those who rule over us"), but most changes were stylistic in nature. The bishops used the occasion to mute the harsh tone of the Butler-General and, even more importantly from a pedagogical standpoint, to rephrase the answers, so that they formed complete sentences that can stand alone, apart from the question. For example, the Maynooth Catechism answers the question quoted above about the purpose of human existence by saying, "God made us to know, *love and serve* Him here on earth; and to see and enjoy Him for ever in Heaven." The answer incorporates the question, making it a complete statement that can easily be memorized. It was a technique found earlier in the Westminster Catechism of the Presbyterians and later in the Baltimore Catechism published by the U.S. bishops.

All three editions of the Butler Catechism remained in use well into the twentieth century. A few dioceses continued to use the original Butler, others used the Butler-General, and a majority adopted the Maynooth Butler. It also lived on in the Baltimore Catechism, which was heavily dependent on it. James Butler's catechism, conceived at the end of the eighteenth century, showed the influence of the Enlightenment, both its positive and negative aspects, and addressed specific Irish concerns regarding civic and social responsibilities. In the nineteenth century, a reaction against the Enlightenment, as will be seen in the next chapter, produced a catechism very different in spirit if not in form.

NOTES

1. F. H. McAdoo, "The Irish Translation of the Book of Common Prayer," *Eigse: A Journal of Irish Studies* 11 (1965) 250–57.

2. My description of Irish catechisms relies on Patrick Wallace's Ph.D. dissertation, *Irish Catechesis—The Heritage from James Butler II, Archbishop of Cashel 1774–1791* (Washington: The Catholic University of America, 1975). Wallace lists eleven Protestant catechisms in circulation in Ireland from the sixteenth through the nineteenth centuries; see p. 168.

3. See T. B. Scannell, s.v. "Doctrine," in *Catholic Encyclopedia* (1908).

4. *Catechismus, seu Doctrina Christiana, Latina Hibernica, per modum Dialogi, inter Magistrum et discipulum, Explicata per R.D. Theobaldum Stapletonium, Sacerdotem Hibernum, cum Charactere Romano;* see Wallace, *Irish Catechesis,* 80f.

5. Froinsias O'Maolmhuaidh, *Lucerna fidelium,* critical edition edited by Pádraig O'Suilleabháin (Dublin: Institute for Advanced Studies, 1962).

6. See Dhotel, *Les origines du catéchisme moderne,* 217, 224, 225, 279.

7. F. M. N. O'Kenny, *The Galway Catechism of Christian Doctrine newly Collected and Augmented for the use of the Three Kingdoms* (Paris: M. Langlois, 1725). See Wallace, *Irish Catechesis,* 89 n. 41.

8. *The Catechism or Christian Doctrine By the Way of Question and Answer* (Paris: James Guerin, 1742). Quoted in Wallace, *Irish Catechesis,* 92.

9. Wallace, *Irish Catechesis,* 93 n. 56.

10. *A Justification of the tenets of the Roman Catholic Religion and a refutation of the charges brought against its clergy by the Rt. Reverend the Lord Bishop of Cloyne by Dr. Butler.* See Wallace, *Irish Catechesis,* 57.

11. Wallace, *Irish Catechesis,* 59–60.

12. Another question, dropped from the Butler-General, reappeared: "By whom was Ireland converted to the true faith?" Answer: "Ireland was converted to the true faith by St. Patrick, who was sent by Pope Celestine, and came to our island in the year 432."

# TEN

# From the Enlightenment to Neoscholasticism: Towards a Uniform Catechism

To appreciate the significance of the catechism written by Joseph Deharbe (1800–1871), it is important to understand its origins. At the beginning of the nineteenth century Catholic theologians were wrestling with the issues raised by the Enlightenment. Church leaders and statesmen alike were attempting to restore ecclesiastical and political structures in the wake of the French Revolution and the Napoleonic Wars. Although Catholics were not of one mind as how best to do it, they were intent on reaffirming their tradition and maintaining continuity with the past.

It was against this background that Joseph Deharbe, S.J., composed one of the classic catechisms in the Catholic tradition. For generations it served as a paradigm for what catechisms should be: precise, concise, complete, orthodox. On the one hand, it represented a reaction against the proliferation of catechisms born of the notion that each diocese and linguistic group should adapt catechesis to the local Church. On the other hand, it linked catechesis to Scholastic theology. The result, as we have already seen in the case of the Penny Catechism in England, was to blur the distinction between personal faith and the systematic presentation of Church teaching; between revelation and theology.

Before describing Deharbe's catechism in detail, it will be helpful first to give a few examples of the kinds of catechisms against which he reacted, and then to say a word about Neoscholasticism and its impact on catechesis.

### Enlightenment Catechisms

The Deharbe catechism represented a reaction not simply, or even principally, to the number of catechisms in circulation. At the beginning of the nineteenth century there was little agreement regarding catechesis itself. Theologians and pastoral ministers debated the content. Catechists proposed different methods. Catechisms incorporated approaches that were often at odds with one another.

A legacy of the eighteenth century were catechisms that embodied the spirit and addressed the agenda of the Enlightenment. The Enlightenment, an amorphous movement that peaked about the time of the American Revolution, is generally associated among English-speaking peoples with the Age of Reason. Its theology was irenic in the sense that it sought to establish a consensus on the basis of reason and natural law. Its pedagogical principles were borrowed largely from Jean Jacques Rousseau (1712–88) and Johann Heinrich Pestalozzi (1746–1827). In the catechetical field, it shifted emphasis from memorization to "understanding," and from doctrine to moral teachings. Catechists were encouraged to use the Socratic method in order to evoke a response from their students based on the students' own religious sense. Moral teaching, always an element in catechesis, had traditionally been seen as an aspect of Christian doctrine. The Enlightenment recognized the importance of ethics to private morality and civic well-being, but it sought to ground ethics in natural law rather than Christian doctrine.

One of the best known "Enlightenment catechisms" was the programmatic work by Vitus Anton Winter, *Religios-sittliche Katechetik (Religio-moral Catechetics)*. In Winter's scheme there was little place for revelation and the supernatural. Doctrine *(Religionslehre)* ought to be preceded by lessons on the science of nature, natural law *(Rechtslehre)*, and moral teaching *(Sittenlehre)*. Catechesis regarding the person of Christ should emphasize his earthly ministry, the benefits he brought to humanity by his moral teachings, the pattern of his life, and the heroic example of his suffering. When teaching about the sacraments, the catechist should avoid useless disputes, for example, the differences among Christians on the Real Presence in the Eucharist, and explain only their purpose and correct use.

## The "Imperial Catechism"

Another catechism, very different in spirit and purpose from the Enlightenment catechisms, deserves mention because it reflects particular needs of the Restoration period. The *Catechisme à l'usage de toute les Églises de l'Empire français* (1806) or, as it was popularly known, the "Imperial Catechism," was designed to serve political as well as religious goals. Napoleon I, who commissioned it, ordered that it be used "in all the churches of the French empire." According to the arrangement agreed upon by the French government and the papacy in 1801 for drawing new diocesan boundaries, the liturgical rites in all dioceses were to be uniform and there was to be a single catechism for the entire country. In effect, it meant a suppression of local liturgical customs, and a departure from the practice that allowed, and even encouraged, each diocese to compile its own catechism.

The papacy's objective in giving grudging approval to the new arrangement was to restore order and rejuvenate the Church after the Revolution. Napoleon, for his part, seemed convinced that religion insures the well-being of individuals and consolidates the power of the state, and thus he saw the catechism as a political instrument. In compiling the catechism, the Director of Cults inserted a series of questions and answers in the section explaining the Fourth Commandment that emphasized obedience to authority and the respect owed the emperor and his office. The text of the catechism was completed in 1803. Although Pope Pius VII refused to approve it, the more malleable papal legate, Cardinal Caprara, in order to save the Concordat, endorsed it. (It should be noted that despite its official approbation, bishops, pastors, the general public, and printers, hurt financially, resisted the imposition of a single catechism on the entire nation.) In 1814, with Bonaparte's downfall, King Louis XVIII suppressed the Imperial Catechism, allowing each bishop to provide the catechism he thought best for his own diocese.

Based on the catechisms of Jacques Bengine Bossuet and Claude Fleury, the Imperial Catechism had a preface that outlined "sacred history," describing events from the creation of the world to the triumph of the Church under Constantine. The body of the catechism followed tradition in organizing the material in three parts, but they were more sharply delineated than was the general practice: doctrine, based on the articles of the Creed; morals, an explanation of the Ten Commandments and precepts of the Church; and worship, including the sacraments and, in an appendix, a description of liturgical feasts. In all three parts an asterisk marked the questions and answers that were deemed most important. This tripartite division was copied by other catechisms long after the Imperial Catechism itself had fallen into disuse. Its most lasting influence, however, was probably the encouragement it gave to individuals who were promoting a uniform catechism as a means to insure Catholic unity.

## The Revival of Scholasticism and the Tübingen School

At the beginning of the nineteenth century, Catholics reacted strongly against the ideas and spirit of the Enlightenment which, many (including Deharbe) thought, was responsible for the French Revolution and the subsequent upheavals that had beset Europe. Theologians, especially in Germany, looked back to medieval Scholasticism for answers. The underlying issues raised by the Enlightenment concerned the need for revelation, the prowess of reason, and the relationship between nature and the supernatural. Most theologians believed that Thomas Aquinas's metaphysics and theology of grace had to be the foundation of any Catholic response to these challenges, but there was a small group at the University of Tübingen who sought an alternative to Thomism.

The Tübingen theologians, of whom the best remembered are Johann Sebastian Drey and Johann Adam Möhler, were leaders in the revival of Catholic thought in Germany. They manifested a strong attachment to Catholic orthodoxy and loyalty to the Church. They shared the Enlightenment's low esteem for Scholastic philosophy and theology, and sought to develop a different methodology that would give fresh expression to a Catholic theology of revelation and the role of the Holy Spirit in the Church, the bearer of Christ's living tradition. Rather than emphasizing fixed forms and unchangeable doctrine, they stressed the development of doctrine. They distinguished between the content of faith and the manner in which it was expressed.

It was common for German theologians of the time to differentiate between dogmatic and practical theology. Under the latter heading they grouped moral, ascetical, and mystical theology, and such areas as homiletics and catechetics. The leader among the practical theologians in the Tübingen School was Johann Baptist von Hirscher (1788–1865), professor of moral and pastoral theology at Tübingen where he taught for two decades before moving on to the University of Freiburg im Breisgau. Gerald McCool describes Hirscher as "the most antischolastic of the Tübingen theologians and one of the least acquainted with scholasticism."[1] It was at Freiburg that he published a work criticizing the catechisms of the Counter-Reformation as too abstract and the catechisms of the Enlightenment as too moralistic. For Hirscher, the central theme of catechesis is the kingdom of God. He argued that catechesis should present Christian doctrine as a message of salvation, relying not on definitions but, in so far as possible, on biblical examples and historical narrative. He emphasized the need to take into consideration the emotional life of the child and cautioned against overwhelming the learner with too much information and too many facts. He attempted to give concrete form to his ideas in a catechism published in 1842.

Although Hirscher's ideas stirred a lively debate, his catechism was, at best, only a modest success. The first two books treat of God, creation, and redemption. The next three treat of the individualization of the kingdom of God in souls and its interior and exterior manifestation, that is to say, justification, sanctification, and the Church. The sixth and last book treats the kingdom of God in the life to come. According to Josef Jungmann, Hirscher's "plan was too unusual, and the presentation too heavy,"[2] and furthermore, it appeared at a time when Neoscholasticism was cresting in Germany and Rome.

## Joseph Deharbe, The Man and His Times

Joseph Deharbe's career overlapped that of Hirscher. It is also significant that he was a contemporary of Joseph Kleutgen, S.J. (1811–83), "the greatest of the early Jesuit neo-Thomists,"[3] and a vigorous critic of Hirscher. Another Deharbe contemporary was Joseph Denziger (1818–83), editor of the famous *Enchiridion symbolorum et definitionum (Handbook of Creeds and Definitions)* which, up to Vatican II, was a standard reference and, for many, the definitive canon of orthodox Catholic teaching. As a group, the Jesuits, revitalized after being suppressed for almost forty years, took the lead in the Neoscholastic revival in Germany and Rome, promoting positivist theology with its emphasis on conciliar definitions, decrees, and papal declarations.

Born in Strassburg in 1800, Deharbe entered the Society of Jesus in 1817, at a time when it was undergoing a revival. He taught for eleven years at Jesuit College in Brig, Switzerland, until he was assigned to pastoral work about 1840. When the Catholic cantons were defeated in a civil war in 1847, the Jesuits were banned from Switzerland and Deharbe barely escaped with his life. It was while preaching parish missions and catechizing, first in Switzerland and later in Germany, that he came face to face with the problem of the catechism. He saw with concern that people were losing their faith and abandoning the Church. Convinced that the number and diversity of catechisms was a principal cause of poor religious instruction, he felt the need for a single catechism that everyone would use.

In 1847, probably with episcopal encouragement, Deharbe published his *Katholischer Katechismus oder Lehrbegriff, nebst einem kurzen Abriss der Religionsgeschichte von Anbeginn der Welt bis auf unsere Zeit: Für die Jungend sowohl as für Erwachsene (A Catholic Catechism or Manual with a Brief Summary of the History of Religion from the Beginning of the World to Our Time for Youth and for Adults)*. His name did not appear on the first edition and so it was known initially by the place of publication, the "Regensburg [Ratisbon] Catechism." It was an immediate success. Deharbe succeeded in presenting a masterful precis of Neoscholastic theology in the form of questions and answers. The original version had more than a thousand questions. Subsequently, Deharbe published two shorter versions for children and for use in schools. Although he recognized that some of the terms would be difficult for youngsters, the wording in the abridgements is the same as that in the original. Question followed upon question in a logical sequence that reflected the systematic exposition of the seminary manuals. It addressed the mind, and made little attempt to speak to the heart.

Although the spirit of positivist theology and Neoscholasticism pervades Deharbe's catechism, it is also reminiscent of Fleury's *Catéchisme historique*. Both are divided into two parts. Deharbe first presents "A Short History of

Religion," divided into three parts: from the creation of the world to Christ; the life of Christ; from the ascension to the pontificate of Pius IX. It had an apologetic purpose similar to the *demonstratio christiana* and the *demonstratio catholica* that prefaced the Neoscholastic textbooks used in seminaries. It argued that by reason of antiquity Christianity is the true religion, and by reason of continuity with the past, the Catholic Church is the authentic expression of Christianity. The main point was to present Protestants as innovators, and to blame the rationalists and freethinkers for the chaos and misery of the French Revolution. "Enlightenment was their word when they abolished religion; *Liberty* and *Equality,* when they murdered their fellowmen. . . . In the year 1799, Napoleon, in quality of First Consul seized upon the sovereign power; but he did not venture to govern a people without Religion. He therefore restored the Catholic religion in France . . ."[4] And as in Fleury's *Petit catéchisme,* study questions accompanied the text (e.g., "How many people are said to have been slaughtered during the Reign of Terror?" "Did Napoleon remain a faithful son of the Church?").

Despite Deharbe's claim to have adopted the structure "prescribed" by the Roman Catechism, the main body of the catechism followed an outline that was closer to the threefold division of Robert Bellarmine's catechism: faith (Creed), Commandments, and the means of grace, that is, sacraments and prayer. The anti-Protestant attitude inherent in Neoscholasticism is reflected in the apologetic tone which was not at all attenuated in the English translation, first published in London in 1862 and shortly thereafter in the United States. The Reverend John Fander acknowledged this polemical character in his introduction to the English text:

> The dogmatical and moral explanation of the Christian Doctrine itself is comprehensive and plain, and is adapted to the present wants of youth, being proved in full from Holy Scripture, Tradition and the General Councils. It is at the same time controversial inasmuch as the objections made against it by Infidels, Heretics, and Innovators, are *solidly* refuted; and, therefore, it may justly be called a *full* Catechism of the Catholic Religion.[5]

The authority of the Bible is cited to confirm the Church's teaching, but it is not the only source of that teaching. In response to the question (1.7), "How did Divine Revelation come down to us?" Deharbe states the Neoscholastic position clearly and succinctly: "Divine Revelation came down to us, partly by *writing,* that is, by Holy Scripture or the Bible; partly by *word of mouth,* that is, by Tradition." Ultimately, the faith of the Catholic Christian rests on Church authority: "He must believe all that God has revealed, and the Catholic Church proposes to his belief, whether it be contained in the Holy Scripture or not"

(1:20). Deharbe repeats the cautions of the Council of Trent in putting down the following conditions for reading the Bible in the vernacular: ". . . we should have the learning and piety requisite for it; and . . . the translation should be accompanied with explanations, and that both should be approved by the Church" (1:28).

Deharbe concludes most sections with an "application," but these applications have little to do with the practice of virtue or experience of prayer. For example, at the end of the introductory section on the "acceptance, object and rule of faith," he echoes Ignatius of Loyola's "Rules for Thinking with the Church": "In matters of faith, never trust your own judgment, but always humbly submit to the decisions of Holy Church; for when you believe what the Church teaches, you believe the Word of God."[6]

German bishops promoted Deharbe's catechism in its various versions as an excellent basis for the uniform catechesis that many had been looking for. In 1850 the bishops of Bavaria mandated its use in their territories, and in a short time it became the standard text in use among German-speaking Catholics (except in the Austro-Hungarian Empire). It was also in 1850 that Bishop Purcell introduced Deharbe's catechism into Cincinnati which, by this time, had a sizeable German Catholic population with flourishing parochial schools. At the same time he approved "the Regensburg Catechism, long in use in Germany," he decreed that other German catechisms were not to be reprinted. The popularity of Deharbe's catechism soon spread throughout the United States. Bishop Patrick N. Lynch of Charleston, South Carolina, edited his own version of Fander's translation along with a shortened form. At least two Polish versions were printed and circulated in the United States for use in parochial schools.[7] The 1908 edition of the *Catholic Encyclopedia* described the second half of the nineteenth century as "the era of Deharbe's Catechism."[8]

## The Triumph of Neoscholasticism

Deharbe's catechism stands in stark contrast to that of Hirscher. Although they were more or less contemporaries, their works reflect two fundamentally different approaches to catechesis. The abstract, theological, and, at times, technical terms that suffused Deharbe's text were very dissimilar from Hirscher's language, which was inspired by the Bible and the Church Fathers. Even more importantly, Hirscher had sharply criticized the Imperial Catechism because its tripartite division obscured the vital unity of the Christian mystery; yet the same division reappeared in a modified form in Deharbe's catechism. In making the kingdom of God the focal point of his own catechism, Hirscher highlighted the point that catechesis is not so much concerned with imparting religious knowledge as it is with teaching a way of salvation.

Despite the fact that Deharbe is known to have been an effective preacher and an accomplished catechist, he made no attempt to adjust his presentation to his audience. His catechism was criticized, even by those who used it, because it did not take the ability and background of the learner into account. Josef Jungmann, who presents a favorable picture of Deharbe's work, nonetheless complains about the text's unenlightened pedagogy. (In the wake of Vatican II, however, it is now evident that it was not Deharbe's pedagogy so much as his theology that needed to be reassessed.)

In 1879 Pope Leo XIII published the encyclical *Aeterni Patris* which represented the triumph of the Neoscholastic movement. The encyclical dictated the method and content of philosophical and theological instruction in Catholic seminaries, and fixed the pattern of the Church's understanding of its own history and tradition. In effect, it affirmed the approach to revelation, faith, and ecclesiology in Deharbe's catechism and established it as the model for others to follow. As the next chapter shows, the number of catechetical texts continued to multiply in the United States, but for all their apparent differences, most were made of the same wood. The popular image of the catechism, even in the minds of bishops, was no longer the traditional four pillars but hundreds of questions and answers. The pedagogy, with children as the prime audience, fostered memorization, and the Neoscholastic theology presented a picture that was clear and self-sustaining. No distinction was made between Christian doctrine and the way it was expressed, and once Neoscholasticism became the official theology of the Church, any deviation was considered suspect if not heretical.

### NOTES

1. Gerald McCool, *Catholic Theology in the Nineteenth Century* (New York: Seabury, 1977) 188.

2. Josef Jungmann, *Handing on the Faith* (New York: Herder, 1959) 30.

3. McCool, *Catholic Theology*, 4.

4. Joseph Deharbe, *A Full Catechism of the Catholic Religion*, trans. John Fander, 2d American edition (New York: The Catholic Publication Society, 1875) 53.

5. Ibid., v.

6. Ibid., 76.

7. Carmody provides this information and adds that neither Polish version carries Deharbe's name, *Roman Catholic Catechesis*, 66.

8. T. B. Scannell, s.v. "Doctrine," *in Catholic Encyclopedia* (1908).

ELEVEN

# Vatican I to Baltimore III:
# The American Experience

The Roman Catechism, commissioned by the Council of Trent, gave an authoritative explanation of Catholic doctrine and practice. It insured orthodoxy and encouraged uniformity of expression in response to Protestant Reformers. It provided a resource for preachers and parish priests who were in turn called upon to adapt it to the age and particular circumstances of the learners. Consequently it caused a proliferation of "small catechisms," handbooks of instruction for the use of children and "simple folk."

The number of catechisms burgeoned to the point that it caused a reaction. In 1742 Pope Benedict XIV recommended the use of Cardinal Bellarmine's catechism throughout the Catholic world. Pope Clement XIII in 1761, protesting against the rationalistic methods of the Enlightenment, urged a uniform method of catechizing that would employ the same words and expressions.[1] Even before Napoleon attempted to impose the Imperial Catechism in France, Empress Maria Teresa commissioned Johann Ignaz von Felbiger to compile a catechism that she imposed throughout Austria and Bohemia. As early as the First Provincial Council of Baltimore (1832) the bishops of the United States expressed a desire for a single catechism. (The English bishops in 1859, as we saw in an earlier chapter, recommended the Penny Catechism for exclusive use in their jurisdictions.)

By the time preparations for the First Vatican Council got underway, there was much support for a uniform catechism. When the council convened in December 1869, the Commission on Church Discipline was ready with the draft of a constitution proposing a small catechism for the universal Church. The first paragraph of the *Schema constitutionis de parvo catechismo* read as follows:

> Just as all members of the Church of Christ, spread over the whole world, should be of one heart and soul, so too should they have but one voice and tongue. And since different methods and ways of transmitting to the faithful the essentials of faith are known to create no little inconvenience, we

shall by our own authority and with the approval of this council, see to it that a new catechism is drawn up in Latin, modelled after the Small Catechism of the Ven. Cardinal Bellarmine. Compiled at the command of the Holy See, it is highly recommended to all the local ordinaries. Its use by all will facilitate the disappearance in the future of the confusing variety of other short catechisms.

The schema went on to direct that the catechism be translated into vernacular languages, that priests explain it, and that copies be put in the hands of all the faithful "who can easily commit it to memory." It closed urging, "as strongly as we can," that all clergy charged with the care of souls make use of the catechism of the Council of Trent. "In this way," it said, "there will be one common rule for transmitting the faith and for training the Christian people in the works of piety."

The proposal elicited a spirited debate that dominated the proceedings in the early months of the council.[2] The discussions revealed diverse views regarding both episcopal rights and responsibilities and approaches to catechesis. Bishops who agreed on the need for a standard catechism offered a variety of reasons: a uniform catechism would be a great convenience, a bond of unity, and a remedy for what was perceived as confusion and ignorance regarding Catholic teachings. Bishops who opposed *De parvo catechismo* argued primarily on the basis of their own pastoral experience and the traditional right of the diocesan bishop to develop a catechism for his own people. They contended that the real issue was not a catechism but problems of catechesis—the manner of instruction, the need to adapt to local and individual situations, and the competence of the catechists.

Vatican I recessed on 22 February 1870. When it reconvened at the end of April, the council fathers had in their hands a revised draft of the schema. In presenting the new text for a vote a spokesman for the Commission on Discipline made it clear that the schema was concerned only with a catechism to be used in elementary instruction. The new draft also made it clear that, "Although the use of the aforementioned short catechism is to be faithfully upheld, bishops will still be free to issue in separate form whatever catechetical instructions they deem appropriate."

With these clarifications *De parvo catechismo* was overwhelmingly approved: 491 voted in favor *(placet);* 44 favored it with reservations *(placet juxta modum);* and 56 opposed it *(non placet).* After some minor revisions were made in light of the reservations *(modi),* the edited constitution ran about 400 words.[3] The final text was read in the aula but, before a definitive vote could be taken, the council again recessed because of the outbreak of the Franco-Prussian war, never to reconvene.

The action of Vatican I undoubtedly influenced the decision of the Irish bishops at the national synod in 1875 to call for "a national catechism." The "Maynooth Catechism" (1882), another revision of Butler's catechism, was the result. The American bishops followed suit. In the Third Plenary Council of Batimore in 1884, they authorized a national catechism for the United States.

## The American Experience

The only bishop from the United States who took a vocal part in the debate over the catechism at Vatican I was Jean-Pierre Marcellin Augustin Verot, vicar apostolic of Florida and later bishop of Savannah. After coming to the United States from his native France in 1830 he taught at St. Mary's College in Baltimore and was engaged in pastoral ministry throughout Maryland. One of many bishops in the United States to author a catechism, he intervened twice in the discussions on *De parvo catechismo*. His first intervention addressed the original draft of the schema. Speaking in support of a common catechism, he cited the experience of immigrants to the United States who came from their native lands with very different catechetical training and religious practices. He said a standard catechism would insure greater uniformity and a clearer knowledge of Christian doctrine. His second intervention addressed the revised text. He proposed that the vote be only provisional on the grounds that (1) the council fathers were not voting on a specific text, and (2) the bishops might find it more difficult to arrive at a consensus on a uniform text than they suspected. Again he cited the experience of the U.S. bishops who had been trying in vain for several decades to agree on a common catechism.

The first catechism to be published in the United States came to be known as the "Carroll Catechism," after John Carroll (b. 1735; d. 1815), the first U.S. bishop, a native of Upper Marlboro, Maryland (consecrated, 1790). The title page describes it as *A Short Abridgement of Christian Doctrine. Newly Revised for the Use of the Catholic Church in the United States of America. To Which is added a short daily exercise.* In substance it is the text of Challoner's *Abridgement* of the Doway Catechism (1759 and 1772). The revisions, minor in character, are mostly in the chapter "A Daily Exercise for Christians," and it omits Challoner's chapter "The Christian's Rule of Life." The only significant addition comes at the end: "A Fuller Instruction concerning the Holy Eucharist and Communion translated from the French Catechism of John Joseph Languet, formerly Archbishop of Sens."[4] From his student years at St. Omer's and his later visits to England, Carroll had opportunity to learn of the catechetical works in France and England at first hand.

Many bishops in the newly independent United States were French or educated in the Sulpician tradition. They were formed in the tradition that saw catechizing, including the authorization of catechisms adapted to the needs of their flocks, as an essential part of their ministry. Jean Baptist David compiled catechisms for the diocese of Bardstown, Kentucky, and Jean Lefebvre de Cheverus introduced an English translation of Fleury's catechism into Boston shortly after being named bishop there in 1812. Slovenian Frederic Baraga of Sault Ste. Marie and Marquette, Michigan, translated a collection that included prayers, hymns, and a catechism for the Ottawas (1823), and later rendered it in Ojibway for use by the Chippewas. Neapolitan Joseph Rosati, first bishop of St. Louis and apostolic administrator for New Orleans, commissioned a catechism for the Louisiana Territory, the *Catéchisme de la Louisiane* (1829). Bohemia-born John Nepomucene Neumann composed a catechism for German-speaking immigrants in Philadelphia and in 1850 John Baptist Purcell imported the Deharbe catechism for the use of the German-speaking Catholics in Cincinnati.[5]

In 1826, eleven years after Carroll's death, Archbishop Ambrose Maréchal, the third bishop of Baltimore, approved *A Short Catechism for Use of the Catholics in the United States of America.* He rearranged the order and added hymns at the end, but chapter for chapter it was identical to the Carroll Catechism. In 1832 the first diocesan synod of Philadelphia proposed the use of the Carroll Catechism. Buffalo's first bishop, John Timon, published *A Short Abridgement of the Christian Doctrine; Newly Revised and Augmented* in 1851. Before being named bishop of Buffalo, Pennsylvania-born Timon spent a number of years as a missionary in Texas, so he was able to write,

> Having, from long experience in teaching catechism, a deep conviction that answers which contain not a full sense in themselves, but which depend for a meaning upon the question, leave generally but vague impressions on the minds of children; we sought to arrange a catechism which would be free from this objection, and perused many catechisms full of learning, some of them even too profound, but none which, in our judgement, combines in so small a space more information, sweeter simplicity, and holier unction than the catechism of the Venerated Archbishop Carroll.[6]

When the issue of a uniform catechism came up at the First Plenary Council of Baltimore (1852), it was proposed that the Carroll Catechism, with minor revisions, be submitted to the Holy See for approval and adoption.[7]

Another foreign influence on the American catechetical tradition was the archbishop of Cashel, James Butler II. It was to be expected that the Irish clergy who emigrated to the United States would have brought with them, if not the text, at least the memory of one edition or another of the Butler Catechism. Its influence was widespread and, as will be evident below, persistent.

Within months after taking up his residence as bishop of Charleston, South Carolina, Irish-born John England set to work on a catechism. An entry in his diary for 1821 reads, "On the last week of Lent was published a Catechism which I had much labor in compiling from various others and adding several parts which I considered necessary to be explicitly dwelt upon under the peculiar circumstances of my Diocess *[sic]*."[8] It is evident from the first series of questions and answers alone that one of the sources England used was the Butler Catechism. The new material he introduced and the phrasing of his answers addressed issues that everyday Catholics were likely to face in Protestant North America. The innovative features in England's catechism caused his colleagues Bishop Jean Baptist David, coadjutor of Bardstown, and Bishop Henry Conwell of Philadelphia, both of whom were to compose catechisms of their own, to write to Archbishop Maréchal, criticizing it.

### The "Vexed Question of a Uniform Catechism"

Archbishop Maréchal was among the first to express the need for a common catechism for the United States. In response to England's own complaints about the catechism published by Conwell, Maréchal suggested that the disagreements would end only when the entire country used the same catechism. Writing to Cardinal Cappellari, prefect of the Sacred Congregation for the Propagation of the Faith, in 1827, Maréchal described the catechisms of Conwell, England, and Benedict Joseph Flaget of Bardstown, Kentucky, and expressed fear of what might result from a "multiplicity of discordant catechisms."

Despite pressure from his suffragan bishops Maréchal refused to convene a synod. His successor, Archbishop James Whitfield, however, convened the First Provincial Council in the first year of his episcopate. It lasted just over two weeks, 3-18 October 1832, and passed thirty-eight decrees regulating various aspects of Church life and discipline. The thirty-third decree prohibited the "promiscuous" use of "unapproved catechisms and prayerbooks" and directed that a catechism adapted to the needs of U.S. Catholics be prepared and issued with the approbation of Rome. According to custom, the decrees were submitted to the Holy See for approval. In approving the decree on catechisms, the Congregation for the Propagation of the Faith inserted a clause stating that the proposed catechism would be based on that of Cardinal Bellarmine. Nothing was done to implement the decree, and bishops continued to compile and authorize catechisms for use in their own dioceses. (At the second diocesan synod of Philadelphia in 1836, Irish-born Bishop Francis Patrick Kenrick proposed that the catechism of James Butler be officially adopted for English-speaking Catholics in the diocese.)

The next twenty years was a period of rapid growth in numbers and diversity for the Church in the United States. By the time the First Plenary Council of Baltimore convened in 1852 there were six metropolitan sees (Baltimore, Baker City, St. Louis, New York, Cincinnati, and New Orleans) and twenty-six suffragan sees. Early in the proceedings Kenrick, now archbishop of Baltimore and the presider, appointed a three-man committee to settle the "vexed question of a uniform catechism in English." Two of the three committee members, Timon and Bishop Martin Spalding of Louisville, were authors of catechisms; the third member was Bishop Ignatius Reynolds of Charleston. They consulted with Neumann regarding the best catechism for German-speaking Catholics. The council adjourned on 20 May and on 20 September Spalding sent to Fenwick a "condensed" critique of Timon's catechism in which he complained of its shortcomings.

The formal decrees of the council did not address the matter of the catechism, but the pastoral recommendations contained a proposal for a single catechism. The suggestion was made that, "the extensively and favorably known catechism of the Venerated Archbishop Carroll, after having received some few merely verbal and unimportant emendations, be submitted to the judgment of the Holy See, for general use in this country." In the final version of the decrees and acts of the council, approved in Rome, the reference to the Carroll catechism was omitted, replaced by a recommendation that Bellarmine's catechism be the model.

The recommendations of the committee did not have any immediate results, but some time later there appeared a work described on the title page as *"A General Catechism of the Christian Doctrine,* prepared by order of the First Plenary Council of Baltimore for the use of Catholics in the United States of America, approved by the Most Rev. M. J. Spalding, D.D. Archbishop of Baltimore." The catechism was a slightly revised version of the work published by Spalding in 1852 when he was bishop of Louisville which, in turn, was based on the Carroll catechism.

It is difficult to fix this catechism in the sequence of events because it carried no date of publication. Spalding succeeded Kenrick as archbishop of Baltimore in 1864. The Second Plenary Council of Baltimore met in 1866 and reaffirmed the position of the previous council on catechisms. Under the heading "De disciplinae uniformitate promovenda" ("Promoting Uniformity of Practice"), it repeated the recommendation about the importance of a standard catechism for all the dioceses. Spalding favored adopting a catechism written by Monsignor John H. McCaffrey (1865), the president of Mount St. Mary's Seminary in Emmitsburg, Maryland, but it was strongly opposed by Timon and Verot who found it too brief and obscure. Instead of McCaffrey's work, the bishops seem to have agreed on Spalding's catechism.

### The Catechism of Baltimore III

Almost twenty years passed between the Second and Third Plenary Councils of Baltimore. However they understood the decrees of the earlier council, bishops continued to compile and authorize the publication of catechisms. In the interim the First Vatican Council met (1869–70). Verot compiled three catechisms in this period. In 1864 he published a small catechism that he later revised and incorporated in a larger work that ran 108 pages. This second volume, published in 1869, was unique in several ways. It began with a selection of prayers "that all children must commit to memory." This was followed by "The Smaller Catechism—for young children and illiterate persons." The next section, simply titled "Catechism," consisted of eleven chapters of more detailed questions and answers. Next, in the tradition of Fleury and Bossuet, there was "A Short History of Religion." Then there followed three specialized treatises, a "Short Catechism—for Converts from Protestantism," "A Short Catechism for Converts from Infidelity," and "A Short Catechism for Converts from Judaism." The last 29 pages presented a selection of prayers and hymns. In 1873 Verot published a 32-page work titled *Short Catechism of Christian Doctrine on the Basis Adopted by the First Plenary Council of Baltimore for the Use of Catholics.*

In preparation for Baltimore III, Archbishop James Gibbons, who was to preside over the council as apostolic delegate, appointed a committee of bishops to study the question of a uniform catechism in advance of the council. He instructed the committee, chaired by Archbishop Joseph S. Alemany of San Francisco, to give special consideration to three points and report on them to the council:

> 1st. On the expediency of adopting a uniform catechism at the Council.
> 2nd. On naming the catechism which they prefer to be sanctioned.
> 3rd. Whether the Germans, Slavonians, Italians, Spaniards, French, etc., should have a translation of the catechism to be adopted, or whether another catechism should be approved for them.[9]

The catechism committee met several times in the course of the council. In the initial discussions committee members favoring a new catechism prevailed over those who would have adopted the Butler catechism issued by the Synod of Maynooth two years earlier. The committee made its official report to the council on 29 November 1884. After amendments from the floor, the report was incorporated in the *acta et decreta* of the council. The section pertinent to the catechism directed the catechism committee

> 1. To select a catechism and if necessary to emend it, or to start from scratch if they would feel it the necessary and opportune thing to do.
> 2. Let them present this work thus finished to the body of Roman Catholic Archbishops who will re-examine the catechism and will provide that it be published . . .

The report went on to state that the new catechism would be composed in English in order to provide a means of promoting uniformity and would be translated so that it could be used by the faithful of other tongues. It went on to add: "Especially since the children born of German, French, or any other nation frequently come to Catholic Church in a later period, in which churches the Christian doctrine is proclaimed in an English tongue, let us recommend that the youths who understand fully both tongues and who live totally among English-speaking people learn the before-mentioned Catechism in the English tongue."[10]

Eight days later on 6 December  the catechism committee distributed galley proofs of the proposed catechism to the full assembly of bishops. Since the council was to adjourn the next day, the committee requested that the bishops send any suggestions for changes in the text to Bishop John L. Spalding of Peoria as soon as possible. The draft of the catechism that was distributed to the bishops was, according to accounts of the time, prepared by Italian-born Monsignor Januarius de Concilio, pastor of St. Michael's Church in Jersey City, who was present at the council as the theologian of James O'Connor of Nebraska. Later, when the Baltimore Catechism came under a volley of criticism, de Concilio was to downplay his part in the work.

Spalding took up residence in the rectory of the Church of St. Paul the Apostle in New York City until 25 January 1885. The location, a ferry ride across the Hudson from Jersey City, made it possible for him and de Concilio to collaborate. Toward the end of February Spalding wrote to Gibbons: "I have received suggestions from all the archbishops concerning the catechism and have made such changes as seemed desirable."[11] Archbishop John Cardinal McCloskey of New York gave the *imprimatur* on 6 April 1885 and on the same day Gibbons, as apostolic delegate, approved the text. Spalding was granted a copyright for *A Catechism of Christian Doctrine, Prepared and Enjoined by the Order of the Third Plenary Council of Baltimore.*

The Baltimore Catechism is a compilation. The original edition consisted of 421 questions, distributed in 37 chapters, that ran to 72 pages. Compared question by question with other works, only 49 are not found in either the Butler-Maynooth, Verot's, McCaffrey's, or David's catechism. Of the questions unique to Baltimore, 13 relate to the themes emphasized at the truncated Vatican I: the nature of the Church and authority. It explains such terms as *infallibility* and *indefectibility* that were uncommon in earlier catechisms. Unlike the First Provincial and Plenary Councils of Baltimore, Baltimore III did not recommend that the text be sent to the Holy See for approval. Apparently the endorsement of Gibbons, as apostolic delegate, was deemed sufficient. Thus the earlier pressure to use Bellarmine's catechism as the model did not prevail, and the dominant influence on the Baltimore Catechism seems to have been Butler.

Despite the fact that the Baltimore Catechism derived almost all its content from other works, its organization was original. Most of the catechisms of the time followed a sequence of Creed, Commandments, sacraments. Baltimore, closer to the Catechism of the Council of Trent, organized the material under the headings of Creed, sacraments, and Commandments. It dealt with prayer at the end of the section on sacraments and, it must be observed, in a rather perfunctory way.

Using the same *imprimatur* Spalding, within months, published a shorter version, *A Catechism of Christian Doctrine, Abridged from the Catechism Prepared and Enjoined by Order of the Third Plenary Council of Baltimore*. Sometimes referred to as "Baltimore Catechism No. 1," the abridged version reduced the contents to 208 questions, 33 chapters, and 36 pages. Although Spalding dropped some questions and rearranged them within the chapters, the wording in all cases remained the same. Baltimore No. 1, however, never rivaled the original in popularity.

### The Baltimore Catechism: Criticisms and Revision

Initially, the original Baltimore Catechism received a lukewarm reception, and it did not put a stop to the proliferation of catechisms. Benedictine Mary Charles Bryce has counted fifteen new catechisms that appeared with episcopal approval by the turn of the century. The earliest and sharpest criticisms appeared in the *Pastoralblatt*, a German-language monthly published in St. Louis. In a series of articles beginning in September 1885 the writer (or writers) attacked the work for its pedagogical and theological shortcomings. The catechism was said to be unsuitable for children because of its style (dull, repetitive, and replete with incomprehensible terms) and, surprisingly, because it was too *small*. (Children, said the anonymous writer, prefer larger volumes!) Furthermore, because the text described all matters in the same monotonous way, the pupil would not learn to distinguish teachings of greater and lesser importance—what has come to be called "the hierarchy of truths." The critic found the catechism's theology deficient because of the little attention it gave to the Godhead and angels, the absence of any consideration of divine providence, and because the one question it devoted to the resurrection missed the point of its significance.

Most of the shortcomings pointed out in the *Pastoralblatt* are endemic to small catechisms but the writer also attempted to undermine the authority of the Baltimore Catechism. He charged (correctly) that the catechism was published before the Congregation for the Propagation of the Faith approved the acts and decrees of the Third Plenary Council of Baltimore. Furthermore, the final text was not sent to the bishops for their review and approbation.

Ten years after its publication the archbishops of the country acknowledged that the catechism "in its present form seems unpopular." They moved to poll the bishops of the country "as whether the present catechism should be revised or another catechism prepared as a substitute for the one now in use."[12] The archbishops took up the catechism as the first item of business the following year. According to the minutes of the 1896 meeting, "From the reports of the various Provinces, it was evident that all the Bishops of the country were in favor of some changes while the majority recommended a *revision* of the present catechism." They appointed a committee to undertake the revision. Even after several years, however, the committee could not come up with a satisfactory solution. The minutes for the 1902 meeting report that the committee members "found themselves unable to offer an adequate remedy because they knew no existing catechism which they could fully recommend; secondly, even if a proper catechism were prepared, the Board of Archbishops has no authority to order its general use."

Despite the fact that it gradually gained acceptance in most dioceses, dissatisfaction with the Baltimore Catechism continued. In 1934 the Congregation for the Council (the congregation that had the responsibility of implementing the decrees of Trent, including oversight of the catechism) issued the decree *Provide sane concilio* which dealt with the care and promotion of catechetical instruction. It provided the immediate stimulus for the long talked-about revision of the Baltimore Catechism. The bishops' committee for the Confraternity of Christian Doctrine, chaired by Bishop Edwin O'Hara, then of Great Falls, Montana, assumed the responsibility for the revision.

The CCD committee enlisted the services of the Reverend Francis J. Connell, C.SS.R., professor of moral theology at The Catholic University of America, to assemble, synthesize, and edit the suggestions sent in by the bishops. The committee prepared four drafts between October 1936 and June 1941 when *A Catechism of Christian Doctrine*, a revised edition of the Baltimore Catechism, was published. A few months later, a revised edition of Baltimore No. 1 appeared, followed by a First Communion edition in October 1943. Subsequently Archbishop John T. McNicholas of Cincinnati, a member of the bishops' CCD committee, working with Connell, edited an enlarged version—Baltimore No. 3—for the use of adults (1949). This last had the same questions as the revised Baltimore, but the answers were more expansive and included pertinent biblical quotations.

The revised Baltimore Catechism added some material. The original text had 421 questions in 37 chapters; the revised edition had 499 questions in 38 lessons. The 38th chapter, a new addition, was intended to remedy a notable deficiency in the original text. It consisted of a series of questions on each of 8 petitions in the Lord's Prayer. The revised edition added another 16 questions in an appendix titled "Why I Am a Catholic," based on the classic tract "De vera religione" ("The True Religion") found in the manuals of Neoscholastic theology used in seminaries.

The revised edition also reordered the sequence of the parts. The 1885 edition organized the questions around the Creed, the sacraments and the Commandments—the three parts that gave rise to the phrase "creed, cult, and code." The 1941 edition reordered the sequence to "creed, code, and cult." Connell justified the change stating: "This seems a more logical division—what we must believe, what we must do, and the chief supernatural means to aid us to believe revealed doctrine and to obey the law of God. It is this order that is followed by most Catechisms, although the Catechism of the Council of Trent was arranged according to the plan followed by the original Baltimore Catechism."[13] The change in order reflected a very different understanding of sacrament and sacraments from that of Trent if not from that of the compilers of the original text. In the new arrangement, sacraments, like prayer, appear as means, "channels," of grace. But in reality they are more than instruments of salvation: sacraments, like the Church itself, are symbols that embody the reality they signify.

The 1941 text of the Baltimore Catechism was not greeted with any more enthusiasm than the 1885 edition. In addition to individuals who opposed change on principle, many critics took the occasion of the publication of the revised edition to rehearse the inadequacies of catechisms in general. There was nothing new to allegations about the revised text's pedagogical inadequacies and theological shortcomings, most of which are limitations of the genre. The criticisms, however, were presented in a different context. Between the two editions of the Baltimore Catechism, kerygmatic theology and biblical studies brought a fresh approach to the Scriptures and to the presentation of doctrine and morality; the liturgical movement had retrieved the ancient understanding of liturgy and catechesis; and people were beginning to understand the sacraments and the Church itself as more than conduits of grace. The editor of the revised Baltimore Catechism took none of these new developments into account.

This revised version continued in print to the time of Vatican II, but by then it had already been displaced by textbooks in many parishes. The textbooks echo formulas that go back beyond Baltimore to Butler, Carroll, Challoner, Bellarmine, and, even more, to Canisius. They attempt, moreover, what the catechism genre does not, namely, to encourage learners to bring questions born of their own experience into the discussion of God, Church, and Christian living.

NOTES

1. Maurice Simon, *Un catéchisme universel pour l'Église catholique du Concile de Trente à nos jours* (Leuven: University Press, 1992) 77.

2. This account is based on the research of Michael Donnellan, *Rationale for a Uniform Catechism: Vatican I to Vatican II* (Ph.D. diss., The Catholic University of America, Washington, 1972). Also see Simon, *Un Catéchisme Universel*, 64–129.

3. See Appendix A for the full text.

4. Bishop Languet (1677–1753), a staunch opponent of Jansenism, wrote a series of short catechisms on the sacraments. See J. Carreyre, "Languet de Villeneuve de Gergy, Jean-Joseph," in *Dictionnaire de théologie catholique*. The full text of Carroll's Catechism was transcribed by Thomas E. Wrangler and reprinted in *The Living Light* 31:1 (Fall 1994) 62–78.

5. For a detailed account of catechisms written by bishops in the United States, see Mary Charles Bryce, *Pride of Place: The Role of the Bishops in the Development of Catechesis in the United States* (Washington: The Catholic University of America, 1984). Charles Carmody provides additional bibliographical information, *Roman Catholic Catechesis*, passim.

6. Quoted in Bryce, *Pride of Place*, 63.

7. Charles J. Carmody, "The 'Carroll Catechism'—A Primary Component of the American Catechetical Tradition," *Notre Dame Journal of Education* 7 (Spring 1976) 76–95.

8. Quoted in Bryce, *Pride of Place*, 34.

9. Quoted in ibid., 88. The other members of the committee were: Louis de Goesbriand of Burlington, Stephen Ryan of Buffalo, Joseph G. Dwenger of Fort Wayne, John L. Spalding of Peoria, John J. Kain of Wheeling, and Francis Janssens of Natchez.

10. See full text in Appendix B.

11. 23 February 1885. Quoted in Bryce, *Pride of Place*, 90.

12. Quoted in ibid., 94–95.

13. Quoted in ibid., 108.

TWELVE

# The Dutch Catechism:
# Harbinger of a New Genre

The ninety years that separate the First and Second Vatican Councils witnessed great advancement in the field of catechetics. During this period adult catechesis came to the fore. As seen in the previous chapter, Vatican I approved, but never promulgated, a constitution that called for a uniform catechism to be used throughout the Catholic world. As its title, *Constitutio de parvo catechismo*, suggested, it was to be a "small catechism"—a catechism for children. Vatican II, by contrast, rejected the notion of a uniform catechism and shifted the emphasis to adult catechesis. It was a move that gave rise to a new genre of catechisms.[1]

By way of preparing for the Second Vatican Council, bishops from around the world sent in proposals on many subjects. Bishop Lacointe of Beauvais, France, anticipating that many of his brother bishops would propose to return to the unfinished project *De parvo catechismo* of Vatican I, urged instead the compilation of a catechetical directory that would establish principles and general norms to serve as guidelines for catechesis. He argued that a single catechism for the universal Church was not possible or, at least, not proper.

Lacointe's proposal notwithstanding, the central commission that functioned as a steering committee instructed the preparatory commission "de disciplina cleri et populi Christiani" ("on the way of life of clerics and Christian people") (1) to draw up plans for a new catechism containing the principal elements of the sacred liturgy, Church history, and social teaching; and (2) to emphasize the importance of adult catechesis. Although this latter commission recommended a catechetical directory instead of a catechism, it highlighted the importance of adult catechesis. And in the end, the council fathers took the position that a uniform catechism for the entire Church was not feasible (*non expedire*). The Decree on the Pastoral Office of Bishops, *Christus Dominus*, sanctioned "a directory for the catechetical instruction of the Christian people in which the fundamental principles of this instruction and its organization will be dealt with and the preparation of books relating to it" (no. 44). When the General Catechetical Directory was published in 1972, it underscored the importance of adult catechesis in an often quoted statement: "Shepherds of souls . . . should also remember that catechesis for adults, since it deals with persons who are capable of an adherence that is fully responsible, must be considered the chief form of catechesis. All the other forms, which are indeed always necessary, are in some way oriented to it" (no. 20).

### Post-Vatican II Catechisms

While work was going forward on the general directory the Italian hierarchy was carefully laying the groundwork for a renewal of catechesis. The bishops had recognized, even prior to Vatican II, that the Catechism of Pope Pius X, widely used in Italy, no longer satisfied the needs of the times. The bishops began by issuing a foundational document setting down principles governing the aims, agents, and methods of catechesis that anticipated the spirit and vision of the general directory.[2] The next step was to publish a *Catechismo per la vita cristiana* ("Catechism for the Christian Life"), consisting of six individual catechisms adapted to the various age groups from infants to adults.[3] Following the principles laid down in their foundational document, the bishops decreed that the language should speak to the modern mind and make revelation intelligible in contemporary culture. The catechism should present the whole of Christian doctrine, ordering the content around the mystery of Christ, "the living center of catechesis." It should also treat, where appropriate for the age level, themes of concern in today's world: peace, freedom, social justice, cultural and political affairs, international cooperation for peoples in developing countries, and, in particular, the human and social problems of Italy.

The first book in the series *Il catechismo dei bambini (A Catechism for Infants)* was published in 1973. Running to 165 pages, it was not intended for use by small children themselves, but for clergy, religious and lay teachers, parents and future parents. Although each of the catechisms takes a different approach, each presents a unified vision of the Christian message. The catechism for adults *Signore da chi andremo? (Lord to Whom Shall We Go?)*, for example, is built around the theme of the kingdom of God. It is developed in relationship to the Holy Trinity: part 1 describes the mission of Jesus who announces the kingdom and calls people to conversion; part 2 describes how the Church is called into being and grows by the action of the Holy Spirit in word and sacrament; part 3 describes how the kingdom, a "project of love and responsible action in the world," moves through history until it reaches fulfillment and brings humans into communion with the triune God. All the catechisms in the series draw on biblical and liturgical sources and the documents of Vatican II as primary means in forming a "mentality of faith."

## The Dutch Catechism

Similarly, the bishops of the Netherlands, before the Second Vatican Council ended, also commissioned a catechism. *A New Catechism: Catholic Faith for Adults,* published in 1966, was innovative in several respects and, as a result, it evoked a bitter reaction from individuals and groups tenacious of the traditional ways. The Dutch Catechism, as it came to be known, gave opponents of *aggiornamento* a concrete target. People who had very little in common except their disenchantment with Vatican II's reforms joined in a coalition against the Dutch Catechism and everything it represented.

The idea for a new catechism began to take shape in the Netherlands in the 1950s.[4] Up to that time the catechism in general use was a 1948 revision of a work originally compiled in 1910. In the form of questions and answers, it was the required text in schools as well as the standard text for the instruction of adult converts. The 1948 revision was a great improvement, but school teachers still found it inadequate. To address the needs of their students they developed lesson plans and supplementary materials, including audio-visuals, that incorporated some of the new developments in theology and liturgy.

Meanwhile others, led by the Augustinians at Culenberg, shifted their attention to adults. The Catholic Action movement encouraged discussion groups and faith reflection along the lines of the Christian Family Movement in the United States. The *Una Sancta* movement, under the aegis of the Missionaries of the Sacred Heart, endeavored to provide ongoing instruction for converts. Father Nicholas G. M. Van Doornik, M.S.C., superior of the Una Sancta House in The Hague, together with two of his confreres, published a catechism for adults based on outlines and methods that they had developed in their ministry. Translated into English as *The Triptych of the Kingdom. A Handbook of the Catholic Faith* (New York: Newman Press, 1954), it is said to have pioneered a new genre of adult catechisms.

In 1956 the Dutch bishops petitioned the Higher Catechetical Institute at Nijmegen to undertake a thorough review of the 1948 catechism with an eye to producing a new work better suited to the needs of the times. The commission appointed to do the study reported back that it was necessary first of all to make a clear distinction between a catechism for children and a catechism for adults. Despite the commission's strong reservations, the bishops decided on a catechism for children, and the Nijmegen institute worked on the project into 1961. At one point the institute, in an effort to get guidance as to what should be included in the catechism for children, conducted a poll to find out what adults knew and what they felt they should know about their faith.

## Controversy Begins

The Dutch, aware of the work of the preparatory commissions, did not wait until the council was over to act. In July 1961 the hierarchy instructed the Nijmegen institute to compile a catechism for adults. By the following March the institute submitted a detailed outline to the bishops who solicited input from a broad range of experts. Theologians, exegetes, psychologists, sociologists, priests, and parents—more than 150 people in all—sent in thousands of suggestions and recommendations. On the basis of this initial consultation, the institute produced the first draft of the catechism that was then circulated to an even larger group of consultants—individuals and institutions. The second consultation evoked another 10,000 responses. A four-man committee, assisted by another 20 consultants drawn from the original group of 150, was charged with sifting through and analyzing the recommendations, and preparing another draft. The text was then revised by a review commission working in collaboration with theologians Willem Bless, S.J., Edward Schillebeeckx, O.P., and Piet Schoonenberg, S.J.

*De nieuwe Katechismus* was published 9 October 1966 with the *imprimatur* of Cardinal Bernard Alfrink, archbishop of Utrecht and primate of the Netherlands. The ink was hardly dry before a group of Dutch Catholics, without notifying the bishops, began planning an appeal to the pope regarding the catechism. The petition they sent to Pope Paul VI was the occasion, if not the motive, for Rome's intervention. A report prepared for the pope by a secret commission, named in Rome in February 1967, recommended that the Dutch bishops rework certain passages in the catechism that were open to ambiguous interpretation. And thus began a controversy that attracted the attention of the secular press throughout Europe and North America.

A colloquium to discuss the troublesome passages was arranged for April 1967 at Gazzarda in Northern Italy. Bless, Schillebeeckx, and Schoonenberg came from Holland; Edouard Dhanis, S.J., Benedict Lemeer, O.P., and Jan Visser, C.SS.R., came from Rome. The Roman theologians had sent a memorandum identifying twelve major points they wanted to discuss, and they arrived in Gazzarda with an additional list of points of lesser importance they sought to add to the agenda. The Dutch theologians refused to address the additional points, preferring to concentrate on the major issues. In anticipation of the report from the Gazzarda colloquium Pope Paul VI formed a commission of cardinals, including Cardinal Alfrink, to advise him regarding the catechism. The cardinals' report, forwarded to the Pope in January 1968, identified some points that they felt should be reviewed, but it did not speak of errors or heresies.

Reports of the controversy, rumor and innuendo fueled the curiosity of the public and made *A New Catechism* a best-seller. Publishers, anxious to capitalize on the notoriety, were hurriedly readying translations. Cardinal Alfrink, however, announced in a radio interview that it would not be possible to grant the *imprimatur* to translations of the catechism until modifications requested by Rome were included. Nonetheless in October 1967 an English translation of the catechism was published by Herder and Herder in the United States with the *imprimatur* of Robert F. Joyce, bishop of Burlington, Vermont, and in England by Burns and Oates, but without an *imprimatur*.[5] Like the Dutch original it sold well.

Two years later, in 1969, Herder and Herder published a second edition, unchanged from the original except for a sixty-page "supplement" by Dhanis and Visser that cited the concerns of the commission of cardinals appointed to examine *A New Catechism*.[6] Dhanis and Visser edited and expanded many passages and presented alternative wording to address the points raised by the cardinals. They concluded the supplement by quoting the final remark of the commission:

> Though the preceding comments are not negligible, either in number or seriousness, they nonetheless leave by far the greatest part of the New Catechism untouched, with its admirable pastoral, liturgical and biblical character. So too they support the praise-worthy intention of the authors of the Catechism, which was to present the eternal good news of Christ in a way which is adapted to the mentality of the people of our times . . .

A side-show had become the main attraction. The points of dispute diverted attention from the overall merits of the catechism itself.

### The *New* in *A New Catechism*

In retrospect, it now seems that, by unduly stressing the catechism's novelty, the carefully chosen title contributed to its own undoing. In the foreword the Dutch bishops present the work as an effort "to render faithfully the renewal which found expression in the Second Vatican Council," and explain why it is called *A New Catechism*. "We hope," they said, "to present anew to adults the message which Jesus of Nazareth brought into the world, to make it sound as new as it is." The whole of the Catholic faith remains the same but "the approach, the light in which the faith is seen, is new . . . [presented] in a form suitable to the present day." Traditional catechisms presented brief formulations that could easily be memorized. *A New Catechism* sought to engage present-day questions, to promote unity among Christians, and to reach out to "all our fellowmen, who live in the same world as we do with its cares and yearnings." Critics, friendly and unfriendly, saw the catechism as redefining the task of catechesis. Catechesis is no longer a mere handing down of the message, but an "illumination," by way of the message, of every aspect of life. The negative reaction of readers who held Vatican II's attempts at *aggiornamento* suspect or who had little sympathy for the ecumenical movement or who denigrated the challenges of contemporary culture was understandable.

The brief essay that follows the foreword, "How to Use this Book," explains the structure of *A New Catechism,* justifies the choice of non-technical language, and identifies its intended audience as "mature readers." The foreword indicates that the catechism can be used for personal study and reflection as well as being a text for discussion groups. And it suggests ways that it can be used as a "reference work."

As if in anticipation of the controversies that were to ensue, the authors request "both Catholics and non-Catholics" to remember, "Misunderstandings are always possible, and a book which covers as many subjects as this one can give rise to many of them. We ask our readers to see each word in the context of the whole gospel message. This means that no passage can be read properly unless the preceding and following pages are taken into account."

## The Contents of the Catechism

*A New Catechism* is divided into five unequal parts. If the chapter titles and subheads are read in sequence, as the catechism itself suggests, one has in effect a short summary of the Christian message. The plan of the book, beginning with the human condition, guides the reader through a presentation of salvation history to its final fulfillment in God's own being:

1. "The Mystery of Existence" examines the human predicament, that who we are and what we do contains both question and answer, grandeur and misery, our longing for happiness and our quest of the good and true.

2. "The Way to Christ" is subdivided into two sections. First, it describes "the way of the nations": the religious quest in ancient cultures, the great religious traditions of the Far East and Islam, humanism and Marxism and "the Spirit of God in the Whole World." Second, it describes "the way of Israel," giving a synopsis of God's wonderful works in Israelite history, revelation, covenant, messianism, the presence of God in the Law and Wisdom. It also calls attention to Israel itself as a unique phenomenon. It explains the origin, structure, and the literary genres of the Bible, and the various senses of Scripture.

3. "The Son of Man" outlines the life, ministry, message, and authority of Jesus. It explains the meaning of the passion, death, and resurrection in the context of Holy Week and the celebration of Easter. The sending of the Spirit

and works of the Spirit bring this part to a close. It ends with a reflection on the liturgy of Pentecost and the Church year.

4. "The Way of Christ," the longest part by far, begins with an overview of Church history and a discussion of the Church's mission. It describes the Church's hierarchical structue and priestly nature. It presents the theology of conversion, redemption, and grace in the context of the Church's sacramental life, and explains the personal and social responsibilities of Christians in relationship to the Commandments. The failures of Christians are identified as sin, and the sacrament of penance is presented as the means of forgiveness.

5. "The Way to the End" reflects on the last things in light of Christian hope in the resurrection, the "new creation," and the transcendent God for whom "all things were created."

The supplement in the second edition identifies the points that the commission of cardinals found misleading, inadequately explained, or simply neglected. The first deals with creation, specifically with the creation of pure spirits—angels and devils—and the human soul. Almost a third of the supplement consists of an alternate text explaining issues surrounding the nature and transmission of original sin. The emphasis in the catechism on the symbolic meaning of the virgin birth is not enough; catechesis must consider the truth of this mystery in the full context of the incarnation and Mary's perpetual virginity. In the area of Christology, the supplement calls for greater clarity in explaining the satisfaction that Jesus offered to the Father, and insists that the traditional explanation of the Eucharistic sacrifice be included. Out of concern lest readers of the catechism be misled regarding the infallibility of the Church and knowledge of the sacred mysteries, the supplement, quoting Pope Paul VI, stresses that "faith is not only a search, but a certainty." It calls for a clearer explanation of the ordained priesthood and the office of bishops, especially the pope. It also suggests modification in the wording of texts that dealt with a number of specific issues in dogmatic (e.g., the consciousness of Jesus) and moral theology (e.g., the indissolubility of marriage).

No catechism is without limitations, but the harsh criticism aimed at the Dutch Catechism can be explained only in terms of a larger context. From a distance of time it is now clear that the issue was less a new approach to *catechesis* than it was a new *theology* that attempted to engage modernity. Subsequent events suggest that the controversy had less to do with the Dutch Catechism as such than it did with Dutch theologians.

## "A New Genus of Catechism"

In 1976, almost ten years after the publication of the Dutch Catechism, the German bishops commissioned a catechism for adults. The project, at one point near collapse, received new life when Cardinal Josef Ratzinger, then chairman of the Commission for the Faith of the German Episcopal Conference, enlisted the services of Professor Walter Kasper of the Catholic faculty at the University of Tübingen to draft the test. An English translation of the *Katholischer Erwachsenen-Katechismus* (1985) was published in the United States as *The Church's Confession of Faith: A Catholic Catechism for Adults* (San Francisco: Ignatius Press, 1987).

The German Catechism begins with a chapter on the human search for meaning and revelation. The Nicene Creed provides the structure for the three principal parts of the first volume under the headings of "God the Father," "Jesus Christ," and "The Work of the Holy Spirit." In the third part the German Catechism presents the Church as "Sacrament of the Spirit," and under the heading "The Communion of Saints: Through Word and Sacrament" it introduces the general notion of sacrament and explains each of the seven sacraments. The moral teaching of the Church is reserved for the second volume. The German bishops take the position that a catechism is a confessional document as well as a book of instruction.

Addressing the German episcopal conference in the spring of 1984, a few months before the catechism for adults appeared, Kasper described its development and situated it in the history of catechesis. Although he cited the Catechism of the Council of Trent as "the best model"—*mutatis mutandis*—for the undertaking, Kasper acknowledged that the emergence of "a new genus of catechism" provided immediate precedents for the German Catechism. He cited by way of examples the Dutch Catechism, the ecumenical *Neues Glaubensbuch* (published in English as the *Common Catechism*), and the adult catechism issued by the Evangelical (Lutheran) Church in 1975. (In 1985 Kasper served as special secretary for the extraordinary synod of bishops that recommended a catechism for the universal Church.)

The new German work corresponds to the large catechisms of Luther and Canisius—a catechism for catechists, "those transmitting the faith," rather than for catechumens or students. Kasper took the position that "many of today's catechists are, practically speaking, still catechumens themselves and they must be 'met' where they are." Thus the new catechism could not avoid "stressing some thought-provoking topics if it is not to by-pass the problems of this target group." A great deal of theological work went into the catechism; "but at all times," Kasper said,

> its compilers made an honest effort to preserve room for differing theological schools and directions within this creed which is binding on all Catholics. In order to keep this free space open, since that is indispensable for the life of the Church, it was impermissible to have this catechism pass prior judgment on any of the numerous, profoundly important, questions

in theology which are legitimately and even necessarily, being raised today.[7]

An example of such a question is the ordination of women to the priestly office and to the sacramental diaconate.[8] Church teaching "binding on all Catholics" is set off from discussions of theological questions open to speculation and further reflection by the use of type fonts, the former indicated by a large type face, and the latter set in a smaller type (the difference is more pronounced in the German edition).

Even as work on the *Catechism of the Catholic Church* was getting underway, the episcopal conferences of Spain and Belgium published national catechisms. In 1986 the Spanish bishops published *Esta es nuestra fe. Esta es la fe de la iglesia*. It begins with an introduction that outlines God's covenant with humanity as it is seen to unfold in the Old and New Testaments. The main body of the work, divided into three parts, explains the Creed, the sacraments and liturgy, and basic principles of Christian morality. An appendix contains traditional prayers and Catholic devotions. Addressed first to young people and then to adults—parents, parish priests, catechists, and all who are responsible for catechesis—the bishops want the faithful to read and re-read *Esta es nuestra fe* throughout their lives as a means of keeping alive the faith they profess, of helping to celebrate the mysteries of salvation in the liturgy, and of witnessing by their works the commitment they made in baptism.

In 1987 the bishops of Belgium introduced a *Livre de la foi* as an instrument in their effort to evangelize their country anew. Known in the United States by its English title, *Belief and Belonging* (Collegeville, Minn: The Liturgical Press, 1990), *Livre de la foi* is also intended to be a catechism for adults. It has three main chapters: to know the faith (Apostles' Creed), celebrate the faith (liturgy and sacrament), and live the faith (holiness and Christian morality). Less than half the length of the volume published by the German bishops, the Belgium Catechism is intended for a mass audience and (as one would expect in largely Catholic Belgium) individuals whose culture has brought them into contact with the Church. Handsomely illustrated with color plates, it presents fundamentals of the Catholic faith without venturing into disputed theological issues or questions of biblical interpretation.

Close upon the publication of the Belgium Catechism was the *Catéchisme pour adultes* authorized by the bishops of France (1991). Five years in the making, it was the outcome of a resolution made by the episcopal conference in 1985 to undertake the compilation of "a work for adults, a work primarily intended for catechists," that would constitute "an organic and complete exposition of the faith." Although it is dominated by the theme of covenant, the *Catéchisme pour adultes* follows the general structure of the Creed. The first of its seven chapters explains the act of faith. The second chapter, titled "God of the Covenant," presents the revelation of God as Father and Creator who interacts with human beings in a history marked by sin and the promise of salvation. This chapter introduces the notion of revelation, the Scriptures, and tradition. The third chapter, "The New Covenant in Jesus Christ," is the centerpiece of the work. Chapter four treats "The Church, People of the New Covenant"; chapter five, "Sacraments of the New Covenant"; chapter six, "The Law of the Way of the New Covenant"; and chapter seven, "The Fulfilment of the New Covenant in the Kingdom of God."

Each of these catechisms, the Dutch Catechism included, seeks to offer a comprehensive vision, showing that the gospel message and the Church's teaching is still vital in today's world. The story in all of them is the same, but each tells it with a distinctive slant, aimed to appeal to a particular audience. Together they redefined the catechism genre, making the adult catechism the source and standard for children's catechisms, reversing a century-long convention that made the Penny Catechism and the Baltimore Catechism the benchmark of Catholic teaching. The Dutch, German, Belgium, and French catechisms provide a context for the use and interpretation of the *Catechism of the Catholic Church*. In justifying the decision to call this last a "catechism" rather than a compendium of Catholic doctrine, Ratzinger cited the Dutch and German catechisms.[9] The three are comparable in size and, in so far as they are comprehensive statements that can be used as reference works for understanding the truths of faith, they are compendiums of Catholic doctrine. The term *catechism*, however, better describes their purposes and aim, namely, to present the Christian message in a way that calls the baptized and non-baptized to commit themselves to the gospel message so that their faith "becomes living, explicit and productive through formation in doctrine and the experience of Christian living" (canon 773, *Code of Canon Law* [1983]).

NOTES

1. Maurice Simon gives a detailed report of the actions taken and not taken by Vatican II regarding catechisms: see *Un catéchisme universel*, 132–284. For a briefer account see Berard L. Marthaler, *Catechetics in Context: Notes and Commentary on the General Catechetical Directory* (Huntington, Ind.: Our Sunday Visitor, Inc., 1973) xvi–xxx.

2. Berard L. Marthaler, "The Renewal of Catechesis in Italy," *Religious Education* 65 (1971) 357–63.

3. John E. MacInnes, "Italy's *Catechism for the Christian Life:* More than Meets the Eye," *The Living Light* 18 (1981) 334–44. The Italian episcopal conference published a second edition with some revisions, 1991–94.

4. This account relies heavily on Leo Alting von Geusau and Fernando Vittorino Joannes, *Il dossier del catechismo olandese* (Verona: Arnoldo Mondadori, 1968).

5. The *imprimatur* appeared only in the first printing of the American edition. Subsequent printings continued the notice on the dust jacket, "Authorized Edition of the 'Dutch Catechism,'" noting on an inside page that the original Dutch edition had the *imprimatur* of Bernardus Cardinal Alfrink.

6. The commission's concerns were reported in *Acta Apostolicae Sedis* 60 (1968) 687–91.

7. Walter Kasper, "The Church's Profession of Faith: On Drafting a New Catholic Catechism for Adults," *Communio* 11 (1984) 61, 63.

8. With regard to the ordaining of women to the priestly office, the German Catechism, citing the 1976 declaration of the Roman Congregation for the Doctrine of the Faith, says "it does not seem possible." With regard to the ordination of women to the sacramental diaconate, it states, "More discussion is needed, however, as is a consensus in the entire Church" (p. 247).

9. See the summary of Cardinal Ratzinger's report to the Synod of Bishops. 25 Oct. 1990 in *Origins* 20:22 (8 Nov. 1990) 358.

THIRTEEN

# The 1985 Synod of Bishops:
# Catechisms Universal and Local

In Rome, on 24 November 1985, Pope John Paul II convened an extraordinary assembly of the Synod of Bishops to commemorate the twentieth anniversary of the Second Vatican Council. The most significant action taken by the assembly was a recommendation that led in time to the publication of the *Catechism of the Catholic Church*. The wording of that resolution, as we shall see below, is significant. It called for "a catechism or compendium of all Catholic doctrine regarding both faith and morals [to] be composed, that it might be as it were, a point of reference for the catechisms or compendiums that are prepared in the various countries." The resolution was a result of the proposal made by Cardinal Bernard Law of Boston on the floor of the synod for a "conciliar catechism." Suggestions of this kind had been put forward many times in the years after Vatican II, but none was ever acted upon.

Before describing the development and structure of the *Catechism of the Catholic Church* in the next chapter, it is well to recall that the decision of the Second Vatican Council, alluded to in the previous chapter, *not* to mandate a catechism had not satisfied everyone. Despite the publication of the General Catechetical Directory many individuals and factions continued to be preoccupied with a crisis in the post-Vatican II Church, real or perceived, that they attributed to disarray in religious education.

### The General Catechetical Directory on Catechisms

The first general assembly of the Synod of Bishops, itself a creation of Vatican II, met in the fall of 1967 when the uproar over the Dutch Catechism was at its peak.[1] In his inaugural address to the synod, Pope Paul VI summoned the bishops to insure the integrity of the Catholic faith, renew its vigor, and address the dangers that threatened it. As a way of achieving these aims, several bishops proposed a catechism like that of the Council of Trent; some proposed a revised edition of the Tridentine catechism that would incorporate the teachings of Vatican II; others favored a catechism for adults, but they were vague as to its nature and contents. In the end, however, no action was taken on a catechism because most agreed that *Christus Dominus,* in mandating a catechetical directory, had already dealt with the question. The Pope, communicating through Cardinal Jean Villot, then prefect of the Congregation for the Clergy, reaffirmed his support for a general catechetical directory.

The *Directorium catechisticum generale* was published in the summer of 1971, after a protracted consultation with episcopal conferences around the world. The foreword explains that the intent of the directory "is to provide the basic principles of pastoral theology" for effective ministry of the word. "The errors which are not infrequently noted in catechetics today," it says, "can be avoided only if one starts with the correct way of understanding the nature and purposes of catechesis and also the truths which are to be taught by it, with due account being taken of those to whom catechesis is directed and of the conditions in which they live." The task of applying the principles and directives to concrete situations belongs to bishops "and they do this by means of national and regional directories, and by means of catechisms" and other suitable catechetical aids.[2]

In addition to the foreword, the GCD has six parts, subdivided into 134 sections: Part 1 sketches some of the factors, including social change and cultural pluralism, that affect the Church's mission to proclaim the gospel in the modern world. Part 2 relates catechesis to revelation and evangelization, and describes its nature and goals in the context of the Church's pastoral mission. Part 3 gives specific norms for the presentation of the Christian message and outlines its "more outstanding elements." (According to the foreword, the summary is provided "so as to make fully clear" that the goal of catechesis is to present the Christian faith in its entirety.)[3] Part 4 discusses the strengths and limitations of various methods used in catechesis, stressing the importance of formulas (no. 73) and experience (no. 74). Part 5 gives guidelines for catechesis according to the special needs of various age levels. Part 6 is concerned with practical matters such as the formation of catechists, organization, and catechetical materials, including catechisms.

A lengthy paragraph in part 6 describes the purpose and nature of catechisms as well as procedures for compiling them and having them approved:

> The greatest importance must be attached to catechisms published by ecclesiastical authority. Their purpose is to provide, under a form that is condensed and practical, the witness of revelation and of Christian tradition as well as the chief principles which ought to be useful for catechetical

activity, that is, for personal education in faith. The witness to tradition should be held in due esteem, and every great care must be taken to avoid presenting as doctrines of the faith special interpretations which are only private opinions or the views of some theological school. The doctrine of the Church must be presented faithfully. . . .

In view of the great difficulties in putting these works together and the great importance of these witnesses, it is most expedient that:

a) there be collaboration by a number of experts in catechetics and in theology;

b) there be consultation with specialists in other religious and human disciplines, and also with other pastoral organizations;

c) individual local ordinaries be consulted and their opinions carefully considered;

d) limited experiments be tried before definitive publication; and

e) these texts be duly reviewed after a certain period of time.

Before promulgation, these catechisms must be submitted to the Apostolic See for review and approval (no. 119).

It is evident from this paragraph that the GCD was not intended to replace catechisms and, in fact, anticipated their publication.

## The Discussion Continues

The third general assembly of the Synod of Bishops, in 1974, had as its topic evangelization—"the proclamation of the Gospel to people of our time." That assembly witnessed a degree of tension between bishops who recognized the challenges presented by cultural differences and bishops who gave priority to uniformity of doctrinal expression as a means of insuring unity of faith. The latter favored a *catechismus typicus* (paradigmatic catechism) as a necessary means to that end, but they were in a minority. (It should be noted that the Polish-language group favored a catechism, and a member of that group was the cardinal archbishop of Cracow, Karol Wojtyla.)

Paul VI's apostolic exhortation *Evangelii nuntiandi,* issued in the wake of the 1974 assembly, reflected the stance of the majority of bishops when it stated,

A means of evangelization that must not be neglected is that of catechetical instruction. The intelligence, especially that of children and young people, needs to learn through systematic religious instruction the fundamental teachings, the living content of the truth which God has wished to convey. . . . Truly the effort for evangelization will profit greatly—at the level of catechetical instruction given at church, in the schools, where this is possible, and in every case in Christian homes—if those giving catechetical instruction have suitable texts, updated with wisdom and compe-

tence, under the authority of the bishops. The methods must be adapted
to the age, culture and aptitude of the persons concerned . . . (no. 44).

The synod on evangelization touched on many aspects of catechesis, but
the fourth general assembly of the Synod of Bishops in 1977 addressed them
directly. The theme, "catechesis in our time, especially for children and youth,"
provided a context for a discussion of every facet of catechesis and related issues. It provided an occasion for overt lobbying on the part of individuals who
linked what they identified as a "crisis in the church" to the direction of catechesis in the post-Vatican II years. When the bishops arrived in Rome, they
became aware that organized cliques, including an American group, had complained to the Pope and the synod fathers that their bishops were not doing
enough to safeguard the integrity of the Christian message.[4]

Although the issue of catechisms was not mentioned in the outline of
themes *(lineamenta)* proposed for discussion at the synod or in the "working
paper" *(instrumentum laboris)* that set the agenda, it surfaced in interventions
made by bishops from the floor. There was little agreement, however, in the
kind of catechism envisioned by its proponents. Some expressed the desire for
a short catechism that could serve as a fundamental text of Christian doctrine
for youngsters; some called for a catechism that would be a compilation of the
teachings of Vatican II; a few spoke of a catechism to guide catechists; and five
proposed a catechism that would be normative for the universal Church. The
differences became more apparent in the discussion groups *(circuli minores)*.
Eight of the eleven groups that took up the issue of the catechism were divided
on the question, and it was evident that the bishops were far from a consensus
with regard to both the contents and the utility of a catechism for the universal Church. (Cardinal Pericle Felici, head of the Commission for the Revision
of the Code of Canon Law, stated that a new catechism was unnecessary because the Church already had a list of normative beliefs in Paul VI's *Credo of
the People of God.)* In the end, the 1977 synod made no recommendation regarding a catechism.

In his closing address to the bishops, the Pope commented on several of
the synod's recommendations. He took comfort in the emphasis that the assembly put on "systematic catechesis" because "this orderly study of the Christian mystery is what distinguishes catechesis itself from all other forms of
presentation of the word of God." He also endorsed the synod's insistence on
the need for "some fundamental formulas which will make it possible to express more easily, in a suitable and accurate way, the truths of the faith and of
Christian moral doctrine." He said that such formulas—among which he cited
important biblical texts and liturgical texts that serve to express common
prayer—"if learned by heart," greatly aid the stable possession of these truths
and make the profession of faith easier.[5]

### *Catechesi Tradendae* on Catechisms

Paul VI was at work on an apostolic exhortation addressing issues raised by the synod when he died, and it was left to his successor to complete it. In the introduction to *Catechesi tradendae* Pope John Paul II notes that he had participated in the 1977 synod and that "catechesis has always been a central care in my ministry as a priest and as a bishop" (nos. 2, 4). *Catechesi tradendae*, the most comprehensive statement on the catechetical ministry in the Church's annals, set the context for the *Catechism of the Catholic Church*.

*Catechesi tradendae* returns to Pope Paul's emphasis on systematic catechesis. Without denigrating the need of specialized catechesis that targets issues of personal, family, social, and ecclesial life, Pope John Paul writes, "I am stressing the need for organic and systematic Christian instruction, because of the tendency in various quarters to minimize its importance" (no. 21). The handing over of the Creed—the *traditio symboli*—along with the Lord's Prayer in the initiation of catechumens deserves a prominent place in catechesis. Pope John Paul declares that Paul VI's *Credo of the People of God* "is a sure point of reference for the content of catechesis" because it brings together the essential elements of the Catholic faith, especially those that present major difficulty or risk being ignored (no. 28). *Catechesi tradendae* returns to a theme that ran through the 1977 synod, namely, that the Christian faith should be presented in its entirety and that catechists on their own initiative cannot decide what is important and unimportant "so as to teach the one and neglect the other" (no. 30).

*Catechesi tradendae* describes various "ways and means of catechesis," including electronic media, special occasions, the homily, and textbooks and other catechetical materials. In this context John Paul II makes reference to catechisms. They must take "their inspiration from the General Catechetical Directory," which, he says, "remains the standard of reference." And then he continues,

> In this regard, I must warmly encourage the episcopal conferences of the whole world to undertake, patiently but resolutely, the considerable work to be accomplished in agreement with the Apostolic See in order to prepare genuine catechisms which will be faithful to the essential content of revelation and up to date in method, and which will be capable of educating the Christian generations of the future to a sturdy faith (no. 50).

None of the formal actions taken by the Synod of Bishops, including the 1977 assembly, indicated that a catechism for the universal Church was on the horizon. In retrospect, the only hint one finds that the idea still had life is a paragraph of *Catechesi tradendae:*

The ministry of catechesis draws ever fresh energy from the councils. The Council of Trent is a noteworthy example of this. It gave catechesis priority in its constitutions and decrees. It lies at the origin of the Roman Catechism, which . . . is a work of the first rank as a summary of the Christian teaching and traditional theology for use by priests. It gave rise to a remarkable organization of catechesis in the Church. It aroused the clergy to their duty of giving catechetical instruction. Thanks to the work of holy theologians such as St. Charles Borromeo, St. Robert Bellarmine and St. Peter Canisius, it involved the publication of catechisms that were real models for that period. May the Second Vatican Council stir up in our time a like enthusiasm and similar activity (no. 13).

In light of subsequent events, the foregoing paragraph can be seen to have outlined the scenario for the preparation of the *Catechism of the Catholic Church.*[6]

## The Year 1983

The discussions at the Synod of Bishops were being carried on against the backdrop of the brouhaha that surrounded the Dutch Catechism and a series of minor controversies throughout the Catholic world. In the United States opposition to catch phrases like "continuing revelation" and "experiential catechesis" cloaked a resistance in some quarters to new approaches to biblical studies, liturgical change, and ecumenical dialogue, and reflected nostalgia for the simple world of the Baltimore Catechism. In Germany, Hubertus Halbfas caused a stir with the publication of *Fundamentalkatechetick* (1968), in which he questioned the manner of presenting doctrine and challenged the basic structures and goals of German Catholic education. In Italy the cardinal archbishop of Florence banned the Isolotto Catechism because he felt that it presented Christ as a social agitator and reduced salvation to liberation from oppression and exploitation.[7] The Church in Argentina was divided over the use of *Hoja de Ruta* 5, a catechetical text that dealt with a variety of social issues of concern to youth. The cardinal archbishop of Buenos Aires objected to its use despite the fact that it had been developed under the aegis of the Salesian Catechetical Center and carried the *imprimatur* of the bishop of Quilmes.[8] These and similar controversies fueled the drive for a new catechism for the universal Church.

Several developments in 1983 signaled the continuing concern of Roman authorities over the state of catechesis in the Church. In April the International Council for Catechesis, known popularly by the Italian acronym COINCAT *(Consiglio Internazionale per la Catechesi),* met in Rome. The council, a consultative body of the Congregation for the Clergy, the congregation that oversees pastoral ministry, including catechesis, was at the time "in large measure a self-governing body."[9] One of the agenda items was a consideration of the second draft of the "Schema of Christian Doctrine." The schema had been drafted in 1980 and sent to the members of the council and other consultors for their observations and suggestions. The second draft, though still incomplete, was based on this consultation. In the form in which Cardinal Oddi, prefect of the Congregation for the Clergy, presented it to COINCAT, the schema was a document of nine-and-a-half pages, divided into eighty propositions. It was intended, he said, as a synthesis of the fundamental truths of faith, in the spirit of Vatican II, that would give direction to catechesis. He explained that it was being prepared in response to the widespread demand from bishops, parents, parish priests, and teachers for a reliable and authoritative resource for the contents of catechetical programs.

After discussing it over three days, the members of the council went on record stating they did not believe the schema in its present form would achieve the desired goal. They reaffirmed the need to present the Christian message faithfully, dynamically, and in its entirety. They feared that the schema, once completed, ran the risk of being published and distributed as a basic catechism and thus undermining the doctrinal integrity the congregation was trying to safeguard. COINCAT recommended instead that doctrines that had been omitted or presented erroneously should be dealt with in the context of the third part of the General Catechetical Directory. COINCAT's reservations notwithstanding, Pope John Paul, in his remarks at a private audience for the members of the council (16 April 1983), took a stand that was in substantial agreement with the views expressed by Oddi.

Meanwhile the intervention of the Congregation of the Doctrine of the Faith in two local disputes, the one in France, the other in the United States, clarified the criteria and further regulated the issuance of catechisms. The bishops of France, exploring a novel approach to catechesis for children, had authorized "a Catholic collection of privileged documents of the faith." The short work of 126 brilliantly illustrated pages incorporated the traditional sources for transmitting the faith, giving prominence to the Bible, the Creed, liturgy, and traditional prayers. It also highlighted Church history through the living witness of the saints and contemporary witnesses to the faith. Notes scattered through the text explained technical terms and the meaning of traditional formulas. The novel approach of *Pierres vivantes (Living Stones)* was widely acclaimed by catechists.

The publication of *Pierres vivantes* raised a number of issues, some regarding content, some regarding procedure. With regard to the first, the Congregation for the Doctrine of the Faith objected to the manner in which the work made use of contemporary biblical scholarship, and called for a more "traditional" approach.[10]

The second set of issues had more to do with procedures and the authority of the episcopal conference vis-à-vis Rome. Although the French hierarchy did not advertise *Pierres vivantes* as a catechism, it came under the scrutiny of the Congregation for the Doctrine of the Faith because it was an official publication of the French hierarchy, and intended for use throughout the country.

The issues of procedures and authority were clarified by a series of questions that Oddi addressed to the Congregation for the Doctrine of the Faith. He inquired about the interpretation of *Ecclesiae pastorum*, a decree regulating the prior censorship of books, as it applies to catechetical works. The congregation issued two responses, both dated 7 July 1983. In summary it declared: a national or regional conference of bishops cannot publish national or regional catechisms or catechetical documents, to be in force on the supradiocesan level, without prior approval of the Holy See; nor can episcopal conferences propose and disseminate catechisms at the national level for "consultation and experimentation"; even if he has already approved a national catechism, a local ordinary can give an *imprimatur* to particular catechisms when these have a safe content and clear presentation; an episcopal committee cannot be given the permanent authority to approve or reject catechisms at the national level or for individual dioceses; in addition to an official catechism, other catechisms which have been duly approved by ecclesiastical authority may be used as "subsidiary means."[11]

About the same time in the United States, Anthony Wilhelm's best-selling *Christ Among Us* was under attack. After several attempts to meet the objections of the Congregation for the Doctrine of the Faith proved unsuccessful, Cardinal Ratzinger declared that even with "substantial corrections" the book "would not be suitable as a catechetical text." The principal objection to Wilhelm's work seems to have been one anticipated by the general directory, namely, that the teachings of the faith are not easily distinguished from the sometimes speculative interpretations of theologians. In 1984 Ratzinger asked Archbishop Gerety of Newark to withdraw the *nihil obstat* and *imprimatur* that he had given to Wilhelm's work.

The controversies over *Pierres vivantes* and *Christ Among Us* were already smoldering when Ratzinger became prefect of the Congregation for the Doctrine of the Faith late in 1982 but, as we have seen in the previous chapter, his interest in catechisms predated this appointment.

In January 1983 Ratzinger gave a well-publicized lecture in France in which he said, "It was an initial and grave error to suppress the catechism and to declare obsolete the whole idea of catechisms." The abandonment of the catechism, he said, has contributed to the fragmentation of the proclamation of the Christian message, a certain arbitrariness in the way faith is explained, and a calling into question of some of its parts. Specifically he expressed concern about the preeminence given to method at the expense of content in religious instruction, and the prominence given to theologians at the expense of the Church's magisterium. The denigration of the magisterium means "that the borders between theology and faith are slowly fading, that church teaching disappears and theological teaching remains the sole form of interpreting the Christian gospel." He held up the Catechism of the Council of Trent, built around the four pillars of catechesis—Creed, sacraments, Commandments, and the Lord's Prayer—as the model catechism.[12]

## The Synod of 1985

It is not surprising, given the ongoing controversies over catechetical texts, that the extraordinary assembly of the Synod of Bishops in 1985 once more took up the issue of catechisms. In his summary of the responses to the questionnaire sent out by the general secretariat in preparation for the 1985 synod, Cardinal Danneels, *relator* of the synod, noted that in some countries there was evidence of a kind of selective Christianity which suggested a lack of integrity and organic structure in catechesis. Some episcopal conferences suggested a catechism that would meet the needs of the post-Vatican II Church in the way that the Roman Catechism addressed the needs of the Church after the Council of Trent.

In their interventions at the assembly itself, about half the bishops had something to say about catechesis—often noting progress and advances in cultural adaptation—but only a few mentioned a catechism. Cardinal Bernard Law, archbishop of Boston, was the first to advocate a universal catechism along with a plan to bring it into being: "I propose a Commission of Cardinals to prepare a draft of a Conciliar Catechism to be promulgated by the Holy Father after consulting the bishops of the world. In a shrinking world—a global village—*national* catechisms will not fill the current need for clear articulation of the Church's faith."

The following day Bishop Ruhuna of Burundi requested "a model catechism, inspired by Vatican II." The Latin patriarch of Jerusalem, Giacomo Beltritti, as he had in previous meetings of the synod, advocated a single catechism for children to be used in the entire Church, adaptable to the need of various countries.

When the synod discussion shifted to small study groups, divided according to languages, the proposal for a catechism began to crystallize. The Italian-language group recommended the publication of three works to promote the knowledge of Vatican II: a "catechism of the faith" directed toward believers; a "book of Christian faith," for non-believers; and a "book of moral doctrine" for everyone. The English-language study group A urged "a compendium of Catholic teaching from which each country could draw its own teaching documents." Similarly the French study group B recommended "a catechism or compendium" containing the teachings of Vatican II. It added that the catechism should take care to present Jesus Christ as the object and center of catechesis and that the gospel should be presented as a way of life and not as an ideology.

The Spanish-language group B wanted the Holy See, after consulting with the conferences of bishops, to undertake the preparation of a reference work of Catholic teaching, a compendium of synthetic formulations of faith and morals. They made it clear that they were asking not for a detailed catechism but for a synthesis of all Church teaching regarding faith and morals presented with the new pastoral insights of Vatican II. The Latin study group recommended a universal catechism according to Vatican II similar to the one published after the Council of Trent. In what could be read as a putdown for the General Catechetical Directory, the Latin group urged that Pope Paul VI's profession of faith be taken into account because, they said, it must be regarded as the principal directive in producing new catechism texts.

The reports of the study groups are especially important for understanding the basis and intent of the recommendation that appeared in the final report of the extraordinary synod: there should be "a catechism or compendium of all Catholic doctrine regarding both faith and morals . . . a point of reference for the catechisms or compendiums that are prepared in the various regions. The presentation of doctrine must be biblical and liturgical. It must be sound doctrine suited to the present life of Christians (II, B.4)."[13]

The wording of the resolution as it was forwarded to Pope John Paul II steered a careful course between the Scylla of uniformity and the Charybdis of cultural diversity. In the context of both the interventions of individual bishops and the discussions in the various language groups, it is evident that the "catechism or compendium" requested by the synod of 1985 was to be quite different from the small catechism proposed at Vatican I and rejected by Vatican II in favor of the General Catechetical Directory. The recommendation of the extraordinary synod envisaged a work for mature readers, primarily catechists, teachers, and other pastoral leaders charged with the instruction of the faithful.

The recommendation seemed simple and straightforward but, as will be explained in the next chapter, decisions regarding the form and function of the proposed catechism proved to be more complex than the planners anticipated. It took seven calendar years and uncounted working-hours on the part of commissions, writers, translators, bishops, and others involved in a broadly based consultation process before the final text of the *Catechism of the Catholic Church* saw the light of day in 1992.

NOTES

1. The standard work on meetings of the synod is G. Caprile, *Il Synodo dei vescovi*, 8 vols. (Rome: La Civiltà cattolica, 1966–86). Also see Simon, *Un Catéchisme universel*, 284–408.

2. General Catechetical Directory (Washington: United States Catholic Conference, 1971) 1–2. A photostat copy of the USCC translation is reprinted in Berard L. Marthaler, *Catechetics in Context* (Huntington, Ind.: Our Sunday Visitor, 1972).

3. The outline of the "more outstanding elements" was assimilated almost immediately in the U.S. document *Basic Teachings of Catholic Religious Education*, then in progress of being written. See Charles C. McDonald, "The Background and Development of 'The Basic Teachings' Document," *The Living Light* 10:2 (Summer 1973) 264–77.

4. Simon, *Un Catéchisme universel*, 326.

5. An English translation of Pope Paul VI's closing address can be found in *The Living Light* 15:1(Spring 1978) 98–101. See Simon, *Un Catéchisme universel*, 339.

6. This paragraph was cited in the "provisional text," the draft of the catechism sent to the bishops of the Catholic world for their input and suggestions in the fall of 1989. See chapter 14.

7. For a summary of these and other significant developments in catechetics from 1965 to 1985, see the report of a Joint Committee of the National Conference of Diocesan Directors of Religious Education, Catholic Theological Society of America, College Theology Society, and Canon Law Society of America under the title "The Approval of Catechisms and Catechetical Materials," in *The Catholic Theological Society of America: Proceedings of the Forty-First Annual Convention*, Chicago, 11–14 June 1986, pp. 199–204.

8. Reported by Dafne de Plou in *Latinamerica Press*, 11 February 1988, p. 6.

9. See Wilfrid H. Paradis, "Report on the Fifth Meeting of the International Catechetical Council, Rome, April 11–17, 1983," *The Living Light* 20:2 (1984) 150–70.

10. In the first edition, *Pierres vivantes* began the account of salvation history, not as "traditional" works had done with Genesis and the story of creation, but with Exodus and the Israelites coming to see themselves as God's people. Similarly it began its account of salvation in the New Testament, not with the infancy narratives and the gospel accounts of Jesus' ministry, but with the descent of the Holy Spirit at Pentecost as described in the Acts of the Apostles.

11. See *CTSA Proceedings*, 204.

12. For an English translation of Cardinal Ratzinger's address, see "Sources and Transmission of the Faith," *Communio* 10:1 (Spring 1983) 17–34.

13. *The Extraordinary Synod—1985* (Boston: St. Paul Editions, n.d.) 51–52.

FOURTEEN

# The *Catechism of the Catholic Church:*
# The Old and the New

Pope John Paul II describes the *Catechism of the Catholic Church* (CCC), published in November 1992, as containing "both the new and the old because the faith is always the same yet the source of ever new light." The contents of the catechism, he writes, "are often presented in a 'new' way in order to respond to the questions of our age." The "old" is represented by the "traditional order" that arranges the material according to the fourfold division of Creed, sacraments, Commandments, and prayer found in the Catechism of the Council of Trent. The point of this chapter is not to explicate the text of the catechism, but to identify its chief purpose and audience, and to describe the order and arrangement of the material. Even a cursory glance at its table of contents sustains the Pope's assertion that the *Catechism of the Catholic Church* follows in the tradition of the catechism approved by Pius V. A closer reading of the work, however, demonstrates that the selection and ordering of the material are more innovative than at first appears.

By reason of size alone the *Catechism of the Catholic Church* is unique. It is half-again as large as the Heidelberg Catechism, and a third larger than the catechism of Trent. In the original French edition the text (without indices) runs to 581 pages; the English translation printed in the United States, 688 pages; and the one published for use in the United Kingdom and Ireland, 610 pages. In accord with the customary practice of Church documents, the 2865 paragraphs are numbered for ease of citation. (The numbers in parentheses in this chapter refer to specific paragraphs.) Another innovation is the reliance on different typefaces to distinguish the character and importance of the paragraphs. The catechism itself explains that the use of small print in some passages indicates "observations of an historical or apologetic nature, or supplementary doctrinal explanations" (20). Quotations from patristic, liturgical, magisterial, and hagiographical sources, "intended to enrich the doctrinal presentations," are also in small print and indented (21). This use of lengthy quotations is another original feature of the CCC. At the end of "each thematic unit" there is a series of short texts under the heading "In Brief" that summarize the main points of the foregoing section (22); they are either in italics (as in the French and English editions) or indented (as in the U.S. edition).

The catechism puts a new spin on an old wheel in the importance it gives to pictures. The use of the visual arts—paintings and sculpture—in catechesis can be traced to the catacombs, the source of three pictures in the CCC. Medieval churches had their murals and stained glass windows; Byzantine churches, their mosaics; and monasteries, their illuminated manuscripts, the source of a fourth picture in the CCC. Luther's catechism used woodcuts to illustrate the text, a practice copied by Peter Canisius and many others to the present time. As if to emphasize the importance of the visual arts in catechesis, the CCC includes a colophon on the title page and four color plates. Publishers were directed to include the pictures, even at considerable expense, because they are integral to the text of the catechism.[1] The catechism itself explains how the pictures express characteristic aspects of the catechism as a whole and each of the four parts.

## The Development of the Text

The synod of bishops that proposed "a catechism or compendium of all Catholic doctrine regarding both faith and morals" adjourned in December 1985, and the following July, Pope John Paul appointed a commission to oversee the work. It was made up of twelve cardinals and bishops, including representatives of "the most important curial offices and all the major cultural areas of Catholic activity." Cardinal Ratzinger, prefect of the Congregation for the Doctrine of the Faith, chaired the commission which numbered among its members Cardinal Bernard Law of Boston who had introduced the proposal at the synod.* As the CCC began to take shape, Ratzinger and others closely connected with the work gave progress reports in various forums.[2] The commission of cardinals published an "informative dossier" describing the principles that guided the work of the writers and editors.[3] Taken as a whole, these reports

---

* In addition to Cardinals Ratzinger and Law, the members of the Commission were Cardinal Prefects Baum (Congregation for Catholic Education); Lourdusamy (Congregation for the Oriental Churches); Tomko (Congregation for the Evangelization of Peoples); Innocenti (Congregation for the Clergy); and Bishops Stroba (Archbishop of Poznam, Poland); Edelby (Greek Melkite Archbishop of Aleppo, Syria); D'Sousa (Archbishop of Calcutta, India); De Sousa (Coadjutor Archbishop of Cotonou, Benin); Schotte (titular Archbishop of Silli and General Secretary of the Synod); Benítez Avalos (of Villarica, Paraguay). The list was published in the *L'Osservatore Romano*, June 6, 1986, and in the *Dossier Informativo* which indicated that Bishop Noujem substituted for Archbishop Edelby.

and the dossier present a rather detailed account of the procedures followed by the commission, the issues faced by the writers and editors, and the rationale for the contents of the catechism.

From the time the commission set down to work, it considered and approved ten schemas and drafts in various stages of development on the way to the finished catechism:

1. A rough outline *(Adumbratio schematis)*, Feb. 1987
2. A preliminary prospectus, May 1987
3. A first draft *(Specimen ou Avant-projet)*, May 1988
4. Revised draft. Provisional Text *(Projet révisé. Texte provisoire)*, Nov. 1989
5. An emended text, March 1991
6. A "pre-definitive" text, May 1991
7. A corrected version of the "pre-definitive" text, Aug. 1991
8. Definitive text, Dec. 1991
9. Completed project, Feb. 1992
10. *Catechismus Ecclesiae Catholicae*, April 1992

It was at the meeting of May 1988, when the commission considered the first draft, that the members decided to add an epilogue on the Lord's Prayer. In February 1989 John Paul II received the commission and the editorial committee in an audience. He reaffirmed the importance of their work and proposed the idea of the "in brief" summaries. He suggested that the catechism include "some basic formulas drawn from Scripture, tradition and the church's magisterium that, easily memorized, summarize in a simple and concise form the truly important themes, properly respecting the order and hierarchy of Catholic doctrine."

According to the original timetable, the commission planned to have finished its work by the 1990 assembly of the Synod of Bishops, but it was the end of 1989 before the text was far enough along to submit it to the bishops of the world for their suggestions, amendments, and opinions. The response of the bishops was overwhelming; they sent in twenty-four thousand suggestions *(modi)* on ways to improve the text. As a result parts 3 and 4 were expanded, or more accurately, part 3 was rewritten and part 4 was added. It took a considerable amount of time to examine all the *modi* and to decide which to include and in what form. After that it was largely a matter of polishing the text and preparing it for publication.

## The Catechism Genre

When the members of the commission met for the first time, in November 1986, they faced a series of decisions that would define the character and scope of their work. Guided by little more than the mandate of the 1985 synod, the commission had to settle on (1) what the synod intended when it proposed "a catechism or compendium," (2) who it was intended for, (3) what authority it would have, (4) who would write it, and (5) in what language it would be written. The issues were closely related, and the way one was settled had ramifications for another.

The first question concerned the genre itself: What is the proper form and the function of a catechism? The synod and the Pope had called for a "catechism or compendium of all Catholic doctrine." Is a catechism the same as a compendium? If not, how do they differ? The members of the commission recognized that the ordinary faithful, and even some specialists in catechetics, associate a catechism with questions and answers, but they were also aware of the tradition of "large catechisms" *(catechismi majores)*, like that of Trent and Luther's German catechism. The commission recognized the limitations of small catechisms *(catechismi minores)* designed for use in parish and school catechesis. No single work of this latter kind could respond to the greatly different cultures and circumstances throughout the Catholic world. Furthermore, the question-answer approach, generally found in small catechisms, whatever its pedagogical value, is not conducive to "proclamation."

From the start the commission favored a *catechismus major,* but it was necessary to explain how it would differ from a compendium. To the commission, a "compendium" suggested "a whole collection of volumes intended for the shelves of the learned and not for the ordinary reader."[4] A catechism, on the other hand, is not a scholarly work but an instrument of evangelization. Even the word *catechism (kata,* again + *echein,* to resound), implies a proclamation of the Christian message that echoes over the centuries to people of today.

Although the *Catechism of the Council of Trent* was held up as the model, the early schemas for the projected catechism called for only three parts: the Creed, the sacraments, and the Commandments. (One recalls that the Spanish catechism *Esta es nuestra fe,* and the Belgian *Livre de le foi,* both had three parts.) After much discussion the commission resisted proposals that would have systematized the contents of the catechism around a single central concept. At one point, for example, they had thought of making the kingdom of God the unifying principle, but in the end they acknowledged that "the best way to organize the content of catechesis will emerge from particular concrete circumstances and cannot be imposed on the whole Church through the common catechism."[5] They agreed that the catechism should focus on the essential elements that are conditions, recognized already in the early Church, for admission to baptism and the communal life of Christians. In the context of the catechumenate, ancient catechesis focused on conversion of life; the *traditio et redditio symboli*—the "handing over" to those preparing for baptism the Creed and the Lord's Prayer—and the candidates in turn making them their own and professing them publicly before the community; and the post-baptismal mystagogy which deepened their participation in the sacramental life of the Church and their understanding of Christian moral teaching.

The ancient praxis confirmed the advantages of the fourfold division of the Trent catechism—the confession of faith, sacraments, Commandments, and prayer—as the structure of the new catechism. In later drafts these elements, taken together, were seen to form an organic whole and have an inner unity (18). Yet while emphasizing the cohesion and unity of the parts, the commission resisted editorial conceits that would make it look as if the catechism were imposing a doctrinal "system." Furthermore, they feared giving the document an appearance of "ecclesiocentrism" that would make Church teaching seem a kind of ideological construct different from reality. The catechism presents *truth,* not simply *truth claims,* and confesses the faith as reality and not merely as the content of Christian awareness.[6]

As work went forward and in the course of the consultation with the bishops of the world, the focus and functions of the catechism were sharpened. The informative dossier published by the commission speaks of the catechism "as an instrument to convey the essential and fundamental content of Catholic faith and moral teaching in a complete and summary way—*non omnia sed totum.*" It goes on to say that the catechism "is characterized by its concerns for essentials, its conciseness, sobriety, incisiveness and clarity." In one of the many interviews that Bishop Christoph Schönborn, O.P., the secretary of the drafting committee and a principal editor of the catechism, has given since its publication, he explained:

> The literary genre of the catechism is an organic, complete and synthetic exposition of the Christian faith. This Christian faith contains parts that are essential and parts, let us say, that are secondary. There is a center and a periphery. The dogmatic value of the different elements that constitute a catechism depends on the proximity of such or such as an affirmation to the center of our faith. This center is the affirmation of the mystery of the Most Holy Trinity, the mystery of Christ, of the Holy Spirit and of the Church.[7]

Questions of methodology and style became very concrete when it came to deciding on how to begin the book. What should be the starting point? As Ratzinger put it, "Should we follow a more 'inductive' method, starting from man in the modern world and finishing with God, Christ, and the Church, which would involve structuring the text in a more 'argumentative' manner allowing for a constant unspoken dialogue with today's issues—or should we start from the faith itself and argue from within its own logic, i.e. testifying rather than reasoning?"[8] The members of the commission opted for the latter approach. Circumstances of the times would inevitably shape aspects of the catechism, but the commission concluded that there is no such thing as a "uniform world situation." After going back and forth several times, the members recognized that it is vital to maintain dialogue with today's world and social realities, but they left it to the local Churches to respond to specific issues. The task of adapting catechesis to the sociocultural and ecclesial circumstances of particular countries can be best handled by national catechisms. The catechism itself says that the "adaptation of doctrinal presentations and catechetical methods required by the differences of culture, age, spiritual maturity, and social and ecclesial condition" are "the responsibility of particular catechisms and, even more, of those who instruct the faithful." It calls such adaptations "indispensable" (24).

### The Authority of the Catechism

The commission sought to create an instrument that could be a rallying point for Catholic unity without imposing unacceptable uniformity or seeming to endorse the opinions of one theological school or interest group. Their aim in outlining the fundamentals of Church teaching which unite Catholics was to establish the parameters of pluriformity in practice and diversity of expression. And at the same time, the members of the commission struggled to avoid projecting the notion they were compiling a "tool for the censorship of theological research."

Cardinal Law's initial proposal at the 1985 synod called for a "conciliar catechism," but the dossier explicitly states that the CCC "cannot be called the 'Catechism of the Second Vatican Council', since it was not mandated by the Council." Nonetheless it is "dedicated to the full and faithful expression and implementation of the teaching" of Vatican II, and draws on the council's documents much more extensively than the Catechism of the Council of Trent drew on the council that mandated it. The "Index of Citations" at the end of the CCC indicates the heavy reliance of part 1 on *Dei Verbum,* the Constitution on Revelation, and even more on *Lumen gentium,* the Constitution on the Church. Part 2 draws deeply on the Constitution on the Liturgy, *Sacrosanctum concilium;* and part 3 makes frequent reference to *Gaudium et spes,* the Constitution on the Church in the Modern World.

Pope John Paul set the agenda when he charged the commission to produce a catechism that would not be a substitute for diocesan or national catechisms, but would serve "a point of reference" for them. "It is not meant to be therefore, an instrument of flat 'uniformity,' but an important aid to guarantee the 'unity in the faith' that is an essential dimension of that unity of the church . . ." And just as diocesan and national catechisms are to find in the new catechism "a point of reference," the Pope said that the projected catechism, "in its turn, will have to have as a constant point of reference the teachings of the Second Vatican Council."[9] From the outset the commission made a conscious effort to link catechesis to evangelization, emphasizing throughout the central nucleus of the Christian proclamation, namely, God's plan of salvation realized in Christ. The authors of the catechism were sensitive to ecumenical concerns, and sought to reflect the open and constructive dialogue with non-Christian religions found in *Nostra aetate,* Vatican II's Declaration of the Church's Relationship to Non-Christian Religions. The catechism is especially keen on reminding the faithful that Christianity, beginning with its founder, is deeply rooted in the Jewish tradition.

The magisterial authority of the catechism is implied in the apostolic constitution *Fidei depositum* with which Pope John Paul introduced the text to the world. *Fidei depositum* declares the CCC "to be a sure norm for teaching the faith." It will foster ecclesial communion and "support ecumenical efforts . . . showing the content and wondrous harmony of the catholic faith." In the spirit of Vatican II, the CCC offers no new doctrinal definitions, but seeks to present an authoritative and comprehensive statement of what the Church believes and teaches. Ratzinger comments on *Fidei depositum,* saying, "The individual doctrines that the catechism affirms have no other authority than that which they already possess. What is important is the catechism in its totality: it reflects the Church's teaching; anyone who rejects it overall separates himself unequivocally from the faith and teaching of the Church."[10]

## The Audience

At a time when parish priests were the principal catechists, the Council of Trent had designated its catechism *ad parochos*— "for the use of pastors." But to whom should a post-Vatican II catechism be addressed? The commission, recognizing that today many more people share in the catechetical ministry, opted to prepare the new catechism for the use of bishops who, by reason of their office, have the responsibility of overseeing the whole of catechesis. The catechism is thus designed to serve as a reference tool in the preparation of programs and catechetical publications in the local Churches. By directing the catechism primarily to bishops, their collaborators, and publisher-editors of catechetical materials, the commission wanted it to be accessible to everyone in the Church (11). The laity, imbued with the *sensus fidelium,* are not and have never been merely passive recipients of doctrine. Quoting *Lumen gentium,* the catechism declares that Christ fulfills the prophetic office in today's world, "not only by the hierarchy," but also by the laity. Further "lay people who are capable and trained may also collaborate in catechetical formation, in teaching the sacred sciences, and in use of the communications media" (904, 906). It was the intention of the commission to create a resource that would benefit all the faithful on their way to maturity of faith.

### The Writers and the Language

Once they determined the guiding principles and parameters of the work, the commission had to face the question of who would do the actual writing of the text. The decision to give the task to seven diocesan bishops rather than specialists was dictated by a desire, on the one hand, to emphasize the pastoral character of catechesis, and on the other hand, to witness to the catechism's collegial and magisterial character. Ratzinger speaks of the catechism as a papal document but, he says,

> the new catechism offers an excellent example of the reciprocal interaction between papal sovereignty and collegiality. . . . The pope is not talking over the heads of the bishops, but invites his brothers in the episcopate to sound out the symphony of faith together. He stamps the result with his authority, which then guarantees the juridical value of the book. This authority is not something imposed from the outside, but brings the common witness to the forefront.[11]

Each of the seven bishops was assigned a particular section. Bishop José Estepa Llaurens, military ordinary for Spain, and Bishop Alessandro Maggiolini of Carpi, Italy, were given the task of drafting the first part dealing with the confession of faith. The section dealing with the sacraments was entrusted to Bishop Jorge Medina Estevez, apostolic administrator of Raneagua, Chile, and Archbishop Estanislao Esteban Karliç of Parana, Argentina; and the section on morals to Bishop Jean Honoré of Tours, France, and Bishop David Konstant of Leeds, England. The seventh member of the group, Archbishop William Levada of Portland, Oregon, was asked to compile a glossary of terms.

The first three sections had been planned from the beginning, but when members of the commission were reminded of the central place the Lord's Prayer had in traditional catechesis, they looked for a writer who could draw on the rich heritage of the Eastern as well as the Western Fathers. Thus it came to be that the "epilogue" explaining the Lord's Prayer that appeared in the provisional text was composed in Beirut by Jean Corbon, a priest of the Maronite rite and a member of the International Theological Commission.[12]

Later the commission engaged polyglot Bishop Schönborn to serve as editorial assistant. It was his task to coordinate the work of the writers and the commission, and serve as editor of the text. A professor at the University of Fribourg, Switzerland, Schönborn specialized in patrology. In the course of the work, he was appointed as auxiliary to the archbishop of Vienna.

The language of the catechism presented unexpected problems. The first draft, completed in 1987, used Latin. When it was sent to forty consultants in different parts of the world, it became apparent that not all had equal facility in Latin, and, consequently, language was often a source of misunderstanding. Thus it was agreed that French would be the working language in subsequent drafts because all the writers were to a greater or lesser degree able to express themselves in it. The plan is to publish a definitive text—the *editio typica*—in Latin only after the French text and approved translations in the chief national languages have been in circulation for some time. The *editio typica* will take account of observations "made in the first phase of the reception of the catechism." Subsequently translations in the national languages will be revised on the basis of the definitive text.[13]


## Old Facade, New Interior

The image of structuring the catechism on the "four pillars" of catechesis (13) conjures up a picture of a Roman *palazzo* built in the Renaissance and modernized after World War II. The facade and foundations remain unchanged, but the interior has been remodelled. So it is with the *Catechism of the Catholic Church:* old and new at the same time.

The blueprint for part 1, the longest part of the catechism, is the baptismal Creed. The CCC, in the tradition of medieval catechesis, follows the text of the Apostles' Creed, "a faithful summary of the apostles' faith" (194), "which constitutes, as it were, 'the oldest Roman catechism.'" On the other hand, it admits to making "constant references to the Nicene Creed which is often more explicit and more detailed" (196). Sensitive to the cause of ecumenism and concerned for the traditions of the Eastern Churches, the CCC acknowledges that the Nicene Creed is commonly accepted by "all the great churches of both East and West" (195).

The CCC, according to the custom dating back to Ambrose, identifies twelve articles in the Creed, "symbolizing the fullness of the apostolic faith by the number of the apostles" (191). It does not, however, make mention of the other medieval tradition, found in such disparate works as *The Lay Folks' Catechism* and the catechism published by Juan Zumárraga in Mexico, which identified fourteen articles. Luther's Small Catechism emphasized the Trinitarian structure of the Creed. The Catechism of the Council of Trent also acknowledged the threefold division of the Creed, but it organized the material under the headings of twelve articles. The CCC, by contrast, subordinates the twelves articles to the ternary structure of the baptismal profession of faith. Making a deliberate effort to emphasize the work of the persons of the Holy Trinity in the mystery of creation, redemption, and sanctification (190, 426, and *passim*), it organizes its presentation of doctrine in three chapters. This is the core of Christian faith, and all other doctrines are a development of this nucleus. Thus "even by its structure," writes Ratzinger, "the catechism shows the hierarchy of truth of which the Second Vatican Council spoke."[14]

It is in the third chapter, "I Believe in the Holy Spirit," that one sees most clearly the influence of the Second Vatican Council. There is no precedent in other catechisms for the rich pneumatology and ecclesiology presented here. Unlike Calvin's catechism (and the General Catechetical Directory), which considered the Church as a fourth part of the Creed, the CCC states that the article concerning the Church "depends entirely on the article about the Holy Spirit," and that "the church is, in a phrase used by the fathers, the place 'where the Spirit flourishes'" (749). It introduces the Church's call to be missionary by proclaiming the gospel always and everywhere. At the same time it outlines an open and constructive vision of non-Christian religions along the lines of *Nostra aetate.*

The work of the Trinity, celebrated in the paschal mystery, provides the foundation of part 2 (1076–1134). Inspired by Vatican II's Constitution on the Liturgy and drawing much of its material from the revised sacramental rites, part 2 of the catechism is similarly both old and new: old in the sense that it revives ancient symbols and rites and retrieves the rich sacramental theology of the early Church Fathers, new in the  sense of the categories it uses to explain the liturgy. The CCC asks: who celebrates? how is the liturgy celebrated? when and where is it celebrated? The catechism describes "becoming a Christian" as a journey whose principal stages are outlined in the *Rite of Christian Initiation of Adults* (1229–33).

The CCC, following *Lumen gentium,* is traditional in presenting the Eucharist as "the source and summit of the Christian life," so that "the other sacraments, and indeed all ecclesiastical ministries and works of the apostolate," are bound up with it and oriented toward it (1324). The catechism echoes the disputes of the Reformation (quoting Vatican II's Decree on Ecumenism) in stating that Churches "separated from the Catholic Church, 'have not preserved the proper reality of the eucharistic mystery in its fullness, especially because of the absence of the sacrament of Holy Orders'" (1399). On the other hand, it reflects issues raised in ecumenical dialogue. Although intercommunion is not possible for the Catholic Church (1400), "Christians not in full communion with the Catholic Church, who ask for them of their own free will," may under certain circumstances receive the sacraments from Catholic ministers (1401). The catechism explicitly recognizes that "through ecumenical dialogue Christian communities in many regions have been able to put into effect a *common pastoral practice for mixed marriages*" (1636).

Another novel feature of the CCC is the explanations it gives of sacramental practice and ritual in the Eastern traditions. This is most evident in the presentation of confirmation-*chrismation* (1289–92). "A certain communion *in sacris*" with Eastern Churches that are not in full communion with the Catholic Church suggests that Eucharistic intercommunion, "given suitable circumstances and the approval of Church authority, is not merely possible but is encouraged" (1399).

Implied in the recognition of the Eastern tradition are broader principles that had fallen out of the catechetical tradition after the Chinese rites controversy in the seventeenth century. "The mystery of Christ," declares the CCC, "is so unfathomably rich that it cannot be exhausted by its expression in any single liturgical tradition" (1201), and the celebration of the liturgy "should correspond to the genius and culture of the different peoples" (1204).

Part 3 of the catechism was thoroughly reorganized and enlarged in the wake of the negative reaction to the provisional text in 1989–90. The CCC continues the old catechetical tradition that dates back to Augustine of presenting the Decalogue in the framework of the twofold commandment of love of God and love of neighbor (2055). In this tradition the one table of laws that Moses brought down from Mount Sinai reveals the first three commandments that concern love of God; the other table contains the seven that describe love of neighbor (2067).[15] The catechism situates the Ten Commandments in the context of the Exodus, "God's great liberating event at the center of the Old Covenant," and finds in them "the conditions of a life freed from the slavery of sin" (2057).

Noticeably new in the CCC is an emphasis on social responsibility. Catechisms have always labeled behaviors inimical to personal dignity or harmful of other individuals as sinful and outlined general principles of distributive justice. No previous catechism, however, had anything like the chapter in the CCC, "The Human Community" (1877–1948), that describes "the communal character of the human vocation" and the obligation to participate in the political life of society. The new catechism, inspired by the Pastoral Constitution on the Church in the Modern World of Vatican II and the social encyclicals of recent popes, especially John Paul II, sketches a comprehensive vision of the common good that identifies "three essential elements": respect for the inalienable rights of the human person, including freedom of conscience and religious freedom; social well-being and requisites that are necessary for a truly human life, that is, "food, clothing, health, work, education and culture, suitable information, [and] the right to establish a family"; and finally, "peace, that is, the stability and security of a just order" (1905–09). A passage from Pope John Paul's encyclical *Centesimus annus* explains how modern industrial society, "with its new structures for the production of consumer goods, its new concept of society, the state and authority, and its new forms of labor and ownership," has caused the Church to address economic and social matters "with the assistance of the Holy Spirit in the light of the whole of what has been revealed by Jesus Christ" (2421–22).

Part 3 states that "the beatitudes are at the heart of Jesus' preaching" (1716), and sketches some of their main points. It outlines a catechesis of the "human virtues" that helps one "grasp the beauty and attraction of right dispositions towards goodness" and the "Christian virtues" of faith, hope, and charity, but other traditional lists prominent in the catechetical tradition receive only passing mention: the seven capital ("deadly") sins and sins that cry to heaven (1866–67); the seven corporal and seven spiritual works of mercy (2447); the seven gifts of the Holy Spirit (1831). The precepts of the Church, five in number, are given a new rationale in that they are said to be "set in the context of a moral life bound to and nourished by liturgical life" (2041).

The basic plan of the fourth part of the CCC, "Christian Prayer," is much like that of the Catechism of the Council of Trent. In the first section it discusses the importance of prayer, drawing on the example of such biblical figures as Moses, David, and Elijah, but mostly on the examples of Mary and Jesus. It explains types of prayer, various ways of praying, and obstacles to prayer. Like the Tridentine catechism, the CCC devotes a second section to a reflection on the Lord's Prayer in general and to each of its seven petitions.

The basic plan of part 4 is hardly new, but it draws on sources that (at least for the Western Church) are fresh and links prayer to life in the contemporary world. Pope John Paul's directive that the presentation of doctrine should be "biblical" is evident throughout part 4, and especially in the prominence it assigns to the psalms (2585ff.) and to Mary. It points up Mary's "unique cooperation with the working of the Holy Spirit" in her own prayer (2675), her Fiat and Magnificat (2617ff.), and in the Church's prayer to the Mother of God, "centering it on the person of Christ manifested in his mysteries" (2675). Prayer to Mary "has found a privileged expression in the *Ave Maria*," and the CCC (unlike the catechism of Trent) provides a reflection on the text (2676ff). Mention has already been made of the fact that Maronite theologian Jean Corbon authored the original draft of part 4, a fact that is evident in the frequent references to Eastern traditions, especially with regard to Marian prayer forms.

### The Catechism in Summary

The CCC quotes Tertullian saying the Lord's Prayer "is truly the summary of the whole gospel" (2761). By the same token, one might say that the reflection on the Lord's Prayer in part 4 summarizes the main themes of the catechism. The experience of the Trinity in Christian life is proof that the Father "sent the Spirit of his Son into our hearts, crying, *'Abba!'* Father" (2766, 2789). The Lord's Prayer is an integral part of all liturgical traditions and its "ecclesial character" is especially evident in the sacraments of Christian initiation (2768). The first of the three petitions center on God, "*thy* name, *thy* kingdom, *thy* will" (2804), and by them "we are strengthened in faith, filled with hope, and set aflame by charity" (2806). The reflection on the petitions of the Lord's Prayer, notably "thy kingdom come," reveals Christianity's eschatological character, the "end-time," that is, "the time of salvation that began with the outpouring of the Holy Spirit and will be fulfilled with the Lord's return" (2771).

The other four petitions concern us in our present world, but not merely as individuals. They underscore the solidarity of the human family: God is *our* Father, we pray "give *us* . . . forgive *us* . . . lead *us* not . . . deliver *us* . . ." (2805). Although "thy kingdom come" refers primarily to the reign of God that will come with Christ's return (2818), the petition "give us this day our daily bread," a reminder of "the drama of hunger in the world," according to the catechism, "cannot be isolated from the parables of the poor man Lazarus and of the Last Judgment" (2831). The newness of the kingdom, already at hand, "must be shown by the establishment of justice in personal and social, economic and international relations, without ever forgetting that there are no just social structures without people who want to be just" (2832; see 2820).

The concluding doxology, "For the kingdom, the power and the glory are yours, now and forever," a reprise of the opening petitions, affronts the pretentious claim of Satan to bestow kingship, power, and glory. To which we add, "Amen," an affirmation of our faith in the prayer and the mystery of salvation that Christ has revealed to us.

The CCC embodies Pope John Paul's vision of what a catechism should be and do. In *Fidei depositum,* he writes:

> A catechism should faithfully and systematically present the teaching of Sacred Scripture, the living Tradition in the Church and the authentic Magisterium, as well as the spiritual heritage of the Fathers, Doctors, and saints of the Church, to allow for a better knowledge of the Christian mystery and for enlivening the faith of the People of God. It should take into account the doctrinal statements which down the centuries the Holy Spirit has intimated to his Church. It should also help illumine with the light of faith the new situations and problems which had not yet emerged in the past.

The CCC, built on the traditional four pillars of catechesis—Creed, sacraments, Commandments and the Lord's Prayer—presents them "often in a 'new' way in order to respond to the questions of our age." And precisely because each generation (not to mention individual) must respond anew to the message of the gospel, the CCC will not be the last in the long tradition of catechisms described in these chapters. Nor is it intended, in the words of Pope John Paul, to replace duly approved catechisms, but it is to serve as "a sure and authentic reference text for teaching catholic doctrine and particularly for preparing local catechisms." (For the complete text of *Fidei depositum,* see Appendix C.)

NOTES

1. *The* [London] *Tablet,* 28 May 1994, p. 672. The English edition prepared by the publishing house Geoffrey Chapman for the U.K. and elsewhere adds four color plates that illustrate both the catholicity and the contemporaneity of the faith: Jacob Epstein's *Madonna and Child* from the former Heythrop College in London; an aboriginal carving by George Mung Mung of Australia showing Mary carrying the infant Jesus in her womb; Evie Hone's stained-glass window of the Beatitudes from Manresa House, Dublin; and an African crucifix by James Chikasa of Malawi.

2. The progress reports that Cardinal Ratzinger gave to the successive assemblies of the Synod of Bishops are especially informative. See *Origins* 17:21 (5 Nov. 1987) 380–82; 20:22 (8 Nov. 1990) 356–59. See also Joseph Ratzinger, "The *Catechism of the Catholic Church,* and the Optimism of the Redeemed," *Communio* 20:3 (Fall 1993) 469–84.

Members of the editorial committee also reported on the work in various forums, e.g., William Levada, "Catechism of the Universal Church: An Overview," *Origins* 19:40 (8 March 1990) 645, 647–51; Alessandro Maggiolini, "Il *Catechismo o compendio* della fede e della morale per la Chiesa universale," *Communio* 13 (1990) 92–100; Jean Honoré, "Le Catéchisme de l'Église Catholique," *Nouvelle revue théologique* 115 (1993) 3–18; Christoph Schönborn, "Major Themes and Underlying Principles of the *Catechism of the Catholic Church (CCC),*" *The Living Light* 30:1 (Fall 1993) 55–64; William Levada, "The New Catechism: An Overview," *Origins* 23:42 (7 April 1994) 733–41.

3. *Dossier informativo* (Libreria Editrice Vaticana, 1992). The text also appeared in *Il Regno-Documenti* 37 (1992) 450–56. For an English summary see *The Living Light* 29 (Summer 1993) 82–84.

4. Ratzinger, "The *Catechism,*" 473.

5. Ibid., 479.

6. Ibid., 481.

7. *Catholic World Report* (December 1992) 57–58.

8. Ratzinger, "The *Catechism,*" 475.

9. *Origins* 16:26 (11 Dec. 1986) 487–88.

10. Ratzinger, "The *Catechism,*" 479.

11. Ibid., 478–79.

12. Ibid., 477.

13. Ibid.

14. Ibid., 482.

15. The CCC cites Augustine's *Sermo* 33, but the catechetical tradition more likely depends on Augustine's *Enchiridion*. The catechism's assertion, albeit in small print, that "ever since St. Augustine, the Ten Commandments have occupied a predominant place" in catechesis is open to question; see Johannes van Oort, *Jerusalem and Babylon. A Study into Augustine's "City of God" and the Sources of his Doctrine of the Two Cities* (Leiden: Brill, 1991) 343.

FIFTEEN

# *Post Scriptum:* The CCC in English

Pope John Paul II gave formal approval to the text of the *Catechism of the Catholic Church* on 25 June 1992, and before the year was out bookstores were doing a brisk business selling the French edition and Italian and Spanish translations. The Anglophone world, however, had to wait almost two years, until June 1994, before an authorized English translation became available. The reasons for the delay were varied and sundry. They included controversy over the principles that should guide translation (a dispute that dates back at least to the time of St. Jerome), organized opposition, and different views about the purpose and function of catechisms.

Wanting to disseminate the catechism as quickly and widely as possible, the commission of cardinals and bishops that supervised its compilation established procedures for translating it even before the definitive text was approved. Responsibility for the English translation was given to American cardinals Law and Baum, both members of the commission, and British bishop Konstant, a member of the editorial committee. At the outset they agreed that a standard translation for all English-speaking Catholics would promote a common vocabulary in catechesis. They engaged the services of the Reverend Douglas Clark, a priest of the diocese of Savannah, Georgia, whose studies in Rome gave him a solid grounding in classical and modern languages, and a broad knowledge of biblical, patristic, and theological sources. Clark was charged with producing an idiomatic translation that, while remaining faithful to the French original, would be attractive to English readers. During the year (January 1992–February 1993) he spent translating the catechism, Clark submitted his work for review to two groups of editorial advisors, one in the United States, the other in the United Kingdom.[1]

Konstant is quoted as saying, "to take into account the inevitable tension between accuracy and literalness, and also to attempt to produce a text that draws its readers on both because of its compelling style and because of the nature of the subject matter" is a "well-nigh impossible task."[2] And the task was made more complex by the desire to make one translation serve the entire Anglophone world (some twenty-one countries). The translation of the catechism text presented one set of problems, the translation of the quotations found in the text, another set. The original *Catéchisme de l'Église catholique,* as already noted, is replete with passages, many lengthy, translated into French from the Scriptures, the liturgy, the documents of Vatican II and, to a lesser extent, the Code of Canon Law. Those responsible for the English translation thought it desirable to substitute wherever possible standard translations of these texts or, where none could be found, to translate them from the original language rather than from the French translation. The English-speaking world, however, does not have translations of religious works, except liturgical texts, that are standard and universally accepted. There are several approved translations of the Bible, two approved translations of the Code of Canon Law (British and American), and no official translation of the documents of Vatican II. In the end, Clark was instructed to follow the general principles set down in *Comme le prévoit* which the International Commission on English in the Liturgy (ICEL) had used to guide their translations of liturgical texts. *(Comme le prévoit* was published by the Consilium for the Implementation of the Constitution on Sacred Liturgy.) Clark was further directed to use the New Revised Standard Version (NRSV) for biblical quotations, the translation of the Canon Law Society of America for the canons, and to translate Vatican II documents from the authorized Latin texts.

### Inclusive Language

The choice of the NRSV for biblical quotations was dictated chiefly by two considerations: First, it had been approved for liturgical use by the Congregation for Divine Worship and was accepted in the United States, the United Kingdom, Canada, Ireland, and other English-speaking countries;[3] and second, it uses "inclusive language." The group responsible for the translation of the catechism, prompted by pastoral concerns, opted to follow *Criteria for the Evaluation of Inclusive Language Translations of Scriptural Texts Proposed for Liturgical Use,* a document published by the National Conference of Catholic Bishops (of the United States). These criteria directed, among other things, that references to human beings should avoid generic terms like *men, sons,* and *brethren* that have come to be regarded as gender-specific so as not to seem to exclude women. Instead, generic terms like *people, humans,* and *persons* should be used. Similarly, plural pronouns, because they are inclusive, should replace male pronouns in the singular. The NCCB criteria, "in fidelity to the inspired Word of God," insists on referring to the persons of the Trinity by the traditional "Father, Son and Holy Spirit," with the corresponding masculine pronouns. In short, the rule-of-thumb was to follow Church usage when it came to "vertical language," that is, language naming God and his attributes and activities, and to use inclusive terms when speaking of humans. But a consistent use of inclusive language in doctrinal tracts, never easy, demands a rethinking of grammar as well as a translation of words.

The decision to write the *Catéchisme de l'Église catholique* in French, which at one time seemed like a good idea, compounded the problem for the English translator. Its frequent use of *homme,* for example, when translated as "man" in English sounds sexist despite the fact that it was not intended to be so by the original. Like other Romance languages, French does not have a neuter gender. Thus a singular possessive like the English *its* is rendered as either masculine or feminine according to the gender of the thing or person possessed (thus *sa mère* can mean "her mother" or "his mother").

Similarly, the decision to adopt the general principles of *Comme le prévoit* was the cause of unforeseen difficulties. *Comme le prévoit* seemed to provide the translator with ready-made guidelines that had already been tried and tested. But in the opinion of some, they were found wanting. Groups and individuals unhappy with the vernacular liturgical texts found Clark's translation of the catechism to embody everything they disliked about the translations of the liturgical texts produced under the aegis of ICEL. Further, at the very time that Clark had finished his translation using the New Revised Standard Version of the Bible, the National Conference of Catholic Bishops was seeking, in the face of organized opposition, Rome's approval for a new translation of the Sunday lectionary that utilized the NRSV. These factors, compounded by the commercial interests of at least one American publisher, restive under the restrictions set down by the National Conference of Catholic Bishops for the dissemination of the CCC, who sought to market his own translation of the catechism, and the widespread misrepresentation of Clark's work in some circles, first delayed and eventually caused his translation to be aborted.[4]

After some months of transatlantic editorial tinkering that failed to produce a satisfactory compromise, the task of reworking the English translation was given over to Archbishop Joseph Eric D'Arcy of Hobart (Australia), assisted by the Reverend John Wall, a lecturer in English at the University of Tasmania. After receiving Clark's translation in April 1993, they spent the next three-and-a-half months editing it and suggesting revisions. Rome then sent their revisions "to various consultants for comment."[5] D'Arcy acknowledged that Clark's style was smoother and more readable, but he defends the changes that he and Wall made, saying they do "better justice to the French." Because the CCC is primarily written for people who have to teach the faith, D'Arcy says, "They've got to have the stuff transmitted to them as close to the original as possible, not only in words but in sequence of thought and so on."

It may be, as D'Arcy maintains, that when the translation left his hands, "eighty per cent of Clark" was still there, but other changes make it read like a very different work. In the approved translation, quotations from Scripture are taken from the Revised Standard Version (RSV), and texts of Vatican II are quoted from Austin Flannery's translation. The RSV, authorized by the National Council of Churches (1946–52), is based on the Authorized Version (that is, the King James Bible). The NRSV (1990), a major revision of the RSV, abandoned "thou" pronouns and overtly sexist language. The different tone that the use of the RSV gives to the catechism is readily illustrated (to cite only one example) by the translation of Genesis 1:27-28 and 5:1-2 in paragraph 2331:

| **Clark's Translation** | **Authorized Translation** |
| :---: | :---: |
| [NRSV] | [RSV] |
| God created the human race in his image, "male and female he created them." He blessed them and said, "Be fruitful and multiply." When God created them, "he made them in the likeness of God. Male and female he created them, and he blessed them and named them . . ." | "God created man in his own image . . . male and female he created them"; He blessed them and said, "Be fruitful and multiply"; "When God created man, he made him in the likeness of God. Male and female he created them, and he blessed them and named them Man when they were created." |

Archbishop William Levada, a member of the seven-man editorial committee that produced the text of the CCC, had concurred in the decision to undertake an English translation that used inclusive language, but in the end concluded that "the translation of a doctrinal text such as the catechism into an 'inclusive' English translation is always difficult and may not even be possible."[26] He acknowledges that inclusive language was not the only consideration in judging Clark's translation unacceptable, and he questions whether the principles that guide the translation of liturgical texts should be the same as those which guide the translation of catechisms. Like D'Arcy he believes that faithfulness to the French text should be the ultimate norm.

The full story of the English translation of the CCC has yet to be written. The public controversy that centered on the issue of inclusive language distracted people from consideration of other important issues. It side-tracked discussion of the purpose and function of catechisms. It left unresolved questions about the normative value of the French text which, the commission of cardinals and bishops has said, is not the *editio typica*. It silenced discussion about the pastoral and pedagogical implications of using one translation of the Scriptures in the catechism and another in the lectionary. It did not explore the norms that are to guide "the adaptation of doctrinal presentations and catechetical methods required by the differences of culture, age, spiritual maturity, and social and ecclesial condition" of those to whom the CCC is addressed (24).[7]

Pope John Paul asked for a work that would present "sure teaching adapted to the actual life of Christians." In the spirit of the Second Vatican Council, the CCC proposes no dogmatic definitions and unfurls no condemnations; its language is descriptive rather than prescriptive, irenic rather than polemic. The commission of cardinals and bishops and the editorial committee responsible for the text planned it as a pastoral work, an instrument of evangelization, a means to renew the proclamation of the gospel message. Only time will tell whether the language in the English translation as it now stands abets or hinders these lofty goals.

NOTES

1. Clark spells out principles that guided his work and gives the names of the editorial advisors in "On 'Englishing' the Catechism," *The Living Light* 29 (Summer 1993) 18–28.

2. Quoted by Clark, ibid., 16.

3. The Congregation for Divine Worship and the Sacraments confirmed the use of the NRSV for liturgical use in 1992, but revoked its approval in 1994. *Origins* 24:22 (10 Nov. 1994) 576.

4. The editors of the *Catholic World Report* (March 1993) linked an article by Helen Hull Hitchcock, "A Sacrifice of Grace," in which she discusses the pros and cons of inclusive language in the lectionary to a short piece, "Trouble with the Catechism," in *The* [London] *Tablet* (13 Feb. 1993) 206. *The Tablet* stated that "clearly there is a real war behind the battle of the pronouns." (Hitchcock herself had not cited *The Tablet* piece.) Michael J. Wrenn and Kenneth D. Whitehead offer a detailed critique of Clark's translation, "Unfaithful to Truth," in *Crisis* 11 (Nov. 1993) 17–24. Another piece, especially critical of Cardinal Law, "American Roadblock: Why Rome Refused a Politically Correct Translation," appeared in *Crisis* (June 1993) 35–36. The writer, using the *nom de plume* "Father Brown," says that resistance to Clark's translation was "spearheaded by Fr. Joseph Fessio (a California Jesuit and publisher) and Msgr. Michael Wrenn (a Manhattan pastor and veteran translator)." Brown credits them with contacting "sympathetic English-speaking bishops in the United States, Canada, England, and elsewhere around the world" to organize "loyal opposition" to the Clark draft.

5. This information comes from an interview that Archbishop D'Arcy gave to Chris McGillion in Sydney, reported in *The* [London] *Tablet* (21 May 1994) 624.

6. William J. Levada, "The Problem with 'Englishing' the Catechism," *The Living Light* 30 (Spring 1994) 18–25.

7. The controversy did not address the kind of issues raised by Cardinal Ratzinger in the address he gave to the eighth plenary session of the International Council for Catechesis, 24 Sept. 1992. See Joseph Ratzinger, "Catechismo e inculturazione," *Il Regno-documenti* 19/92: 585–89.

# The Constitution *De parvo catechismo* Approved by the First Vatican Council[1]

Holy Mother Church has always given special attention to children so that at an early age they might be fully grounded in the duties of their religion. In this the Church has been taught by the precepts and example of her Spouse, our Saviour Jesus Christ. The Council of Trent therefore was not content to tell bishops to see to it that [at least on Sundays and holydays] children are carefully taught the basics of their faith and their duties towards God and towards their parents. It also felt bound to draw up for the faithful some definite form and method of instruction in the fundamentals of the faith which pastors and teachers in all churches should follow. Since the Council was unable to carry this out itself, it fell to the Apostolic See therefore to bring it about and to publish the Catechism for Parish Priests or the Catechism of the Council of Trent. Furthermore, the Fathers at Trent had desired that in the future everyone should use one and the same method of teaching and learning the catechism. The Apostolic See therefore approved the shorter catechism for the instruction of children, drawn up by Cardinal Bellarmine at its own request. This Catechism is heartily recommended to all Ordinaries, parish priests and all others concerned.

At the present time, however, great inconvenience has arisen from the large number of shorter catechisms circulating in different provinces and even in different dioceses of the same province. We propose therefore with the approval of the Council to have a new catechism (in Latin) drawn up which everyone must use so that the diversity of shorter catechisms can in future be

---

1. The translation is taken from Michael Donnellan, *Rationale for a Uniform Catechism: Vatican I to Vatican II* (Ph.D. dissertation, The Catholic University of America, Washington, 1972) 94–95. Donnellan gives the Latin text, pp. 240–42. The phrases in brackets appeared in the revised schema, but were dropped from the draft approved by preliminary vote of the council. The final draft was never acted on.

eliminated. The above-mentioned catechism of Cardinal Bellarmine will be used [as a model] but special note will also be taken of other catechisms already familiar to the faithful.

[Since it is essential that this small catechism, itself a sign of faith, be easily memorizable,] patriarchs or archbishops in their various provinces, after due consultation with their respective suffragans and with the other archbishops of their region and of their language, should see to it that the Latin text is accurately translated into the vernacular.

Bishops will, of course, be free to draw up fuller catechetical instruction for a more complete training of their faithful and for a defense against any particular errors prevalent in their districts. At the same time, for the elementary instruction of the faithful the shorter catechism without any additional modifications must be retained. If the bishops prefer to combine these additions with the text of the aforementioned catechism, they should be careful to keep these clearly distinct from the prescribed text of the catechism.

Finally, it matters little to memorize formulas given in the catechism unless the faithful also have someone to help them understand what these formulas mean, proportionate, of course, to each one's ability to understand. This consideration makes it all the more important that there be but one method for teaching the doctrines of the faith and the ordinary practices of piety. For this reason we heartily recommend, as our Predecessors have so often done before us, the use of the above noted catechism for pastors and for all those upon whose shoulders the burden of teaching resides.

# Decrees of the Third Plenary Council of Baltimore Regarding a Catechism[1]

217. Indeed to all people, but especially to the children and to the uninformed, the mysteries of the Kingdom of God are revealed through the ministry of Holy Mother the Church who always with every fiber of energy urges on this work in order that they may be nourished continually by the milk of heavenly doctrine. Hence, the most holy Council of Trent commanded the bishops that they provide for the teaching to young children of the elementary and basic items of the faith at least on Sundays and other feast days in each of their parishes. She looks with attention to the pastors of souls to feed the lambs of her flock personally. He would be entirely unworthy of the name of Father, if he would unjustly refuse to break bread with his son who is perishing of hunger. Therefore, we wish the pastors of churches or their assistants be present very often at the schools of catechism on Sundays and that they be present even at colleges, high schools, and academies for boys and girls which are not directed by priests. The teachers not marked with the priestly character, either religious or lay, are indeed of a great help in the instruction of youth, but the burden of teaching the word of God is not a mark proper to them. "For the lips of a priestly person will guard knowledge and will seek the law from his mouth" (Mal 2:7).

218. We therefore order the pastor of souls to have a continual and constantly present care for their youngsters, especially at the time when they are being prepared to receive their First Holy Communion, and indeed we order that the pastors themselves or their assistants teach catechism to the previously mentioned students for six weeks and three times each week (at least in a place where they stay or one where they may rather easily have access). No one

---

1. Reprinted from *Acta et Decreta Concilii Plenarii Baltimorensis Tertii* (Baltimore: Typis Joannis Murphy et Sociorum, 1886) 118–20.

should be admitted to the reception of confirmation unless he carefully be instructed concerning those things which have a bearing on the nature and effect of this sacrament. And so we urge the bishop that he would confer confirmation on those youths, and that he either by himself or through his delegate examine those about to be confirmed in Christian doctrine. The pastors over and above this should provide that the boys and girls after their First Holy Communion be instructed through the two following years in Catholic doctrine and their proper Christian duties.

219. It is of great importance that the catechism be completed and be covered in all its numbers. Several catechisms which were used among ourselves, are not adapted sufficiently to the intelligence of youngsters or are faulty for another reason. Especially since many of our compatriots move around and their children attend different schools, everyone knows how great the disadvantage that arises from the variety and number of catechisms which are circulated in these provinces. Having considered this matter for a sufficient amount of time, we have decided that a committee of Roman Catholic bishops should be set up. The bishops of this committee will consider:

> 1. To select a catechism and if necessary to emend it, or to start from scratch if they would feel it the necessary and opportune thing to do.
>
> 2. Let them present this word thus finished to the body of Roman Catholic Archbishops who will re-examine the catechism and will provide that it be published. This catechism is to be published as soon as possible so that all teachers, both religious and lay, may have and possess the book.

Because this new catechism which will be composed in English will be prepared to this end, so that it will not only provide for a means of promoting uniformity by which the above mentioned disadvantages are taken away, but they will be also better adapted to the condition and state of our faithful people, we strongly have in our prayers that the book, having been turned into their idiom, may be used by the faithful of other tongues. Especially since the children born of German, French, or any other nation frequently come to Catholic Churches at a later period, in which churches the Christian doctrine is proclaimed in an English tongue, let us recommend that the youths who understand fully both tongues and who live totally among English-speaking people learn the before-mentioned Catechism in the English tongue.

# APPENDIX C

# Apostolic Constitution *Fidei depositum*

*John Paul, Bishop, Servant of the Servants of God, For Everlasting Memory,*
*To my Venerable Brothers the Cardinals, Patriarchs, Archbishops, Bishops, Priests,*
*Deacons, and to all the People of God.*

GUARDING THE DEPOSIT OF FAITH IS THE MISSION WHICH THE LORD ENTRUSTED TO HIS CHURCH, and which she fulfills in every age. The Second Vatican Ecumenical Council, which was opened 30 years ago by my predecessor Pope John XXIII, of happy memory, had as its intention and purpose to highlight the Church's apostolic and pastoral mission and by making the truth of the Gospel shine forth to lead all people to seek and receive Christ's love which surpasses all knowledge (cf. Eph 3:19).

The principal task entrusted to the Council by Pope John XXIII was to guard and present better the precious deposit of Christian doctrine in order to make it more accessible to the Christian faithful and to all people of good will. For this reason the Council was not first of all to condemn the errors of the time, but above all to strive calmly to show the strength and beauty of the doctrine of the faith. "Illumined by the light of this Council," the Pope said, "the Church . . . will become greater in spiritual riches and gaining the strength of new energies therefrom, she will look to the future without fear. . . . Our duty is to dedicate ourselves with an earnest will and without fear to that work which our era demands of us, thus pursuing the path which the Church has followed for 20 centuries."[1]

With the help of God, the Council Fathers in four years of work were able to produce a considerable number of doctrinal statements and pastoral norms which were presented to the whole Church. There the Pastors and Christian faithful find directives for that "renewal of thought, action, practices, and moral virtue, of joy and hope, which was the very purpose of the Council."[2]

After its conclusion, the Council did not cease to inspire the Church's life. In 1985 I was able to assert, "For me, then—who had the special grace of participating in it and actively collaborating in its development—Vatican II has always been, and especially during these years of my Pontificate, the constant reference point of my every pastoral action, in the conscious commitment to implement its directives concretely and faithfully at the level of each Church and the whole Church."[3]

In this spirit, on January 25, 1985, I convoked an extraordinary assembly of the Synod of Bishops for the twentieth anniversary of the close of the Council. The purpose of this assembly was to celebrate the graces and spiritual fruits of Vatican II, to study its teaching in greater depth in order that all the Christian faithful might better adhere to it and to promote knowledge and application of it.

On that occasion the Synod Fathers stated: "Very many have expressed the desire that a catechism or compendium of all catholic doctrine regarding both faith and morals be composed, that it might be, as it were, a point of reference for the catechisms or compendiums that are prepared in various regions. The presentation of doctrine must be biblical and liturgical. It must be sound doctrine suited to the present life of Christians."[4] After the Synod ended, I made this desire my own, considering it as "fully responding to a real need of the universal Church and of the particular Churches."[5]

For this reason we thank the Lord wholeheartedly on this day when we can offer the entire Church this "reference text" entitled the *Catechism of the Catholic Church* for a catechesis renewed at the living sources of the faith!

Following the renewal of the Liturgy and the new codification of the canon law of the Latin Church and that of the Oriental Catholic Churches, this catechism will make a very important contribution to that work of renewing the whole life of the Church, as desired and begun by the Second Vatican Council.


## 1. The Process and Spirit of Drafting the Text

The *Catechism of the Catholic Church* is the result of very extensive collaboration; it was prepared over six years of intense work done in a spirit of complete openness and fervent zeal.

In 1986, I entrusted a commission of twelve Cardinals and Bishops, chaired by Cardinal Joseph Ratzinger, with the task of preparing a draft of the catechism requested by the Synod Fathers. An editorial committee of seven diocesan Bishops, experts in theology and catechesis, assisted the commission in its work.

The commission, charged with giving directives and with overseeing the course of the work, attentively followed all the stages in editing the nine subsequent drafts. The editorial committee, for its part, assumed responsibility for writing the text, making the emendations requested by the commission and examining the observations of numerous theologians, exegetes and catechists, and, above all, of the Bishops of the whole world, in order to produce a better text. In the committee various opinions were compared with great profit, and thus a richer text has resulted whose unity and coherence are assured.

The project was the object of extensive consultation among all Catholic Bishops, their Episcopal Conferences or Synods, and of theological and catechetical institutes. As a whole, it received a broadly favorable acceptance on the part of the Episcopate. It can be said that this *Catechism* is the result of the collaboration of the whole Episcopate of the Catholic Church, who generously accepted my invitation to share responsibility for an enterprise which directly concerns the life of the Church. This response elicits in me a deep feeling of joy, because the harmony of so many voices truly expresses what could be called the "symphony" of the faith. The achievement of this *Catechism* thus reflects the collegial nature of the Episcopate; it testifies to the Church's catholicity.

### 2. Arrangement of the Material

A catechism should faithfully and systematically present the teaching of Sacred Scripture, the living Tradition in the Church and the authentic Magisterium, as well as the spiritual heritage of the Fathers, Doctors, and saints of the Church, to allow for a better knowledge of the Christian mystery and for enlivening the faith of the People of God. It should take into account the doctrinal statements which down the centuries the Holy Spirit has intimated to his Church. It should also help to illumine with the light of faith the new situations and problems which had not yet emerged in the past.

This catechism will thus contain both the new and the old (cf. Matt 13:52), because the faith is always the same yet the source of ever new light.

To respond to this twofold demand, the *Catechism of the Catholic Church* on the one hand repeats the "old," traditional order already followed by the Catechism of St. Pius V, arranging the material in four parts: the *Creed*, the *Sacred Liturgy*, with pride of place given to the sacraments, the *Christian way of life* explained beginning with the Ten commandments, and finally, *Christian prayer*. At the same time, however, the contents are often presented in a "new" way in order to respond to the questions of our age.

The four parts are related one to another: the Christian mystery is the object of faith (first part); it is celebrated and communicated in liturgical actions (second part); it is present to enlighten and sustain the children of God in their actions (third part); it is the basis for our prayer, the privileged expression of which is the Our Father, and it represents the object of our supplication, our praise and our intercession (fourth part).

The Liturgy itself is prayer; the confession of faith finds its proper place in the celebration of worship. Grace, the fruit of the sacraments, is the irreplaceable condition for Christian living, just as participation in the Church's Liturgy requires faith. If faith is not expressed in works, it is dead (cf. Jas 2:14-16) and cannot bear fruit unto eternal life.

In reading the *Catechism of the Catholic Church* we can perceive the wonderful unity of the mystery of God, his saving will, as well as the central place of Jesus Christ, the only-begotten Son of God, sent by the Father, made man in the womb of the Blessed Virgin Mary by the power of the Holy Spirit, to be our Savior. Having died and risen, Christ is always present in his Church, especially in the sacraments; he is the source of our faith, the model of Christian conduct, and the Teacher of our prayer.

### 3. The Doctrinal Value of the Text

The *Catechism of the Catholic Church*, which I approved June 25th last and the publication of which I today order by virtue of my Apostolic Authority, is a statement of the Church's faith and of catholic doctrine, attested to or illumined by Sacred Scripture, the Apostolic Tradition, and the Church's Magisterium. I declare it to be a sure norm for teaching the faith and thus a valid and legitimate instrument for ecclesial communion. May it serve the renewal to which the Holy Spirit ceaselessly calls the Church of God, the Body of Christ, on her pilgrimage to the undiminished light of the Kingdom!

The approval and publication of the *Catechism of the Catholic Church* represent a service which the Successor of Peter wishes to offer to the Holy Catholic Church, to all the particular Churches in peace and communion with the Apostolic See: the service, that is, of supporting and confirming the faith of all the Lord Jesus' disciples (cf. Luke 22:32), as well as of strengthening the bonds of unity in the same apostolic faith.

Therefore, I ask all the Church's Pastors and the Christian faithful to receive this catechism in a spirit of communion and to use it assiduously in fulfilling their mission of proclaiming the faith and calling people to the Gospel life. This catechism is given to them that it may be a sure and authentic reference text for teaching catholic doctrine and particularly for preparing local catechisms. It is also offered to all the faithful who wish to deepen their knowledge of the unfathomable riches of salvation (cf. Eph 3:8). It is meant to support ecumenical efforts that are moved by the holy desire for the unity of all Christians, showing carefully the content and wondrous harmony of the catholic faith. The *Catechism of the Catholic Church*, lastly, is offered to every individual who asks us to give an account of the hope that is in us (cf. 1 Pet 3:15) and who wants to know what the Catholic Church believes.

This catechism is not intended to replace the local catechisms duly approved by the ecclesiastical authorities, the diocesan Bishops and the Episcopal Conferences, especially if they have been approved by the Apostolic See. It is meant to encourage and assist in the writing of new local catechisms, which take into account various situations and cultures, while carefully preserving the unity of faith and fidelity to catholic doctrine.

At the conclusion of this document presenting the *Catechism of the Catholic Church*, I beseech the Blessed Virgin Mary, Mother of the Incarnate Word and Mother of the Church, to support with her powerful intercession the catechetical work of the entire Church on every level, at this time when she is called to a new effort of evangelization. May the light of the true faith free humanity from the ignorance and slavery of sin in order to lead it to the only freedom worthy of the name (cf. John 8:32): that of life in Jesus Christ under the guidance of the Holy Spirit, here below and in the Kingdom of heaven, in the fullness of the blessed vision of God face to face (cf. 1 Cor 13:12; 2 Cor 5:6-8)!

Given October 11, 1992, the thirtieth anniversary of the opening of the Second Vatican Ecumenical Council, in the fourteenth year of my Pontificate.

NOTES

1. John XXIII, Discourse at the Opening of the Second Vatican Ecumenical Council, 11 October 1962: AAS 54 (1962) 788–91.

2. Paul VI, Discourse at the Closing of the Second Vatican Ecumenical Council, 7 December 1965: AAS 58 (1966): 7–8.

3. John Paul II, Discourse of 25 January 1985: *L'Osservatore Romano*, 27 January 1985.

4. *Final Report* of the Extraordinary Synod of Bishops, 7 December 1985, *Enchiridion Vaticanum*, vol. 9, II, B, a, n. 4: p. 1758, n. 1797.

5. John Paul II, Discourse at the Closing of the Extraordinary Synod of Bishops, 7 December 1985, n. 6: AAS 78 (1986) 435.

# Index of Names and Places